Social Partnership at Work

The collapse of communism and the ensuing process of reform in central eastern Europe have presented a unique laboratory for researchers interested in social change and institutional building. East Germany provides a particularly interesting case, having experienced rapid and radical political and economic transformation, and representing an historically outstanding experiment of the shifting of an entire social system onto a different society.

Social Partnership at Work provides the first comparative, in-depth analysis of workplace relations in east and west Germany. The author examines the success of the institutional transfer of west German labour organisations into east German workplaces in an effort to address questions central to the discussion of workplace relations in transitional economies, including: Can capitalist labour institutions be imposed on a former communist workforce?, What conditions determine the success or failure of these institutions?, Can 'social partnership' between capital and labour be learned?

This book will be of great interest to students and academics in the areas of industrial relations, industrial sociology and political science.

'Carola Frege, in the face of mainstream German pessimism and on the basis of original and well-designed research, shows the workplace in post-Wall eastern Germany for what it is: a transformed and still-changing arena in which eastern workers have actively taken hold of transferred western institutions such as works councils and unions to use for their own collective and individual purposes. In so doing, in a remarkably short period of time following the collapse of communism, eastern workers have taken on attitudes and behaviours very similar to those of their western counterparts. With such persuasive and surprising findings, Frege casts new light on theories of collective action, industrial relations, social psychology, institutional transfer and economic transformation.'

Professor Lowell Turner, Cornell University

Carola M. Frege is a lecturer in Industrial Relations at the London School of Economics and Political Science. She has written widely on the subject of workplace relations in transitional economies, with articles appearing in the *British Journal of Industrial Relations*, *Industrial Relations* and *Economic and Industrial Democracy*.

ROUTLEDGE STUDIES IN EMPLOYMENT RELATIONS

Series editors: Rick Delbridge and Edmund Heery
Cardiff Business School

Aspects of the employment relationship are central to numerous courses at both undergraduate and postgraduate level.

Drawing on insights from industrial relations, human resource management and industrial sociology, this series provides an alternative source of research-based materials and texts reviewing key developments in employment research.

Books published in the LSE/Routledge series are works of high academic merit, drawn from a wide range of academic studies in the social sciences for which the LSE has an international reputation.

Social Partnership at Work

Workplace relations in post-unification
Germany

Carola M. Frege

London and New York

First published 1999 by Routledge
11 New Fetter Lane, London EC4P 4EE

Simultaneously published in the USA and Canada
by Routledge
29 West 35th Street, New York, NY 10001

© 1999 Carola M. Frege

Typeset in Galliard by
BC Typesetting, Bristol
Printed and bound in Great Britain by
Biddles Ltd, Guildford and King's Lynn

British Library Cataloguing in Publication Data
A catalogue record for this book is available from the British Library

Library of Congress Cataloging in Publication Data
Frege, Carola M., 1965–
    Social partnership at work: workplace relations in post-unification
Germany/Carola M. Frege.
        p.   cm. – (Routledge studies in employment; 2)
    Includes bibliographical references and index.
    1. Industrial relations – Germany (East).   I. Title.   II. Series.
HD8460.5.F74   1999
331′.09431–dc21   98-39657
                                                                    CIP

ISBN 0–415–18950–0

For my grandmother, Rosa Elisabeth Frege (1892–1993), who brought history alive by her compelling stories of her life in Berlin, experiencing so much of German history: the rule of Kaiser Wilhelm II, the Weimar Republic, the Third Reich, the Federal Republic of Germany and re-unified Germany.

Contents

PART III
Explaining post-socialist participation in collective activities

Tables and figures

Tables

Figures

Acknowledgements

This book would not have been possible without the collaboration of the officials of the German clothing union GTB (Gewerkschaft Textil Bekleidung), of the management of the case-study company (Bodywear) and finally of all the works councillors and union members who participated in the surveys and interviews. My fieldwork was partly financed by a grant from the Hans-Boeckler-Foundation Düsseldorf (grant 96-791-2) which is hereby gratefully acknowledged.

During the research phase I benefited from communications with numerous scholars and practitioners in the field. I would especially like to thank Ann Denvir, Michael Fichter, Jack Fiorito, Ariane Hegewisch, Richard Hyman, Wade Jacoby, Martin Jander, Bert Klandermans, Volkmar Kreißig, Stephan Lutz, Walther Müller-Jentsch, Evelyn Preusche, András Tóth, Lowell Turner, Wolfgang Streeck and Rainer Zoll.

My greatest debt is, however, to my former Ph.D. supervisors and now colleagues, Ray Richardson and John Kelly: Ray for being a mentor, friend and critic; and John for being a wonderful colleague, who through many enlightening discussions and from his own work influenced many of the ideas contained in this book. I also owe thanks to my other colleagues in the Industrial Relations Department at the LSE, in particular to David Marsden and Stephen Wood for helpful comments on various drafts and to David in particular for encouraging me to publish this research as a book. Special thanks go to my student, Frances Molinaro, for her careful assistance with the bibliography.

I also want to express my gratitude to Guy Kirsch at the University of Freiburg, Werner Müller at the University of Basel, and in particular to Leslie Sklair, my tutor in the Sociology Department at the LSE, who first challenged me to think critically. Finally, a special thanks to Ian M. Taplin for reading and commenting on the entire manuscript in several early and late incarnations.

An earlier version of Chapter 3 'Transforming socialist workplace relations: co-operation or subservience?' appeared in *German Politics and Society*, vol. 15 (1) pp. 65–93, 1997. An earlier version of Chapter 8 'Collective commitment in the east and west' appeared in the *European Journal of Industrial Relations*, vol. 4 (1) pp. 81–102, 1998.

1 Introduction

> As German unification proceeds, the transformation of political and indus-
> trial relations institutions in the East as well as the effect of unification on
> West German institutions will afford an exciting opportunity for researchers
> in the coming years, one that may shed new light on our ideas of institution
> building and transformation. Although the outcome will undoubtedly be
> the expansion of West German institutions, including unions, works coun-
> cils, and industrial relations practices, into the East, the actual functioning
> of these institutions in the new environment is arguably contingent.
>
> (Turner 1991: 242)

Since 1989, changes in the countries of central and eastern Europe have led to
the establishment of a new framework of industrial relations that is part of a
broader process of social, political and economic transformation. Such changes
pose important questions as to how well institutions function when they are
introduced into an unfamiliar national context. In most of these countries
there was a gradual process of institutional innovation in which some traditional
institutions were kept and reformed and other 'western' structures of industrial
relations were copied and adapted to local circumstances. However, the political
unification of the two German states in 1990 was characterised by an *ad hoc*, big-
bang 'institutional transfer' (Lehmbruch 1993) whereby west German institutions were introduced in the east. This involved a wholesale territorial expansion
of west German political, economic, monetary and social institutions (including
massive financial subsidies) into east Germany[1] and resulted in citizens of the
former GDR (German Democratic Republic) abandoning all their hitherto distinctive constitutional and legal provisions. In the words of one commentator,
this amounted to an act of 'unconditional surrender' (van Beyme 1994: 251,
quoted in Hyman 1996: 602).

During the political unification in 1990, west German labour law and collective bargaining arrangements were introduced into the east. In addition, west
German employers' associations opened regional offices, the industrial branches
of the central state trade union (FDGB) dissolved and their west German

counterparts moved eastwards using the infrastructure of the dissolved socialist unions[2] to recruit members *en masse* (e.g. Fichter 1994, 1996; Weinert 1993). Moreover, the Works Constitution Act re-established works councils, the plant-level interest representation of the workforce which had been formerly forbidden (e.g. Jander and Lutz 1991a; Kädtler *et al.* 1997). The combination of collective bargaining by unions and workplace representation by mandatory works councils constitutes the framework of the 'dual system' of German industrial relations or the so-called social partnership model (e.g. Hyman 1996: 602). Its transfer to the east signified an attempt by the dominant western actors (with the consent of the east German population) to solidify west German industrial relations norms in the unified Germany.

The importance of the east German transformation is that it can teach us about the preconditions of a successful transfer of established institutions into a new cultural context, and in particular about the preconditions for the transfer of the German social partnership model. For as Eisen (1996: 33) emphasises, the process of institutional transfer in the east provides empirical findings with regard to the mechanism of institution building which are less easy to uncover in already consolidated societies (also Offe 1994: 43; Turner 1991: 242).

Moreover, the case of the east German transformation has been cited for its wider importance for the economic and political integration of Europe. Lowell Turner (1997: 2), for example, argues that 'in the "new world order" of an increasingly globalized economy, what happens to the [east] German political economy will have wide repercussions for the pace and shape of economic development throughout Europe'. And from a political perspective Rose *et al.* (1993: 3) assume that 'what is happening in [east] Germany today is significant far beyond the boundaries of the Federal Republic of Germany: it is a microcosm of the challenge facing Europe in the 1990s, the challenge of finding a new relationship between the peoples of eastern, central and western Europe'.

Despite its wider theoretical and political importance, research on east Germany has been mainly limited to scholars within the German academic community writing in German. Consequently, east Germany is neglected in most comparative studies on central and eastern Europe (exceptions are Stark 1992a; Stark and Bruszt 1998) and in the international treatment of the German model of industrial relations (exceptions are Hyman 1996; Turner 1997, 1998). This book is an attempt to redress this deficiency.

The primary aim of this book is to evaluate the success of the institutional transfer in the context of industrial relations at workplace level. Specifically, the focus is on the transfer of the west German workers' interest representation system, trade unions and works councils to the east and the extent to which socialist workplace relations have been transformed by such a transfer. Central to these discussions is an evaluation of whether the (west) German social partnership model between management and worker representatives has been successfully established on east German shopfloors.

The success or failure of east German transformation

Opinions about the success or failure of the east German transformation differ widely even eight years after unification, with discussions focusing upon its atypicality, whether or not the transformation is yet complete, and what its consequences are for the resilience of the western system.

One group of authors point to east Germany as a special case whereby 'a degree of institutional stability . . . that is opposite to all we know from other post-socialist societies' (Wiesenthal 1994: 1) has been attained in a very short time period. Wiesenthal (1995: 154) further points to the high level of 'system integration' which east Germany achieved, and the fact that the institutional framework there was reformed in an overall consistent way. This is in stark contrast to the other post-socialist countries, whose institutional and administrational settings still bear characteristics of the old system. This viewpoint is supported by Eisen and Wollmann (1996: 17) and Pohlmann and Schmidt (1996: 192) who agree that the macro transformation in east Germany, measured by stability criteria, was successful. In particular, it is widely argued that the transfer of industrial relations institutions in the east was successfully completed during the first six years after unification (e.g. Eisen 1996: 42; Hyman 1996; Turner 1997; Woderich 1996: 82). Such a transfer has been emphasised by many observers as one of the few success stories of the overall transformation process (e.g. Schmidt 1996a: 11) and as a 'prime example' of a successful transfer (e.g. Ettl and Wiesenthal 1994: 125; Schroeder 1996: 101).

On the other hand, there are those who emphasise the ongoing nature of the transformation (e.g. Eisen 1996: 35; Kollmorgen 1996: 285; Reißig 1996: 248) and who argue that we are witnessing a process of institutionalisation with its own internal dynamics, and whose outcome remains very unclear (e.g. Martens 1994: 311). For example, Kollmorgen (1996) classifies three stages of transformation (revolution, transitional period, structuration period) and argues that east Germany is currently in the last phase which comprises the complex, long-term consolidation of the capitalist restructuring of the society. In other words, the economic transformation is far from being consolidated (e.g. Schmidt 1996a: 9), nor has the internal transformation of east German companies been completed (e.g. Beyse and Möll 1996: 15; Röbenack 1996: 161). Reißig (1996: 253) concludes that the 'system integration' succeeded but the 'social integration' did not.

More specifically, there is the concern in the industrial relations literature that although the formal transfer of the west German industrial relations institutions has been apparently successful, it does not imply that the institutions are working 'properly' (i.e. as in west Germany). A common argument is that east German works councils are too co-operative, and even incorporated into management rather than being independent bargaining partners, and are therefore not able to provide effective interest representation (e.g. Jander and Lutz 1993a; Mahnkopf 1991: 275, 1993: 17). For example, Kädtler and Kottwitz (1994: 19) argue that although the institutions exist, the necessary network of informal and formal norms, habits, co-operation, and forms of conflict resolution between the actors has not yet been achieved in the east (also Reißig 1993: 18). Fichter (1996: 2) talks of the 'uncompleted crucial step from institutional transfer to institutionalisation of industrial relations' and even Wiesenthal (1996: 283) refers to an 'absence of actors' (*Akteurslücke*). Eisen (1996: 44) talks of specific 'socio-cultural legacies' of the socialist system. Offe (1994: 78) emphasises a 'cultural lag' and refers to the lack of actors' legitimisation of their new institutions. Others declare a mismatch between the 'foreign' west German institutions and a different, partly incompatible east German culture (e.g. Dathe and Schreiber 1993; Zapf 1992: 8). Moreover, Hyman (1996: 607) argues that a temporary mismatch is inevitable since 'any comprehensive cross-national transplantation of institutions creates a new regulatory system with whose principles and dynamics the local actors are unfamiliar'.

Finally, some analysts point to the potential negative repercussions of the east German transformation on the west. They stress the strains and pressures of the east German industrial relations outcomes on the stability of the German political economy (e.g. Martens 1996: 174; Mahnkopf 1993; Streeck 1997). Mahnkopf (1993: 27), for example, speaks of a German Mezzogiorno becoming established in east Germany, and concludes that the future of free collective bargaining in Germany is uncertain because of the overwhelming pressures on trade unions in east Germany. In a similar vein, Jacoby (1994: 1) adds that the transformation in east Germany 'may end up leading to the largest institutional break point in post-war west German history. . . . Germany is caught between the political costs of exposing the eastern economy and workers to the full force of the western system and the economic costs of cushioning the blows'. He concludes that 'under the cover of this dilemma, eastern Germany is quietly building a different kind of political economy'. Last but not least, Hyman (1996) foresees an 'easternisation' of the west rather than a 'westernisation' of the east.

There are various reasons for the wide spectrum of opinions on the success or failure of the east German transformation. It might be partly, as Jens Reich cynically claims in *Die Zeit* (1995), that people seem to have their *a priori* normative assumptions about the east German case and hence 'choose whatever empirical evidence they can find which fits their *a priori* defined conclusion' (quoted in Lutz *et al.* 1996: xiii). However, a more straightforward reason for the divergent interpretations is clearly the different reference points. As Seibel (1996: 359) suggests, the notion of 'institutional transfer' implies a comparative evaluation of its success. Hence, if east Germany is being discussed in terms of the current challenges and the future of 'Rhine Capitalism' (Albert 1993), it provokes a different judgement than if its case is debated in the context of the transformation from socialism to capitalism in central and eastern Europe. More importantly, however, is the fact that the debate on the east German transformation is often flawed by a failure to provide a holistic picture which integrates all dimensions of institutional transfer.

Conceptualising institution building

When discussing institutional transfer or institution building it is useful to distinguish between two dimensions of institutions,[3] described by Eisen (1996: 38) as 'structural' and 'cultural'. These are similar to Offe's (1995: 48) functional or external effectiveness and normative or internal socialisation classifications. Others refer to exogenous and endogenous dimensions of the transformation; formal (legal) and substantial (normative); system integration and social integration (e.g. Wiesenthal 1996); or material and cultural (e.g. Hyman 1996: 630).

With regard to the transfer of industrial relations institutions into the east the structural dimension refers to the legal implementation of west German institutions and regulations, including the take-over of the socialist unions, which was indeed successfully completed in a very short period of time. It also refers to the structural fit of these institutions in its new environment at a meso level. For example, are the social partnership institutions appropriate in the specific context of the radical east German economic transformation and its subsequent problems? And does this allow institutional actors to interrelate with each other in the same way as they do in the west?

The cultural dimension is somewhat more complex to describe. Granovetter introduced the concept of the cultural (social) embeddedness of economic institutions (1985) and refers to the need to have functioning institutions embedded in 'appropriate' social relations, or in a 'complementary culture'. Similarly, Jacoby (1995: 2) highlights that a successful institutionalisation 'must be pulled by social actors rather than decreed by policy makers alone'. Roller (1992: 1) specifies 'the cultural component as certain values, attitudinal orientations and behavioural dispositions of the involved actors that are congruent to the institutional structure'. Almond and Verba (1963: 4) refer to the parts of the 'political culture' which are relevant for institutions to survive and be centred around the participatory orientations of citizens. Eisen (1996: 35) describes it as the symbolic–cognitive meaning of institutions, and highlights integrative function of the normative dimension. Finally, Merkel (1995: 41) points to the necessary legitimisation of actors of their institutions.

When adopting these interpretations to the study of labour institutions it seems reasonable to assume that functioning labour institutions rely on appropriate attitudes and behaviour of workers, respectively union members. Union members' commitment seems to be especially essential for the establishment and functioning of unions in post-socialist societies given the dramatic changes that have recently occurred in union–membership relations. Such changes include the switch from 'obligatory' membership of a socialist 'service station' to membership of a modern interest institution as well as the installation of works councils, which are a new institution for most east Germans (a few older workers experienced them before or during the war). If labour institutions are to be effective, union members need to share the values of trade unions, trust their unions and works councils, have solidaristic feelings towards their co-members and be willing to participate in collective action. Without this commitment and support, the functioning of such institutions will be curtailed.

It has been frequently argued that the successful institutionalisation of works councils and also of unions in the east is partly hindered by the lack of a complementary culture of its actors and in particular of workers (union members). In other words, because union members are regarded as being more individualistic and instrumental in the east than in the west, they are more reluctant to engage in collective activities (e.g. Armingeon 1991; Artus *et al*. 1996: 2; Dathe and Schreiber 1992; Eidam and Oswald 1993: 167; Fichter 1996: 16; Gut *et al*. 1993: 50; Hyman 1996: 627; Kädtler *et al*. 1997; Lippold *et al*. 1992; Mahnkopf 1992; Mickler *et al*. 1996: 212; Neubauer 1992; Zech 1993: 28). Indeed, Mahnkopf (1992: 35) writes, 'there is only a small number of members who have an emotional relationship to the union, who identify with the content of union policies and are willing to participate in active and "self-responsible" collective action'. The increasing withdrawal from membership (during 1992 union membership in the east declined by 18 per cent to just under 3.4 million),[4] and the apparent lack of commitment and participation of members is interpreted by many as a sign of an individualistic, instrumental membership (see also Heering and Schroeder 1995: 176; Martens 1994: 314).

In light of the above comments, it seems appropriate to claim that both structural and cultural dimensions are required as criteria of viable, functioning institutions, and thus for the successful institutionalisation or institutional consolidation (Merkel 1995: 39) of the new labour organisations. Thus, institutional transfer and institutionalisation (transformation) are related but analytically different concepts.[5] According to Thompson *et al*. (1990: 21) 'institutions generate distinctive sets of preferences, and adherence to certain values legitimizes corresponding institutional arrangements'. Thus, a formal implementation of west German institutions in the east is a necessary but not a sufficient precondition for a successful transformation. As Hyman (1996: 631) points out, although institutional forms can be transplanted overnight – as was the case with German unification – their outcomes may be very different from those in the country of origin, for their functioning 'must rely on cognitive and moral resources which . . . are not to be created by administrative fiat'.

Resolving the micro/macro impasse

The idea that a complementary culture is necessary for the successful establishment and effective functioning of institutions is consistent with many recent empirical studies (e.g. Almond and Verba 1963; Fuchs and Roller 1994; Roller 1992; Shiller *et al*. 1991). This builds upon Max Weber's (1976: 122) conviction that democratic institutions function best when perceived as legitimate by much of the population. In terms of central and eastern Europe, Mayntz (1994: 23) pleads for research to examine simultaneously both meso and micro levels of the transformation. She highlights the potential tension between institutions and the individual behaviour of the actors during transitional periods and argues that the potential disintegration of both levels should be seen as being mainly responsible for institutional malfunctioning (also Lehmbruch 1993). In a similar vein, Eisen (1996: 39) argues that there is a need for research to reconstruct the transformation process focusing on the interrelationship between the two dimensions of institution building. He concludes that both the structural (formal) and cultural (normative) levels are interdependent and integral parts of a successful societal transformation rather than one being dependent on the other. Thus, actors' behaviour and attitudes are both conditions and consequences of institution building.

Unfortunately, one major deficiency of current research on the transformation of industrial relations in east Germany is the neglect of integrating the cultural dimension of the new institutions into the evaluation of the functioning of the institutions and the success or failure of the overall transformation process. As, for example, Pohlmann and Schmidt (1996: 192) point out, research on the micro levels of the economic (including industrial relations) transformation in east Germany is only just beginning. In particular, there is a lack of research on workers and union members. Most recent research has been preoccupied with the macro and meso (institutional) changes, resulting in an emphasis on the functioning of collective bargaining (e.g. Ettl and Heikenroth 1995; Hyman 1996: 611), union organisations (e.g. Fichter 1994; Mahnkopf 1992) and works councils (e.g. Artus *et al.* 1996; Kädtler *et al.* 1997; Kreißig and Preusche 1994). Sometimes these studies include analyses of opinions and attitudes of union officials, works councillors and also of managers, but rarely of workers or union members themselves. The micro or actor level of employees during the transformation has so far been largely ignored (exceptions are Andretta *et al.* 1994; Alt *et al.* 1994). As Andretta *et al.* (1994: 1) propose, this neglect might be due to the predominance of (macro) labour market problems (see also Dathe and Schreiber 1993: 30). It might be also due to the German academic tradition in the field of industrial relations, which is biased towards the analysis of institutions (e.g. Streeck 1981; Weischer 1993).

Another deficiency of the current research in the east German industrial relations transformation is that the published research on industrial and workplace relations is almost entirely based on expert interviews and/ or case studies of specific companies. More representative, quantitative studies have yet to be produced. In addition, while comparing their findings indirectly with a presumed west German situation, studies so far have not provided an empirically grounded comparative analysis. Indeed, having west Germany as a natural benchmark is clearly a distinguishing methodological advantage for the research on the transformation in east Germany as compared to other central and eastern European countries (see Seibel 1996: 359).

This book begins to overcome these deficiencies by providing a comparative quantitative study, the first of its kind, of the institutionalisation of new interest institutions and of the transforming workplace relations[6] in one specific sector of the east German industry, the clothing industry. Its prime focus is on the cultural embeddedness of these institutions at the micro, workplace level. Utilising survey data of union members in the east and west German clothing sector, it examines east German members' reactions to the labour institutions' efforts to transform themselves into viable, representative institutions.

In a nutshell, the book has three purposes. The first is to describe the institutional transfer of interest institutions and subsequent workplace transformation in one particular industry hitherto neglected in the transformation literature. The primary focus is on the functioning of the newly introduced works councils, a core feature of the German social partnership model at shopfloor level. The key question here is whether works councils are independent, co-operative and effective, rather than subservient, extended arms of management – as frequently argued in the literature – and thus ineffective in representing workers' interests.

The second purpose is to develop a methodology to explore the success of the cultural embeddedness of the labour institutions. This is based on an analysis of unionised workers' attitudes and behaviour towards their new interest institutions. For example, do east German workers accept their new (west German) collective interest representatives, and do they show as much commitment to such institutions as that displayed by their counterparts in the west who are familiar with their operation? Or, as is widely argued in the literature, are east German workers becoming strongly individualistic and hence not supportive of collective interest representation? The comparable data of west German members are used as a benchmark to evaluate the extent of workers' support in the east.

The third purpose is to explore in more detail the extent to which east German union members have different or similar attitudes and behaviour towards their collective interest representation as compared with their western counterparts. Here, the focus is on members' willingness to participate in collective activities, and the possible explanations for variation between individuals. By testing a selection of social-psychological theories associated with the willingness to participate, it should be possible to evaluate whether any of these theories adequately explain participation behaviour in the east German context and to what extent, if any, it differs from that in the west. In other words, are east Germans primarily characterised by an instrumental, cost–benefit approach to participation – as the literature predicts – and do their western colleagues approach collective activities differently, for example based on their identification with the union? Moreover, since these theories have only been tested in western, mainly Anglo-Saxon settings, this case allows us to examine whether the participation theories can also be fruitfully applied to a different, post-socialist context. Finally, since it is very rare for this set of theories to be tested simultaneously, the enquiry should also contribute to the general discussion of the determinants of collective activities.

The empirical part comprises a survey of both works councillors and union members in selected companies throughout the east and west German branches of the clothing and textile union, Gewerkschaft Textil Bekleidung (GTB).[7] In addition, regular interviews with union officials in the east German branch during 1993–4 were conducted together with an intensive case study of a major firm in the east German clothing industry. The latter included taped interviews with all managers and supervisors, works councillors, and a selection of workers during a two-year period (1993–4). Both sets of interviews helped in the design of the questionnaire as well as in data interpretation. This mixture of quantitative, qualitative and documentary methods has rarely been done in previous studies, but is regarded as a sensible methodology in a setting where empirical and theoretical research had to start from scratch (e.g. Giesen and Leggewie 1991; Meier 1991).

Finally, in applying social-psychological theories of collective action, the book tries to circumvent the descriptive character of most studies on transforming societies. It therefore avoids the limitations of most current empirical research on east Germany which is inductive and often lacks a clearly argued theoretical framework.

The clothing industry was selected for several important reasons. First, it represents a critical case study since its external conditions are more likely to evoke non-supportive than supportive reactions in union members. In other words, given the prevailing conditions, one might assume individualism to be the dominant behavioural norm amongst workers and managers alike. This, apparently, did not occur, and needs explanation. Second, this sector has so far been neglected in the industrial relations research on transformation, not only in east Germany but also in other central and eastern European countries. As Bergmann (1996: 258) notes, 'most east German research has so far focused on the metal and energy sector. There is a lack of research on industrial relations in the clothing and textile sector, the chemical or the service sector.'

To return to the first point, using the clothing industry as a critical test case entails discussion of the following four main conditions which have been associated in the literature with passive and individualistic workers. First, the east German clothing industry was (and still is) severely affected by unification and the subsequent exposure to the world market, and is one of the sectors in east Germany that has recovered least well (Küchle and Volkman 1993). For example, between 1990 and 1993 the sector lost 72 per cent of its net production, which in turn led to a dramatic reduction in employment (a decline from 98,215 employees in 1990 to 22,240 in 1995, GTB union statistics). Given the prevailing view that workers in periods of recession act less collectively and militantly than in periods of economic boom (e.g. Ingham 1974; Shalev 1983), such devastating economic and structural conditions should have induced especially low levels of collective activities and negative perceptions of institutional effectiveness amongst workers in the eastern sample. Second, the clothing industry in east Germany now consists of small-sized plants which are seen by some authors as evoking individualism (e.g. Barling *et al.* 1992: 116; Lippold *et al.* 1992: 99). Third, this should be further reinforced in the case of clothing workers who are traditionally (in the western literature) associated with a non-militant union and with a largely inactive, non-committed female membership (e.g. Lawrence 1994). Finally, the clothing union is a relatively unsuccessful union in terms of bargaining outcomes compared to the other unions in the east (e.g. Kittner 1995: 161).[8] In sum, this industry should provide a prime example of non-supportive reactions in union members. However, if the institutional transfer succeeded under such circumstances – and the evidence to be presented argues along this line – there is a strong case to be made that it also worked in other sectors of the industry.

The structure of the book is as follows. The next chapter (Chapter 2) begins by defining 'post-socialist transformation' as a particular form of social change. The chapter then goes on to summarise the socialist system of industrial and workplace relations and workers' attitudes in the former German Democratic Republic (GDR) which presents the basis for the transformation of industrial relations after 1990. Socialist workplaces were shaped by the simultaneous existence of formal bureaucratic regulations and informal networks and practices, producing a sort of 'pseudo-bureaucratic' or 'pseudo-Tayloristic' work organisation. With regard to workers' interest representation, it is argued that most workers did not feel that they were represented by the union organisation. Some workers, however, were able to use their limited passive strength (e.g. due to a labour shortage, and job security) to enter into informal bargaining on certain workplace issues with their supervisors, thus individually representing their interests. A question this study will address is whether these institutional and attitudinal legacies continue and whether the informal networks resist the current institutionalisation of interest representation at the workplace level.

The remainder of the book deals with the post-socialist era of workplace transformation and is organised into three parts: the first considers the institutional setting, particularly the transformation of workplace relations in east Germany; the second examines the cultural embeddedness of new labour institutions; and the third explains participation in collective activities in post-socialism. Part I (Chapters 3–5) analyses the institutional transfer of interest institutions and the transformation of works council–management relations in the east German clothing industry. In particular it deals with the central question of whether works councils are co-operative, incorporated or even conflictual in their relations with management. Chapter 3 starts with a description of the formal take-over procedure of the union branches of the FDGB (the former central union confederation) by the west German unions, of the establishment of the works councils, and finally of the most dominant changes of personnel management in the companies. The rest of the chapter reviews the literature on the development of workplace relations since 1990 by focusing on two principal questions: what are the characteristics of the evolving workplace relations and how effective are the new interest institutions? Most studies of this topic agree on the existence of co-operative attitudes in the newly established works councils but are divided as to whether the relationship between management and works council is co-operative or subservient. In other words, is there real co-operation between two more or less equally strong partners, or is the works council typically subservient and incorporated in management and therefore not effective in representing workers' interests? Both approaches are critically discussed. Chapter 4 analyses the quality of workplace relations in the clothing industry. It describes the wider industrial and workplace relations context of the clothing industry after 1990. This is followed by a detailed analysis of the works councillors' perceptions of their relations with management in a sample of selected companies in the east and west German clothing industry. Two major characteristics of functioning works councils, co-operative relations with management and an effective representation of workers interests, are examined. The questionnaire used for this combines background information on the companies and attitudinal questions on the workplace climate. It provides some initial indication that works councillors' perceptions do not significantly differ in the west and east and that they have in general co-operative attitudes towards management. Overall, the findings suggest that the works council institution in the east is developing, in only a very short time period, in essentially similar ways to works council representation in west Germany. Chapter 5 rounds up the discussion on changing workplace relations by introducing an in-depth, qualitative analysis of the transformation of a major east German clothing company, Bodywear, during the first five transitional years (1989–94). The focus is on the practice of workplace relations; thus it analyses the attitudes and behaviour of the two institutional actors – management and works council. The case study's findings of a harmonious relationship between management and works council (which is clearly not incorporated but quite independent) further support the quantitative findings of the previous chapter.

In sum, Part I explores the institutional transfer of labour institutions in the clothing industry, and finds co-operative workplace relations which do not differ significantly from the ones practised in the west. These findings are in contrast to the widespread assumption in the literature of subservient east German works councils. However, limiting the discussion on the institutional actors at workplace level identifies clearly the need to explore union members' perceptions and reactions towards their new interest institutions in order to evaluate the new institutions' effectiveness in their representative function. This is the topic of the two following parts.

Part II (Chapters 6–8) introduces an alternative but complementary approach to exploring workplace relations through the examination of union members' attitudes and behaviour. Chapter 6 reviews the literature on union member attitudes towards works council, union, management and fellow-workers during the transitional period since 1990. It identifies a major hypothesis of the individualisation of the east German union membership. It then critically discusses the explanations of union members' assumed reluctance to engage in collective activities that are offered in the literature. These explanations either refer to attitudinal legacies of the socialist past or else to the impact of the structural pressures of the transformation, but lack sufficient empirical substantiation. The null hypothesis of this book, which is subsequently tested, is that east German union members are significantly more individualistic, passive and negative about the institutions' instrumentality than their western counterparts. If that were supported one would conclude that the labour institutions had not yet been successful in establishing a supportive culture amongst the people they represent. Chapter 7 is devoted to the concepts and methodology of the union membership surveys which were carried out in the above mentioned clothing firms in the east and west. A scale is developed to test the extent of a supportive culture among union members. Functioning labour institutions are assumed to require three major attitudinal and behavioural attributes of their members: first, a commitment to collective values; second, a willingness to support the institutions actively; and third, a perceived necessity of the institutions and a positive evaluation of their performance. Each is discussed. The chapter finishes by introducing the demographic characteristics of the two survey samples. Chapter 8 discusses the findings of the membership surveys and compares the east and west German respondents in terms of the three dimensions of their cultural support. Central to these findings is that east German members revealed similar attitudes to those of their western colleagues and these were in most cases collectivist rather than individualistic and supportive of unions and works councils. This is in stark contrast to what is argued in much of the existing literature on this topic. Importantly, therefore, this provides the first substantiation for the successful cultural embeddedness of the labour institutions in this particular industry.

Part III takes the descriptive discussion of the membership surveys a step further and analyses the similarities and differences between the western and eastern samples in terms of their reasons for participating in collective action. Investigating people's inclination to collective participation provides a final test of the individualisation hypothesis and analyses whether east Germans reveal a more instrumental approach to participation than their western colleagues. Chapter 9 surveys the theories on participation in collective activities. Here, four major socio-psychological theories (rational choice, social identity, frustration–aggression and attribution) are critically evaluated. The chapter briefly summarises previous studies testing some of these theories together. It will be argued that the social-psychological theories might be complementary rather than independent, competing explanations of people's activism. Chapter 10 tests the different theories of participation in union and works council activities in the east and west German membership samples. It investigates whether any of the four approaches explains participation behaviour in east Germany and to what extent that differs from the west. Two findings stand out. First, in both samples no single theory yields encompassing predictive power. Instead the theories of rational choice and social identity yield the most significant antecedents and are strongly interrelated. In other words, both east and west Germans were primarily guided by collective and instrumental motives. Second, east and west Germans did not significantly differ in their approach to collective action. Thus, the finding that east German members were not exclusively guided by cost–benefit calculations in a context which makes instrumental approaches to collective activities highly probable (according to some arguments outlined before) reinforces the finding that these workers cannot be characterised as being less individualistic than their western counterparts and less supportive of their interest institutions.

The final chapter (Chapter 11) summarises the results with regard to the cultural institutionalisation of the new interest institutions and offers some concluding comments on future scenarios. Whilst much continues to change, and in many ways transformation is an ongoing process, the importance of this study is that it focuses upon a critical juncture in the period of transition. In doing this it allows us to examine the interplay of numerous variables against an unsettled institutional background, in an industry where the compelling evidence suggests a specific set of outcomes, and amongst actors whose behaviour is shaped by multiple, often competing forces.

2 Workplace relations in the former socialist GDR

This chapter outlines the major characteristics of the former socialist workplace relations in east Germany with particular emphasis on shopfloor informal interest representation as well as the attitudes that the workforce had towards their work, management and unions. Describing the past institutional framework and workplace practices helps to illustrate the extent or progress of the transformation of industrial relations.

2.1 Defining 'transformation' of industrial relations

'Transformation' is commonly used as a generic term to describe the various social changes and developments that are ongoing in post-socialist societies (e.g. Kollmorgen 1996: 282). The concept of 'transition' on the other hand has been challenged by some authors as value-laden and deterministic, which implies that these societies are inevitably 'on the road' to capitalism (Stark 1992a). Transformation in this study will be defined as a particular form of social change (e.g. Sztompka 1993a), more specifically as a 'process of changes in significant, typical characteristics of the structure, thus in the dominant institutions of a societal system' (Endruweit and Trommsdorff 1989: 799; Lockwood in Zapf 1969: 124). In other words, transformation describes a significant alteration of social structures, including the manifestations of such structures as embodied in norms, values, cultural products and symbols (Moore in Sills 1968: 366). It is a departure from a relatively stable social structure (Zapf 1994), and as such has a departure point (e.g. the old system of industrial relations) and an arrival point.

Within an industrial relations context transformation describes the changes of the entire industrial relations structure, not only of some actors and regulations but of typical elements and their interaction within the system. In central and eastern Europe, including east Germany, one can observe changes in the labour laws and in the state's role in industrial relations, the emergence of capitalist owners and employers, and the emergence of works councils and western-style trade unions. In addition, the social relations among the actors, their attitudes, norms and habits should change as well.

When speaking of transformation in industrial relations in central and eastern Europe, one needs first to clarify whether an industrial relations system actually existed, which is now being transformed, or whether we are currently experiencing the emergence of something new (for example as Kädtler *et al.* 1997: 17 argue). Answering this question obviously depends on the definition of industrial relations. For example, if one understands industrial relations to be 'the various interrelations between actors, institutions and regulations of capital and labour, as deriving out of an institutionalisation of class antagonism' (Geiger 1949) and stresses the irreconcilability of industrial conflict, then by definition no industrial relations system existed in socialism. The working class owned the means of production and class conflicts could not exist. On the other hand if one adopts a more structuralist definition of industrial relations as 'a network of social, legal, economic rules governing relationships of actors derived from an employment contract' (Schienstock 1982: 14), this can be applied to the socialist societies. Using the term 'transformation' thus inevitably assumes the latter type of definition of industrial relations.

It should be also noted that the term 'transformation' as applied to east Germany will be used for an ongoing process (e.g. Eisen 1996: 44). As indicated in the introduction, although the formal transfer of institutions has been completed and is not being further debated, this cannot be said of the cultural dimension of institutionalisation. The remainder of this chapter describes the starting point of the post-socialist transformation process.

2.2 Industrial relations in the GDR

The general elements of the industrial relations system under the previous socialist regimes in central and eastern Europe are well known and widely documented (e.g. Clarke 1995; Deppe and Hoß 1989; Dittrich *et al.* 1992; Héthy 1994; Széll 1992). Therefore only a brief overview of the formal system will be provided here. In essence, all central and eastern European countries practised the Stalinist model of industrial relations. This model evolved in the Soviet Union in the late 1920s and was introduced in the rest of central and eastern Europe in the late 1940s. The nationalisation of the means of production, along with a centralised planning system including strict norms and instructions for the production and distribution of goods, can be seen as the core elements of this model (Schienstock and Traxler 1993: 3).

Perhaps the fundamental theoretical assumption of this industrial relations system was that it constituted a single homogeneous, 'all-societal interest' system that encompassed all 'classes' (Héthy 1994). This societal interest is claimed to originate from the public ownership of the means of production and from the exercise of power by the working class. Consequently, one would argue from a system-theoretical perspective that the economic and political subsystems of the socialist society were not autonomous, independent areas (as 'ideally' they are said to be in western societies) but were heavily intertwined at formal and informal levels (e.g. Luhmann 1987: 32, 1989; Polanyi 1978). Similarly, the industrial relations actors (state, unions, employers) were seen to be united on behalf of the 'socialist construction' (*sozialistischer Aufbau*) (Héthy and Csuhaj 1990: 10) and could not be identified as being autonomous, independent actors. In other words, this industrial relations system expressed a unitarist view of the interests in society, thus denying the existence of differing/ conflicting societal and enterprise interests of the industrial relations actors. Consequently the exploitation of the working class did not exist in theory. Furthermore, collective labour disputes and conflicts of interests were looked upon as non-existent (strikes as actions of workers against their own interests were superfluous and forbidden by law). If divergences of interests appeared, they were interpreted as manifestations of individual misbehaviour, violations of the law or of the 'socialist morality', or as 'subversion' against the state, and were treated accordingly (Héthy 1991: 126).

In a highly centralised decision-making process the Party worked out the 'one best way' for joint action in industrial relations within the framework of a bureaucratic central planning system and closely supervised the realisation of targets set by similarly rigid bureaucratic control (Héthy 1991: 125). Thus it decided upon such matters as pay levels and the size of the workforce, and relied, in this respect, almost exclusively on legislation and law enforcement, and left no space for any (official) bargaining between the parties.

Within the enterprise, industrial relations formally consisted of three main actors: the Party's (SED = Sozialistische Einheitspartei Deutschlands) enterprise branch, the state union (FDGB = Freier Deutscher Gewerkschaftsbund) enterprise branch (BGL = Betriebsgewerkschaftsleitung) and the directors. In addition there were two minor actors: the secret service branch (Stasi) and the FDJ (state youth organisation).

The Party had representatives in each enterprise. These had four major, legally defined tasks: (i) to strengthen the ideological conviction of its Party members, (ii) to fight against imperialist influences, (iii) the political and ideological education of its members, and (iv) the education of its members in terms of discipline and work ethics (Autorenkollektiv 1978: 339).

The union enterprise branch (BGL) consisted of full-time officials and was subdivided into branches in each department. The role of BGL officials was described in the labour law as that of representing the interests of the workforce and fulfilling its constitutional rights (*Arbeitsgesetzbuch* 1977). The latter comprised the following explicit tasks:

> participating in the fulfilment of the plan, negotiating the work agree-
> ment, supporting the movement 'work, learn, live socialist', organising
> the 'socialist competition' between brigades [brigades = workgroup units],
> supporting the intensification of production and controlling the improve-
> ment of productivity and of the working conditions, participating in the
> vocational and political qualification of the workforce, participating in work-
> ing time/holiday issues, distributing flats and holiday places, improving

health and safety, supporting socialist work discipline, and participating in personnel policies (e.g. employment contracts, dismissals).

The terms 'manager' and 'director' were abolished in the GDR terminology, and instead such people were called 'socialist leaders'. Socialist leaders were by definition 'socialist personalities, who led as commissioners of the working class' (Autorenkollektiv, *Ökonomisches Lexikon*, Vol. H–P, 1978: 395). Their official duties were (i) to fulfil the plan, (ii) to foster the personal development of the workers to become real socialist personalities, (iii) to improve not only workers' working but also their living conditions, and (iv) to collaborate closely with the Party and union branch (*Arbeitsgesetzbuch* 1977).

The three main actors (Party, director and BGL) formed a triumvirate, constituting one single monolithic bloc of power. Their functions were inseparably intertwined. The Party assumed managerial functions on the top state level (e.g. determining production, material, wages), the employer performed state functions related to employment and social policies (e.g. guaranteeing full employment, taking care of the accommodation of its workforce), and the unions acted in the place of managers in operating incentive schemes to promote production and enforce discipline. The directors often had additional Party mandates or other social duties indicating an additional personal interweaving of these areas (see Kreißig 1993). Since the employers had officially no autonomous interests, it turned enterprise managers into the executors of the 'central will' of the economy. They were not free in their decision-making, they depended on the plan, and they were controlled externally by the higher bodies within the combine[1] and the responsible ministry, as well as internally by the union and the Party branch. Without the agreement of the Party branch leader, as well as the official of the state security (MfS), the director (who as an SED member had to comply with the SED directives anyway) could not make any decision. Additionally, the union officials were normally included in the collective decision-making, since they had to guarantee the realisation of the plans. In short, management discretion was limited and managers' prerogatives derived only out of their appointment by the Party and as formal commissioners of the working class. Thus, whereas in capitalist firms structures of control are a consequence of managerial strategies, in socialist firms they were a consequence of state strategies (e.g. decisions to introduce brigades or to start a new discipline campaign were made at the state level).

Since in theory there was a single predominant interest in the enterprise, and since the Party officially represented the working class, there was obviously no need for a representative body of the workers. The trade unions were therefore primarily 'transmission belts' between Party and workforce and 'schools for socialism' rather than representative bodies of worker interests. This union concept was developed by Lenin in the 1920s for socialist societies. The Leninist doctrine of dual-functioning unions, called 'classic dualism', can be seen in the two sets of union functions. First, there was the concern with mobilisation of labour production, thus the management of labour in terms of maintaining discipline, mobilising workers to higher productivity (e.g. via 'socialist competition', 'suggestion schemes'), educating them in the spheres of production, management and ideology. This is summarised in the often quoted Leninist description of unions as 'schools of administration, management and communism'.

Second, there was the concern with the protection of members' rights and interests which meant in essence guardianship of the legal rights of members against managerial arbitrariness and the defence of labour interests when necessary. Legally, participation and co-determination rights of the workers in the GDR were in many areas more advanced than in the west German law (see Belwe 1979: 216; Gill 1989: 379; Lutz 1991: 23; Pirker *et al.* 1990a). The labour law (*Arbeitsgesetzbuch* 1977) nominated the BGL (company union branch) as the holder of company co-determination rights. Thus, the BGL had the right to 'make suggestions and give comments to questions of company planning and management strategy'. In addition, the union branch was in charge of the internal grievance procedure.

Although the notion of dualism between the two functions implies parity, there is widespread evidence that in practice the 'production' function of the socialist union was far more important than the 'protection' function (e.g. Freeman 1993; Kirschner 1991: 1034). This functional bias stemmed directly from the concept of interests that underlies 'classic dualism', thus the absence of 'antagonistic' social conflicts within the socialist society. The unions were told to help resolve any possible minor discord and to ensure that it did not disturb the overriding harmony of relations between labour, management, Party and government. As a consequence the unions had to subordinate the protection of their members' interests to the promotion of Party policy, which axiomatically best served the true long-term interests of all union members.

The notion of unitary socialist interest was also reflected in two organisational tenets of the union. First, the production principle made all those employed (both managers and workers) in one sector eligible for union membership (i.e. socialist unions were industrial unions). Second, the widespread socialist organisational form of 'democratic centralism' was also applied to the union organisation. Thus, it is clear that unions were a highly centralised system of bureaucratic decision-making. Power was highly centralised and in addition became subject to outside control by the Party at all levels. The union remained closely subordinate to the Party. In addition, the close collaboration between management and Party officials within the enterprise severely restricted independent union activity.

Finally, the workforce was officially seen as co-owner of the societal property, and as obedient executors with their primary interest vested in an effective contribution to production and plan fulfilment (Héthy and Csuhaj 1990: 12). In theory they had an institutionalised grievance mechanism (see above) and extensive formal co-determination rights concerning their work and shopfloor decision-making (*Arbeitsgesetzbuch* 1977). The following section will discuss the very different practice that usually occurred.

2.3 Shopfloor reality in the GDR

The formal and informal system of workplace organisation

As with the system of industrial relations, the formal workplace relations of the socialist enterprises were designed in a highly bureaucratic, centralised way (Heidenreich 1991a: 417). Socialist firms were managed according to centrally decided-upon production plans and prices, in combination with the granting of assigned quantities of necessary materials, equipment and employees (see Heidenreich 1991a). The production system, work organisation and personnel policies are described as 'Tayloristic'[2] (e.g. Deppe and Hoß 1989: 84; Heidenreich 1991c; Voskamp and Wittke 1990: 14). Several authors point out that in reality, however, this system was constantly undermined by informal networks of individuals inside and outside the enterprise (e.g. Heidenreich 1991c; Voskamp and Wittke 1991a).

For example, in a western Tayloristic firm the systematic analysis and design of work and production processes might be understood as an attempt to intensify standardisation and productivity. In socialist firms, however, scientific management of the piece-rate system seemed to have had only limited influence on the real processes at the production level. The 'scientific method trainers' seem to have been hindered in their proper working and ended up confirming workers' entitlement to their workplaces and their existing piece-rate payment (Heidenreich 1991c: 423). Such entitlement was made possible by workers' tacit control over the workplace which often enabled them to subvert management oversight and engage in 'faking' behaviour (i.e. piece-rate manipulation). Furthermore, since the hierarchical organisation did not provide sufficient formal cross-co-ordination between the departments,[3] employees had to step in and create linkages themselves within and between the enterprises. In other words, the market which was otherwise absent was nonetheless supplied by a 'quasi-market' of personal contacts, networks and bribery ('I'll help you if you help me') (Fritze 1993b: 186). Thus, the work organisation became 'politicised' and 'personalised' (thus undermining bureaucratic rules and formal organisation by personal contacts and 'connections'). There is widespread evidence that it was especially frequent when shortages in production material deemed it necessary to organise in this way (e.g. Heidenreich 1991c).

In sum, these authors suggest that scientific time-and-motion studies, the piece-rate system and the formal organisation had little real impact on the processes on the shopfloor. There is widespread agreement that a parallel structure of formal, rational, scientific principles of organisation on the one hand, and informal organisational practices on the other, characterised the socialist organisation (e.g. Deppe and Hoß 1989; Heering and Schroeder 1992; Heidenreich 1991c; Voskamp and Wittke 1990). However, there is a division of views among academics as to how to interpret this co-existence of formal and informal organisation.

The system has been described by one group of authors as a 'pseudo-bureaucracy' or as 'pseudo-Taylorism' (Alt *et al.* 1994: 54; Heidenreich 1991b: 18, 1992: 6), 'quasi-Taylorism' (Makó and Simonyi 1987), 'reduced Taylorism' (Deppe 1991), 'double reality' (Weltz 1988), 'divergence between the formal structure and reality' (Voskamp and Wittke 1990: 23), or 'noncontractual relations' (Rottenburg 1991: 306). Clearly, informal sectors are not uncommon on capitalist shopfloors (e.g. Brown 1972; Donovan Report 1968; Hill 1974), but in socialist firms its presence was quite distinctive. Thus, in contrast to the socialist case, informal negotiations in capitalist enterprises exist within and are restricted by the formal industrial relations institutions (Heidenreich 1991b: 15). An important corollary according to these writers is that the position of workers towards management was more powerful than in the west and formal disciplinary rules and motivation strategies were less influential.

Other writers, however, question whether the postulated Tayloristic system was really the official, formal system, since the 'official collectivist ideology is not compatible with the Tayloristic ideology' (e.g. Alt *et al.* 1994: 54; Gensior 1992: 273; Schmidt 1995: 2). In their view the importance of the work collective was fostered by the state ideology which was supposed to integrate the 'whole' personality of the worker. Thus, these authors do not view the informal networks or the work collective as deviating from the official doctrine but as the major official characteristic and thus prefer the term 'bureaucratic paternalism' (Deppe and Hoß 1989: 25) to 'pseudo-Taylorism'.

The strong shopfloor position of workers

Despite the above mentioned differences, there is an overall agreement amongst researchers that informal negotiations existed on the shopfloor – not only in east Germany but in most other central and eastern European countries. Furthermore, such negotiations should be interpreted as an important outcome and also as a source of strength of the workforce at shopfloor level (e.g. Deppe and Hoß 1989; Fritze 1993b; Heidenreich 1991c; Kreißig 1993; Rottenburg 1992). Burawoy (1992: 35) quotes a well-known Hungarian shopfloor joke which illuminates this point well:

> There are three workers: an American, a west German, and a Hungarian. The American eats five eggs and a steak for breakfast and goes to work in his Buick. At work he is exploited. The west German has three eggs and ham for breakfast and goes to work in his Opel. He is also exploited at work. The Hungarian has one egg for breakfast and no meat. He goes to work on a bus but he is not exploited. At work he rules.

The literature defines a 'strong' workforce in terms of its bargaining power in workplace negotiations. Authors generally argue that the strength of the socialist workers' position was fostered by official policies such as a highly stable rate of pay, a high level of indirect income (subsidised rents and goods, as well as company welfare services) and low taxes (5 per cent for blue-collar workers). Moreover, it is said that it was quite common for highly skilled, productive blue-collar workers, especially those doing piecework, to earn a similar if not higher wage than their superiors and white-collar staff.[4] Additionally, there is evidence of workers' bargaining power in informal negotiations. For example, Heidenreich (1991b) notes that working time was often not used productively (some cases report 30 per cent of the working time not being used), work intensity was low, and the frequent disruptions in material flow were used extensively for breaks.[5] Lohr (1992) argues in her study of eight firms in east Berlin that although the socialist enterprise aimed to create a holistic welfare/care system which was intended to produce political conformity, there were various indications that this did not prevent interest negotiations and conflicts on the shopfloor. The workforce frequently regulated their mode of working and their co-operative relationships amongst themselves, largely independently of formal standards. Thus, workers' contact with the company's hierarchy is said to have been mediated above all by their informal negotiating relationships with their supervisors. Major personnel issues (e.g. overtime, piece rates, shift work, breaks) were often informally negotiated between workgroups and their supervisors, who had no real authority.[6] Lohr concludes that conflict regulation was determined not by institutional, written rights and duties, but through the real power positions of the actors and that this was arguably advantageous for the workers, not for the management at that time (1992: 160). In a nutshell, she asserts that the formal interest representation of the union (BGL) was marginal (also Kirschner 1991: 1034; Kreißig 1993: 120). In other words, informal negotiations at shopfloor level provided the interest representation that was otherwise lacking (Voskamp and Wittke 1991a: 32). Authors agree that although the BGL sometimes did provide a route for grievances, it never provided a real 'voice', and thus representation of workers' interests. The union mainly promoted workers' involvement in production, and subordinated any short-term preferences of the workers to the overriding interest of economic growth.

Reasons for informal networks

There are various reasons given for the informal networks and the supposed 'passive strength' of workers. First, they were a result of the permanent shortage of labour in the socialist 'shortage economies' (Kornai 1986) with supervisors dependent on their workforce. Labour, like other production factors, was utilised inefficiently and stockpiled. Due to the 'soft budget constraints', companies had no interest in utilising labour economically and wage costs were in any case low due to the high living-cost subsidies. This made the enterprise dependent on worker compliance when extra work was needed or when production bottlenecks arose. In other words, workers had to agree to work in 'impossible' working conditions with overtime and insufficient material rather than being forced to do so. Second, the extensive legal protection against dismissals (i.e. right to work, job security) suspended traditional management controls and disciplinary measures, and limited the possibilities for motivation policies (e.g. Heidenreich 1992: 8). Third, the low turnover and (geographically) decentralised production units and company social functions (leisure facilities etc.) fostered a very cosy, personal atmosphere and sense of community which supported informal relations. In addition, it has been argued that the supervisors were often former workmates (and often not the best ones, because of the absence of monetary incentives to become a supervisor) (e.g. Alt *et al.* 1994: 84; Heidenreich 1991b: 12). Moreover, the competition between and within the hierarchical levels of the enterprise was low due to small income differences and other 'equalisation' policies (Diewald 1995: 235). Fourth, the GDR's official image as 'the state of workers and farmers' and management being officially the commissioner of workers, added to the social status of the workforce at shop-floor level. Fifth, as mentioned above, management actions were 'personalised' and 'politicised' and thus not always guided by economically rational criteria. Sixth, the limited autonomy of firms forced managers to conform to externally made decisions. Any confrontation with superiors was therefore dangerous in terms of their own career. Accordingly, management feared any industrial unrest amongst their workforce, and this fear took precedence over the aim of increasing labour performance (Fritze 1993b: 201; Kreißig 1993: 111). Furthermore, it is argued that the absence of real interest representation by the unions forced workers to represent their interests on their own. Lastly, the informal negotiations and networks, although they increased the power of workers, were also beneficial for both sides. For management they met the official objectives (ensured worker compliance), and for workers they rendered their work life as comfortable as possible (Voskamp and Wittke 1991a: 31). Thus, there was a practical rationale for working on this slow track, because effort was not rewarded: 'You sometimes worked for four hours and were paid for eight' (worker quote in the Bodywear case study, see Chapter 5).

The research literature speaks of a 'plan fulfilment pact' (*Planerfüllungspakt*) between workers and management/supervisors (Heidenreich 1991c, 1992; Kern and Land 1991; Voskamp and Wittke 1990: 25), or 'emergency communities' (*Notgemeinschaft*) (Senghaas-Knobloch 1992: 300). In some sense both sides profited, but with regard to the economy and society as a whole this practice was not beneficial at all. Although the enterprise achieved considerable flexibility and some kind of worker compliance, the informal contract fostered worker indifference towards production and product quality. Thus, the 'politicisation' of the work organisation is often used by authors to explain the structural inflexibility of the enterprises (despite their strong potential for improvisation) and the aversion to innovation is seen as a major characteristic of socialist firms in the GDR (e.g. Heidenreich 1992: 11). Authors conclude that the informal system was complementary to the formal system but at the same time undermined it. Thus, the informal system increasingly undermined and provided a substitute for the formal system, but paradoxically also stabilised it at the same time.

Problems of this literature

From the above literature on informal networks, five issues merit brief discussion. First, as mentioned above, the literature is entirely based on retrospective data (since GDR scientists did not commonly research the practices of workplace relations), which inevitably implies methodological problems (see Diewald 1995; Marz 1992b; Lange 1992). As Marz (1992b) for example argues, people easily tend to conceive the past in a different, rosier light from what it really was.

Second, it is questionable whether the informal networks also inevitably incorporated informal bargaining arrangements. For example, in this book's case study (Bodywear), informal personal networks existed in former times, yet there is little evidence that workers were also involved in heavy informal bargaining with their supervisors. Moreover, one could argue that much happened in a rather indirect, implicit way. For example, coming to work late is not an indicator of an active, conscious bargaining between the two sides.

Third, one can argue that even if workers had a relatively high degree of control over the production process, it does not necessarily mean they had actual power (see Clarke 1995). For example, they could only escape from potentially dissatisfying working conditions in individual ways (e.g. absenteeism, alcoholism, low motivation, psychological withdrawal and poor discipline), since they had little possibility for collective resistance. In Hirschman's terms (1982), there was no 'voice' available and 'exit' was limited (i.e. the working conditions were not significantly different in other enterprises). Furthermore, one should not think that informal bargaining was always free of problems and friction. Workers were never sure exactly how far they could go and there were obviously conflicts between workers; thus older workers may not have been keen to get overtime work, whereas the younger ones wanted the extra pay (see Freeman 1993b). Finally, some authors state that workers were mainly reacting rather than becoming pro-active (Kirschner 1991: 1035). This can be partly explained by the limited scope of action (e.g. limited bargaining scope at the shopfloor, since much was decided at a higher level, i.e. by the Party; see also Clarke *et al.* 1993: ch. 1). To conclude, several authors have pointed out that the strong position or bargaining power of the workforce on the shopfloor can only be seen as a form of 'passive strength' (Kern and Land 1991; Voskamp and Wittke 1991a) or 'informal power' (David 1992: 130).

Fourth, a related question is that of workers' power. Studies of Hungary have suggested that there was a significant distinction between core and peripheral workers (Burawoy 1985). Core workgroups took the key role in informal negotiating whilst the rest were more passive. Core workers had a strategic function in the production process or were in important departments (e.g. export) with high qualifications; peripheral workers were in less important, less well-paid jobs and found it more difficult to participate in bargaining. With regard to the GDR, Diewald (1995)[7] found that the 'social quality' of the interpersonal networks at the workplace in the retrospective perception of workers varied little between different occupations and income levels. However, as with Burawoy's findings, the perceived (material) usefulness of the networks was seen to vary between job levels and industrial sectors. For example, they were perceived as very useful in the metal industry rather than in industries with lower political status (and hence less bargaining scope), and white-collar workers perceived them as more useful than did blue-collar workers. Moreover, Diewald found that women were less likely to perceive the networks as instrumental than men, a finding which cannot be traced back to job segregation alone. It seems that females were generally less integrated into these networks than males. On the other hand age cohorts did not seem to matter in his sample. Diewald concludes that informal networks did not necessarily even out imbalances but rather increased existing inequalities amongst different types of workers (e.g. skilled/unskilled, male/female).

Finally, the degree to which informal bargaining substituted entirely for official worker representation is still a moot point. Rüthers (1972: 43, quoted in Bust-Bartels 1980) for example mentions that 85 per cent of the conflicts over labour law were regulated by the official conflict commission. There is also evidence of cases where the union branch tried to foster workers' interests. For example, Kreißig (1993: 110)[8] explains that the union branch sought to achieve its ends mainly through collaboration and not confrontation with the directors. Differences had to be settled through amicable negotiation and not by adversarial collective bargaining. Where management really infringed upon members' interests (e.g. health and safety), the union might have protested and referred matters to higher authorities for arbitration. Obviously, there was no room for industrial action, strikes being seen as symptoms of union failure rather than legitimate weapons. However, Kreißig found that in many cases the management agreed to workers' demands in order to avoid unrest and 'scolding' from above. In addition, in some cases the good connections of union officials with the political leaders or union ranks could well undermine the power of directors and Party officials in the enterprise. Nevertheless, Kreißig does not want to suggest that the union branch was anything more than a 'moderator' and 'buffer' for management policies (1993: 120).

In sum, the outlined methodological and contextual problems urge us to avoid too general conclusions on the former socialist workplace relations. Informal networks might have played a larger role in some workplaces than in others and for some workers more than others. However, there can be no doubt that informal networks and a certain degree of workers' bargaining power did exist in most socialist workplaces and that this might cause problems for the current transformation, and therefore the formalisation of workplace relations.

Having discussed the institutional framework of the former industrial relations system, the discussion now turns to the attitudinal legacies of the workforce. The next section summarises workers' reactions to the socialist workplace relations.

2.4 Socialist workers' attitudes

Studies on workers' attitudes towards their work environment were rare in the GDR and there are also not many current (retrospective) studies on this topic. The existing studies will be summarised with regard to four issues: (i) workers' attitudes towards work and management (job satisfaction, them-and-us feelings), (ii) workgroup solidarity, (iii) interest representation and (iv) attribution of workplace problems.

Work and management

Based on the scarce evidence available it seems that workers in the GDR were generally *dissatisfied* with their working conditions (e.g. Miethe *et al.* 1989; Voigt 1973). Miethe *et al.* found 77 per cent of their sample 'totally dissatisfied' with their working conditions in 1989. In 1988, a more detailed, national representative study of employees (IU88, 1988) revealed that 68 per cent of the respondents (1,037 persons) were satisfied with the comradeship at their workplace, but only 43 per cent with their participation rights,[9] 33 per cent with their performance-related pay, and 23 per cent with their working conditions (quoted in Gensicke 1992: 17). Only 39 per cent were satisfied or very satisfied with their work in general. These results became more negative over the years (see IU77 in 1977, also quoted in Gensicke 1992). Voigt (1973: 75)[10] found in 1965 that more than 50 per cent of his construction workers were 'more or less' satisfied with their work. However, when asked about their general associations if they hear the word 'work' (positive, negative, half and half), most workers answered 'half and half'. Asked whether they would generally like to change their job, 40 per cent said no, 25 per cent said yes and 35 per cent were undecided. Voigt compared this with the results of a similar question in a survey of west German metal workers (of the Mannesmann AG) in 1955 which resulted in 70 per cent saying no. He concluded (p. 80) that the construction workers (the best-paid workers in the GDR) had a lower job satisfaction than workers in west Germany. However, this seems to be a hasty conclusion, since the comparability of the surveys is not discussed.

Furthermore, Voigt argued that 'socialist work commitment' (the idea that people should work out of their commitment to the socialist community, not for money or individual ambition) was not established in reality and that workers had instead a highly instrumental approach to work (p. 86). For example, more than 90 per cent of his sample perceived their pay as too low (p. 81). In addition, 71 per cent gave the high pay as a reason for becoming builders, and for slightly more money they would consider changing their job (p. 121). However, dissatisfaction with pay does not exclude a commitment to work and so his conclusion again seems premature. Finally, Voigt (1985: 470) explained the increasing job dissatisfaction during the 1980s by the fact that the qualifications of workers were increasing in the late 1970s and 1980s but not the standards of their

work (also Graf and Miethe 1990: 1003). In addition, an increasing dissatisfaction with the political system and the economic stagnation during the 1980s
was brought into the workplace. Voigt (1985: 467) argued further that the protest manifested itself in a high inclination to escape, a retreat into privacy (and
niches) and an internal withdrawal from work. And Fritze (1993a) proposes
that after years of a planned economy the workforce lost their belief that the
plants belonged to themselves, or that their contribution and effort mattered
or paid off. However, both authors lack direct evidence for their observations.

Overall, one can conclude that the methodology of these studies is somewhat
problematic. For example, the use of very few, broad questions to tackle the
multi-dimensional concept of job satisfaction, the failure to examine causes for
the job dissatisfaction and the small empirical basis all prevent any generalising
of the findings to the whole of the east German workforce. Nevertheless, they
give an idea of the discrepancy between socialist ideology or official propaganda
and the real situation on east German shopfloors. Voigt's study, although not
readily generalisable to the whole east German workforce, provides an especially
interesting case, since construction workers were among the best-paid workers in
the GDR and had a key position in terms of work autonomy.

Some authors argue that *'them-and-us' feelings* (them = management,
us = workforce) did exist in former times (e.g. Haraszti 1974: 151, 1977;
Kern and Land 1991; Voigt 1973: 109). According to Kern and Land,[11] it was
typical for east Germans at their work or in public to make a sharp distinction
between 'top' and 'bottom': between the world above (of politicians, directors
and superiors, all of whom made workers' lives more difficult) and their own
world. Some writers (e.g. Kreißig 1992) argue that this orientation resembled
the them-and-us feelings of workers in west Germany in the 1950s (e.g.
Popitz *et al.* 1957). However, no study has explicitly or in depth dealt with
these feelings. Voigt (1973), for example, based his analysis on just one question
('if there are problems on the building site, what are the causes?', with the
following answers to choose from: 'administration/headquarters, brigade,
supervision of the site, do not know'; result: 74 per cent chose administration).
In addition, one might ask whether this kind of question is an appropriate
measurement of the concept or rather one which measures mere 'causal' attribution. Furthermore, it remains to be discussed whether these them-and-us
feelings existed for the same reasons as in the west (see also Chapter 8). Voigt
(1973), for example, argues that the dichotomy between top and bottom existed
independently of property and class relations, yet again does not provide
evidence.

Work group solidarity

It is well known that work was a central reference point in the socialist countries,
more so than in western countries, and this has consequently left an impact on
workers' former and possibly current mentality (e.g. Diewald 1995: 235;
Gensior 1992: 273; Senghaas-Knobloch 1992). Such a position is, for example,

supported by Voigt (1973: 82) who found that only 30 per cent of his surveyed workers wanted to stop working. This work commitment can still be found today, as for example interviews with workers at Bodywear revealed (see Chapter 5). When asked whether they would want to continue to work if they were to win in a lottery nearly all said yes, since they could not imagine a life without work.

Diewald (1995) explained the importance of the working life by noting that the workplace was a prime social place (i.e. where you met your friends) with this in turn supported by the official social functions of the firm (e.g. company kindergarten, doctors). His data also revealed that the social relations of the workplace (especially the informal networks) were not only important for people's working lives, but also for their private lives.[12] To what extent the former centrality of work evoked a strong 'company identity' (e.g. Allen and Meyer 1990; Guest and Dewe 1991) was not the subject of research in the socialist era. However, some studies have been done on workers' identification with the work collective (*'Arbeitskollektiv'*). There is widespread evidence for this concept in retrospective studies (e.g. Alt *et al.* 1994: section 1.2; Diewald 1995: section 5; Gut *et al.* 1993: 33; Lungwitz 1994: 307) but also in the 'real-time' study of Voigt (1973: 93). Yet, there is a debate as to what extent this 'workgroup solidarity' or 'collectivism' was sustained by official ideologies that invoked work as a form of familial solidarity (see Autorenkollektiv 1983: 77; Diewald 1995: 258), by personnel policies (e.g. brigades or group bonuses) or by the informal networks (e.g. Alt *et al.* 1994: 58; Fritze 1993b: 189). Or, to use Etzioni's terms, it could have been calculative or a form of moral solidarity (1975: 10). Rottenburg (1991: 322), for example, argues for the former, claiming 'it was more conformity and compliance than commitment, more a "mechanistic solidarity" than a real solidarity on the GDR shopfloor' (see also Senghaas-Knobloch 1992). He claims that shopfloor solidarity was a fiction, an 'emergency solidarity' which vanished once people were no longer dependent on each other, and once competition over money and social status started (i.e. after unification). According to Swartz (1990) the perceived community and warmth was merely 'the deceptive community feeling which only a ghetto can evoke'. In other words it was a pure survival instinct which inevitably breaks down after 'liberation'. In short, these writers are sceptical about the quality of the 'emotional' character of the informal networks and argue that the solidarity of the work collective should be better described as a 'cosiness within the cage or prison'. However, none of these writers precisely defines concepts (e.g. solidarity) nor backs them up with anything more than impressionistic empirical data.

On the other hand authors such as Gensior (1992: 273) interpret the informal networks as a real 'work community' and stress the emotional importance of these collectives. The *'Kollektiv'* also stood for comradeship, warmth, friendship and solidarity (see also Alt *et al.* 1994: 54; Gut *et al.* 1993: 33; Schmidt 1995: 5). Finally, Diewald (1995) provided evidence for the co-existence of various, both calculative and emotional, roles of informal networks in people's personal lives. This view is also consistent with his earlier argument that the impact and value of informal networks differ according to the type of worker.

Interest representation

As mentioned above, there is a widespread agreement in the literature that the state socialist union (FDGB) did not provide a satisfactory interest representation. However, empirical studies of workers' opinions are rare. Voigt's (1973) study is one of the few GDR studies that investigated the relationship of worker to union and Party. No current study deals with this issue in detail. Again, his findings are not generalisable, but they nevertheless provide some interesting insights. To his question of whether the FDGB or the Party (SED) represented workers' interests on the site: 74 per cent answered no and only 7 per cent yes. Most said 'they are all in cahoots with each other'. This is in line with an earlier hypothesis that the socialist system lacked an effective institutional interest representation for workers. Furthermore, to the question about what would they say to a colleague who is not a union member, 56 per cent said 'it's his/her own business', 26 per cent 'good', and only 2 out of 911 criticised the colleague.

Assuming that these findings suggest a high degree of disenchantment by the majority of workers in the former workforce (and a lot of anecdotal evidence supports this assumption), the fact that union density in the GDR was extremely high (97 per cent according to Glaesner 1989: 211) is quite remarkable. It tends to support the earlier argument that the main reasons for joining the FDGB lay elsewhere (i.e. in its social functions such as distribution of holiday places).

Causal attribution

There is a large (retrospective) literature on the psychological attribution mechanism of east Germans. According to Stratemann (1993: 16)[13] people in socialist regimes tended to externalise the causes of their problems and circumstances and avoided internal attributions. Externalising also means delegating responsibility to external authorities, another suggested east German characteristic (Alt *et al.* 1993: 31). In other words the cause of a social phenomenon was seen to be largely outside of oneself. This often made sense. For example, decisions about one's career were very much in the hands of the directors and planning committees. Even decisions about which profession one would like to pursue were not purely personal. People learned that most of the important situations in their lives, as well as daily decisions, were more or less out of their control. Marz (1993a: 11) pointed out that people also tended to make external attributions for their own failings/failures. He argued that, knowing what a burden it was to take on individual responsibility in the system, without any incentives or normative pressures to do so, and with the possibility of avoiding this responsibility, people became reluctant to assume it. For example, teachers were responsible for good marks, doctors for health, the work collective for day-to-day well-being, the union for holiday places, the state for social security, and so on.

It seems likely that this habit had an impact on people's personal and social identities. Avoiding personal responsibility makes people dependent on the system and on others, and hinders the establishment of realistic self-perception (Marz 1993a). It has been argued therefore that people often had a theoretical, unreal conception about themselves ('if I only could do as I want, I would . . .'). People's self-esteem and social identity,[14] it was claimed, were mainly based on these hypothetical convictions (e.g. Alt *et al.* 1994: 69; Belwe 1992; Marz 1993b). Besides, the permanent 'double life' (Henrich 1989: 109; Rottenburg 1992: 245) of the formal and informal/private roles made it more difficult to establish a 'normal' social identity (Marz 1992a: 230). Marz added that identity and individuality certainly did exist in the GDR, but that they were typically restricted to the private niches and could not effectively develop in the official work environment. A central question then concerns the implications that the above might have for the current attitudes and behaviour of the east German workers. Thus, it would be no surprise to see today a continuation of 'external' attribution habits and the avoidance of individual responsibility.

Summing up the above section on workers' former attitudes, the few studies provide some evidence that workers in the GDR were dissatisfied with certain working conditions, felt some sort of 'them-and-us feelings' towards management and a certain solidarity with their work colleagues. Most did not feel represented by the union and attributed their workplace problems to external actors. The studies are not generalisable to the whole east German workforce but nevertheless might help to interpret the attitudes of workers after unification.

2.5 Conclusion

This chapter emphasised the bureaucratic, hierarchical organisation of socialist enterprises and work organisation, the 'co-operation' between the three major actors at the top level (triumvirate) and the absence of an effective institutional representation of workers' interests (i.e. by the unions). Shopfloor life was characterised by informal networks and bargaining arrangements and yet was characterised by workers who felt dissatisfied with their working conditions and their official interest representation. In general workers were closely linked to their colleagues, differentiated themselves from the group of directors, and attributed their work problems to external actors. It should be noted that the discrepancy between the theory and practice of socialist workplace relations was by no means unique to the GDR but rather a common phenomenon throughout central and eastern Europe (e.g. Burawoy 1985; Clarke *et al.* 1993).

In sum, the chapter provided an overview of both the official and actual practices of the former socialist workplace relations and serves as a benchmark for understanding the subsequent transformation process. The institutional and attitudinal legacies might also have a continuing impact on the transforming workplace relations. In particular, it seems worthwhile to investigate whether those informal networks were succeeded by the formalisation of interest representation after 1989 and to what extent workers' attitudes have changed during the transformation. The former will be discussed in the following section, the latter in Parts II and III.

Part I

The institutional setting

Transformation of workplace relations in east Germany

Part I discusses the institutional context of the transformation of workplace relations. It starts by giving a broad historical overview of the institutional transfer of the industrial relations actors into the east and also reviews the literature on the institutionalisation of the works council in east German enterprises. Chapter 3 discusses in more detail the industrial relations transformation of the clothing industry and examines one characteristic of the institutionalisation of works councils – its willingness to co-operate with management. The final chapter provides an in-depth qualitative analysis of the organisational transformation and workplace practices of one case study, the largest clothing company of the east German union district.

3 Transforming socialist workplace relations

Co-operation or subservience?

How were the new industrial relations actors established in the east? How did the workplace relations develop? This chapter answers these important questions by describing the institutional transfer of unions and works councils, together with the transformation of management in east Germany after 1989. It further deals with the emerging workplace practices by focusing on the works council, its institutionalisation and its effectiveness in representing workers' interests.

3.1 The institutional context

The acquisition of the FDGB

After a short and failed attempt at self-rescue and reform, the socialist state union (FDGB) formally dissolved and the west German unions moved eastwards, taking over the socialist union infrastructure (e.g. Artus 1996; Fichter 1996; Fichter and Kurbjuhn 1993; Hertle 1990; Hertle and Weinert 1991; Hyman 1996; Klinzing 1992; Pirker *et al.* 1990a, b; Weinert 1993).

For a brief period after the fall of the Berlin Wall it seemed possible that independent trade unions might develop out of the FDGB and these might have merged at a later stage with the organisations in the west (Hyman 1996: 608; Pirker *et al.* 1990a). But this did not happen and the entire FDGB board of directors resigned by the end of 1989 and a special union congress in February 1990 voted for internal reforms of the FDGB. The main reform points were the manifestation of extensive union rights at workplace level, the rejection of the idea of introducing works councils and the decision to make their industrial union branches financially independent (e.g. Pirker *et al.* 1990a: 157). The latter decision opened the way to establish closer links to the parallel union organisations in the west. Observing these developments closely, the west German union federation (DGB) expected 'a thorough process of democratisation and decentralisation to ensue, and also that unions in west and east Germany would find a suitable basis for co-operative relations and possible amalgamation' in the long run (Fichter 1997a: 90). According to Fichter[1] the west German unions had no interest in the rapid acquisition of their socialist counterparts. But, as he goes on to explain, they seemed to have overestimated the political potential of the east German citizens' movement, which was quickly over-whelmed by the popular demand to become part of west Germany and gain access to the Deutsche Mark zone. Thus, after the landslide election victory of the CDU-led east German 'Allianz für Deutschland' in the east German election in March 1990 (the starting point of political unification), a take-over strategy with the goal of 'incorporation' assumed priority in Bonn (e.g. Artus 1996: 22; Fichter 1996: 7). Thus, the election was the turning-point of the reform attempts of the FDGB. The election results were interpreted as a clear plebiscite for a future political unification.

As the movement towards unification gained speed, the DGB unions then faced the choice of either 'mounting a breakneck effort to implement their organisational jurisdiction into the GDR or finding the eastern part of a united Germany virtually devoid of functioning unions' (Fichter 1994: 52). For example, DGB observers expressed the fear that east German union members were increasingly sceptical about the FDGB's efforts to reform itself which had led to increasing numbers leaving the union. Another fear was the scenario of a wage competition between the two countries (e.g. Artus 1996: 26). Armingeon (1991: 34) talks of a '*Zugzwang*' (tight spot) for the west German unions after the institutions of the west German social market economy and the collective labour legislation were extended to the east.

Within only a few months the west German unions then organised the juris-dictional and organisational expansion to the east and the liquidation of the FDGB which led to the successful 'take-over' of the membership. On 8 June 1990 the decision was made (within the DGB) to liquidate the FDGB a few months later (September 1990). The aquisition of the single industrial union branches started during the Summer of 1990 and the successful integration of members took place between Autumn 1990 and Spring 1991.[2]

This process was supported by the west German government, as well as by the west German employers' associations (BDA) which themselves hurried up to install regional subsidiaries in the east (see also Chapter 4) (Wilke and Müller 1991: 267). Thus, in a nutshell, the two social partners developed a common interest in transferring western collective bargaining instruments as quickly as possible to the east. In reaching this consensus the two parties seemed to have removed all doubt regarding the future of their established structures, norms and institutional arrangements in the unified Germany, which could also be interpreted as a move to reduce possible competition from the east (Artus 1996: 25; Fichter 1996: 5; Wilke and Müller 1991: 271).[3] Whatever the case, it required the establishment of employers' associations and trade unions in the east. And Lehmbruch (1996: 128) points to the organisational self-interest of both actors in overcoming uncertainties by drawing upon established regula-tions of the social partnership.

The acquisition strategy chosen by most west German unions is interpreted by many observers as 'a conservative (risk-avoiding) approach designed to retain maximum control over the many uncertainties ahead' (e.g. Artus *et al.* 1996; Fichter 1994: 53, 1997a: 91). It was described by many observers as a 'co-operative take-over' (e.g. Artus 1996: 32). Most unions (including the textile and clothing union GTB) did indeed take a pragmatic stance, arguing that it made sense to take advantage of the existing FDGB infrastructures and resources (buildings, vehicles, etc.). Eventually, the transformation resulted in the complete take-over of both members and union property and assets.[4] It should be noted that in most instances the east German side willingly co-operated (e.g. Artus *et al.* 1996: 32).

That the new union structure in east Germany turned out to be a copy of the western model and did not adapt to the specific circumstances of the eastern *Länder* was in the beginning seriously criticised by academic observers (e.g. Jander and Voß 1991). It was, for example, argued that most union acquisitions were not accompanied by any democratic 'discourse' or learning process or examination of whether there was anything worthwhile which could be kept from the socialist unions. There was also no common approach or discussion amongst the western unions about the possible challenges of the very different historical, cultural and socio-economic legacies in east Germany (Fichter 1997a: 91). Moreover, union leaders ignored grass-roots and shop-floor initiatives associated with the east German citizens movement and rebuffed all efforts by critical voices within their own camp to promote the idea of coupling the expansion process with necessary internal organisational reforms (e.g. Fichter 1997a; Mahnkopf 1991, 1993). However, Fichter argues that in their efforts to stay on top of the complex expansion process, the unions found simply no time for a comprehensive analysis of problems and prospects as a basis for strategy decisions, preferring instead to rely on tried policy options (1997a: 91).

It comes as no surprise that in most cases the new union organisations in the east were staffed by western officials – some of them recently retired; at most, one full-time official in five was an east German (Hyman 1996: 609). This reflected both the inexperience of east Germans in the functioning of the west German institutions, and the suspicions of the political past of former FDGB officials (Hyman 1996).

As a result the western expansion led to large gains in the German union membership in the two years immediately after unification (see Table 3.1). At the end of 1990 the DGB enjoyed a 49 per cent increase in membership (or 3,862,490 new members) (Kittner 1994: 91). This meant that in 1990 only 10 per cent of the east German workers failed to join the new western unions (Lecher 1990: 320). A year later, union density in the east was 42 per cent compared to 30 per cent in west Germany. Since then, membership has been declining throughout the country in the wake of economic recession and – especially in the east – massive de-industrialisation and job losses (Fichter 1996: 11; Wiesenthal 1994: 7). The dramatic increase in total membership was evidently a surprise for the western unions, many of which had expected a massive exodus of FDGB members (see Wilke and Müller 1991: 263). That this did not happen was possibly due to the heightened insecurity and loss of orientation throughout the rapid unification and transformation process. In other words, workers were fearful of the consequences of the introduction of the market

Table 3.1 Membership figures of the DGB

(31.12)	DGB total	DGB west	DGB east*	East per cent of total	West density (%)**	East density (%)
1989	7,861,000	7,861,000	—	—	30.5	—
1990	11,564,923	7,937,923	3,627,000	31.36	30.4	39.4
1991	11,800,413	7,642,587	4,157,826	35.23	29.6	42.2
1992	11,015,612	7,623,865	3,391,747	30.79	28.9	38.2
1993	10,290,152	7,383,500	2,906,652	28.25	27.6	35.2
1994	9,768,373	7,179,123	2,589,250	26.51	26.8	32.0
1995	9,354,670	6,994,292	2,360,378	25.23	26.2	29.5

Notes: * as of 1991 DGB east includes Berlin-west, ** density: membership in relation to labour force
Sources: Amtliche Nachrichten der Bundesanstalt für Arbeit (Sonderheft Arbeitsstatistik) for all years, Fichter (1997b), Kittner (1995); author's calculations

economy (i.e. unemployment, social security) and were convinced that the unions could help. Several authors even claim that there was a widespread belief amongst the east German workforce that west German unions could guarantee a quick improvement of living and working conditions (e.g. Fichter 1994: 56; Mahnkopf 1991) (see also Chapter 6).

Even such a large increase in membership cannot be assumed to have led to an increase in union power, and it is now clear that density figures in east Germany will eventually fall to the comparable west German level or even below (Fichter 1997b; Kittner 1994: 84; Mahnkopf 1993). By 1992, DGB membership had already decreased by 6.7 per cent; whereas the old *Länder* recorded a 0.2 per cent reduction, the new *Länder* showed a decrease of 18.4 per cent (Kittner 1994: 92). A year later, DGB membership dropped a further 6.6 per cent, with east Germany accounting for 64 per cent of the total decrease (*Die Quelle* 1994: 14). Losses among east German members under 25 years of age in east Germany have been particularly high, ranging between 20 and 25 per cent a year since 1992 (Fichter 1996: 13). The loss of members in the east has slackened in the late 1990s but there is still no certainty that a stable level of membership is within reach (Fichter 1996).

The establishment of works councils

As the institutionalised interest representation of the workforce on German shop-floors, works councils were forbidden in east Germany after 1946, when the SBZ (Soviet military zone) government abolished them and – against heavy resistance – replaced them with local union branches, BGL (e.g. Bust-Bartels 1980; Gill 1991; Lutz 1991; Suckut 1982). This was one measure that the GDR state took to change unions' from their traditional socialist defensive role to an industrial–political one within the construction of the socialist economy.

As mentioned above, following the turn-round in October 1989, there was a short period when the FDGB and the BGL tried to reform themselves but without any success. In contrast, a large number of enterprises (no precise numbers are available) established active groups within the workforce or within the BGL. The latter initiated the closure of the old BGL and established so-called 'worker councils'[5] as the new legitimate representation of the workforce. This happened even before the official introduction of the west German Works Constitution Act (BetrVG 1972),[6] and the works council legislation which together with other labour laws (e.g. 'the law against wrongful dismissal', *Kündigungsschutzgesetz*) on 1 June 1990 proved to be the starting point of the economic and currency union between the two German states (*Wirtschafts- und Währungsunion*). Thus, the west German labour legislation was implemented even before the political unification (3 October 1990).

Consequently, all existing 'unlawful' worker councils had to be newly elected under the German law, existing company agreements had to be amended, and works councils were introduced in places where they hitherto had not existed. All this had to be achieved within a two-year period (until 30 June 1992).

In most companies works councils seem to have been established from the mid-1990s onwards (earlier than the transfer of employers' associations and western unions). No data are available, however, on the precise number of east German firms with a works council (according to Niedenhoff of IDW, Institut der deutschen Wirtschaft in Cologne, telephone interview 1994, or Schneider in Kittner 1995).

The literature commonly argues that the activists who initiated the early worker councils were disillusioned by the local union's effort to represent workers' interests, and had lost their last remnants of respect and trust when the unions did not participate in the 'revolutionary' period in the enterprises (e.g. Kirschner 1991). Scholars are, however, divided on the reasons as to why these worker councils were established. The main point of contention is whether they indicate an interest by workers in 'industrial democracy' (improving workers' interest representation), or whether they were merely a vehicle to support management in introducing organisational changes.

One group, the WISOC institute in Chemnitz (e.g. the Ermischer, Kreißig, Lungwitz, Preusche), whose associates have carried out various case studies of companies in Saxony from 1989 onwards, indicate an interest by workers in employee participation, thus 'fulfilling the need of east German employees for self-realisation, to develop their own creativity, to be involved in decision-making processes, for general involvement and information' (e.g. Ermischer and Preusche 1995: 53[7]). They argue that worker councils were 'democratically elected forms of employee "bottom-up" participation, developed for the first time after more than 40 years' (ibid.).

Other authors (e.g. the Berlin/Göttingen project with Kädtler, Kottwitz, Weinert and Jander, Lutz)[8] are more sceptical, arguing that worker councils did not represent a push for democratic reforms in the socialist firms, but instead emerged as a result of political protests against the SED regime (in order to stop the 'red socks' in the enterprises, i.e. to get rid of the Stasi and the Party) and in support of the reconstruction of the enterprise. Industrial democracy is not seen to be the reason for establishing the worker councils, because they were not linked to any civic movements outside the firm and because people aimed for a restructuring process through harmonious workplace relations ('partnership'). WISOC, however, argues that improving employees' voice in the enterprise was one reason for the establishment of these councils.

To conclude, their different interpretations might well be due to their different empirical samples which may be indicative of nothing more than regional differences (Berlin versus Saxony, the centre of civic movement). However, a more likely reason seems to lie in their different understanding of 'industrial democracy', which neither side defines with precision. Furthermore, neither side provides explicit and sufficient evidence to support its views, and therefore to allow a final evaluation.

Management in transformation

Over a period of only four years (1991–4), the east German economy experienced the most rapid and radical restructuring and privatisation process within central and eastern Europe. Privatisation was understood as a once-and-for-all transition, in which productive assets were transferred from the (alleged) public sphere to (alleged) private control (Specht 1993). Any mixed or 'recombinant property' types as are typically found in other transforming countries (e.g. Stark 1995 for Hungary) were not allowed. The privatisation was under the control of a single state privatisation agency, the Treuhandanstalt, which quickly became the most important and most controversial institution in the transformation of socialist combines into privately owned, capitalist companies.

In brief, at its foundation in 1991 the Treuhandanstalt was entrusted with the administration of around 270 combines, employing about 90 per cent of the industrial workforce in east Germany. It thereby took over the assets and liabilities of over 100 billion Deutsche Mark of the east German combines. Its main duty was to decentralise the combines into sellable enterprises, to prepare the enterprises for privatisation (organisational restructuring) and finally to privatise them (paragraph 2 Treuhandgesetz, Article 25 Einigungsvertrag). In 1992, the Treuhand had responsibility for over 5,100 companies (Treuhand prospectus 'Entschlossen Sanieren' 1992: 17). By the end of 1994 and beginning of 1995, the Treuhand had completed its work of privatising most of the firms and was dissolved (being replaced by regional 'holdings'). The eventual sale of 15,000 individual firms produced gross proceeds, however, of only 30 billion Deutsche Mark, and at the time of its dissolution the Treuhandanstalt left a total indebtedness of 256 billion Deutsche Mark (e.g. Brücker 1995: 448).

The outcome of the Treuhandanstalt's work has been critically and divergently discussed in the public arena and in academia. According to some observers, the agency was extremely successful in the formal aspects of privatisation (e.g. Grabher 1995: 43). For example, by mid-1994, 51.7 per cent of firms from the original inventory of 12,335 had been privatised, 12.9 per cent reprivatised, 2.1 per cent transferred to the municipalities and 27.6 per cent liquidated (Treuhandanstalt Information 1994). On the other hand, a 70 per cent decline in industrial production and an almost total de-industrialisation of some parts of the economy led to a decline in job opportunities of almost 40 per cent (of total jobs in 1989) and to mass unemployment (15 per cent unemployment rate in 1994) (e.g. Kempe 1995; Wiesenthal 1994). Another outcome of the privatisation is the dramatic decrease in average company size: two-thirds of firms employed more than 200 employees in 1987; in 1994 two-thirds of firms employed fewer than 100 employees. In other words, three-quarters of the east German workforce worked in firms with 20–499 employees in 1994 (Schmidt 1996b: 232).

The privatisation process clearly influenced the pattern and speed of the organisational restructuring of the enterprises. For example, Grabher emphasises that the radical decomposition of the old formal socialist combines into separate sellable units also resulted in the dissolution of the pre-existing informal firm networks. This is in contrast to other post-socialist countries where they remained a characteristic pattern of the transformation (see Stark 1995 for Hungary). This paralysation of the informal networks in east Germany was a precondition, according to Grabher, for a smooth integration of the east German units into the western corporate networks. This proved to be the most promising route to capitalism since isolated plants, cut off from central research and development, distribution and administrative functions of their combine organisation, had little chance of survival since they were barely equipped with skills and (informal) mechanisms of self-organisation (Grabher 1995: 43–4). This lack of entrepreneurial experience basically resulted from the tight integration of plants in the former combines. Grabher concludes that, in this sense, the tight integration into combines seemed to preclude alternatives to a subsequent tight integration into western corporations (also Heidenreich 1994: 10–14). These corporations are predominantly of west German origin.

In light of the above, it comes as no surprise that west Germany was and is by far the biggest investor in the east. Just 10.7 per cent of investment and 9.1 per cent of job commitments in the privatisation of the east German economy were of non-German origin (Grabher 1993: 3). West German owners and consultants (who were already widely employed by the Treuhandanstalt during the privatisation process) clearly influenced the direction of the restructuring of east German firms (Pohlmann and Schmidt 1996: 202). In sum, both west German capital and the fact that the Treuhandanstalt had already started to invest in the organisational restructuring of the still Treuhand-owned companies – in contrast to the state-owned companies in other post-socialist economies – clearly led to a relatively speedy restructuring process.

Finally, although the privatisation processes were widely followed by academia and public alike, much less is known about the internal modernisation and restructuring process of the privatised companies (e.g. Peiperl and Estrin 1998; Bochum 1996). A large part of the existing research on organisational and managerial transformation deals with the modernisation process of one or more firms or of a whole industrial sector (e.g. Dörr and Schmidt 1992; Edwards and Lawrence 1994; Heidenreich 1993; Küchle and Volkmann 1993; Mickler *et al.* 1996; Niebur 1992; Wittke *et al.* 1993; and various KSPW[9] studies such as Beilicke 1995; Binus and Groß 1995; Brinkmann 1996; Chalupsky and Seifert 1995; Denisow *et al.* 1994; Glotz and Ladensack 1995; Schmidt 1996). Their main purpose is to analyse the effectiveness of modernisation and restructuring in terms of productivity and competitiveness, but are not necessarily concerned with its impact on workers' attitudes and behaviour.

A second stream of research deals with the transforming east German management. Interestingly, the import of west German managers into the east was less severe than initially expected. Thus, the share of east German managers in the top and middle managerial positions of companies in east Germany accounts for 87–9 per cent. If one adds to that supervisory levels, the share of east German managers is 89–93 per cent (Pohlmann and Schmidt 1996: 205).

Much of the research focuses on the demographic characteristics of the new managerial and entrepreneurial elites ('life biographies of the new elites') (e.g. Koch 1993, 1997; Matthäi 1996; Pohlmann and Gergs 1996), and on their current structural constraints and strategic choices (e.g. Glotz and Ladensack 1996; Lang 1994; Pohlmann and Schmidt 1996; Windolf and Wegener 1993). Overall, these studies reveal two major characteristics of east German managers. First, most east German top managers have a managerial background. Thus, most had a middle managerial position in the former combines and are between 45 and 50 years old. For example, in the industrial sector nearly 90 per cent of all east German top managers were former socialist leaders (Pohlmann and Gergs 1996). Second, most east German managers have an academic qualification and their share is even larger than among west German managers (Pohlmann and Schmidt 1996). Moreover, their academic degrees are predominantly in technical or natural sciences. Pohlmann and Schmidt speculate that this educational background will induce a strong scientific–technical perception of their managerial tasks (i.e. engineer culture, '*Technikerkultur*') and how they deal with the production restructuring. There is some case-study evidence to support this hypothesis (Glotz and Ladensack 1996; Köhler 1995; Lang 1994; Windolf and Wegener 1993).

Furthermore, there are a few studies which specifically deal with personnel management issues in the east (e.g. Becker *et al.* 1996; Schuldt 1994). This literature, however, provides in most cases only a descriptive account of the changes of the personnel management functions and personnel policies (e.g. handling of dismissals, new selection processes, building up a personnel department). As far as I know there is no specific research which focuses on managers' changing perceptions and role in collective bargaining and towards workers' interest institutions.

Finally, there are several studies on the changing work organisation (production process) in east German enterprises. These will now be briefly reviewed.

Overall, it is argued that east German enterprises predominantly attempt to adopt the prevalent west German model of a 'flexible quality production' and focus primarily on upgrading their technical equipment rather than, for example, on making their workforce more flexible (Bochum 1996: 42). Two different tendencies are taking shape with regard to the social relations of the production process (management–workforce relations).

One group of researchers argues that we are seeing innovative, socially engaged managers who introduce 'innovative', employee-oriented personnel methods (such as human resource management). Managers are therefore seen to build on the old informal partnerships and networks on the shopfloor and to be attempting to get the workforce to agree to a new 'modernisation pact' instead of the old shopfloor 'survival pacts' (see Bluhm 1992; Kern and Voskamp 1994). This view is supported by the WISOC group. For example, Preusche (1994) argues that east German managers in her sample (twenty-three managers of seven companies in the Saxon metal industry) were, due to their prior social-isation, more 'humanistically oriented' and thus desired harmonious employee relations. Furthermore, Lang (1992: 139) found in his comparative study of (155) west and (291) east German managers a more 'co-operative and social orientation' in the east German work behaviour. In the same vein Stratemann (1993: 21) showed in her study on economically relevant personality character-istics of east Germans that east German managers score a stronger 'responsibility for employees' than their western counterparts.

However, one can argue that this proposed 'social behaviour' does not neces-sarily mean that east German managers will install employee involvement schemes. Neither does it say anything about management's relationship with the works councils. It may equally lead to a patriarchal form of employee rela-tions, with works councils being ignored. It would also be natural to speculate about whether most new management techniques are typically being introduced by the western headquarters rather than on the initiative of east German man-agement. Furthermore, Heidenreich (1993: 94) argues that it is utopian to think that under the current labour market circumstances companies could build on the old 'survival pacts'.

The other, more pessimistic, group of researchers argues that these innovative enterprises are rare exceptions, islands largely cut off from their surroundings, or 'cathedrals in the desert' (Grabher 1993: 18) and mostly to be found in the automobile industry (e.g. Volkswagen in Saxony, General Motors (Opel) in Eisenstadt, see Brinkmann 1996; Mahnkopf 1993: 5;[10] Mickler *et al.* 1996). For these writers the major trend seems instead to be a revival of the Taylorist organisation and control principles. This is in line with the above mentioned evi-dence on the scientific–technical background of east German managers. The argument is that management wants to optimise the already existing Taylorist organisation (as defined in Chapter 2), which was impossible in former times due to the continuous production problems and the powerful position of the workers on the shopfloor (e.g. Lohr 1992). Today, power relations have changed and real Taylorism can finally be practised. There is no need to establish a new 'pact' with the workforce in the continuing devastating labour market situation of the new *Länder*. Several studies support this (e.g. Edeling 1992: 55; Heering and Schroeder 1992: 24; Heidenreich 1991a: 33; Lang 1994; Lohr 1992; Mickler *et al.* 1996; Pohlmann and Schmidt 1996: 218; Voskamp and Wittke 1991b). For example, Heidenreich observes in his study[11] a tendency towards 'structural–conservative' (*strukturkonservativ*), rigid-Tayloristic forms of work organisation. He argues that east German managers have begun to act (for the first time) without any social responsibility, and that especially in crisis situations they often do not inform the workforce about the future of the company and, if they do, do so only to secure obedience. It is claimed that these practices will eventually lead to worker resistance and inflexibility (e.g. Bluhm 1992; Lohr 1992: 165; Voskamp and Wittke 1991a), and instead of creating innovative workplaces, it merely leads to a 'downward spiral' (Kern and Land 1991).

To conclude, one might describe the two scenarios as a 'modernisation' and a 'polarisation' scenario (Jürgens *et al.* 1993). However, it is not possible at this stage to make final evaluations as to whether more Taylorist or more flexible production forms will be the common feature in east Germany and to what extent they will differ from west German plants. Sufficient representative data are not available, and the restructuring of work organisation and personnel management in many companies is still ongoing. The type of production will also depend on the kind of industries which are developing (e.g. at the moment most western firms are establishing only distribution and mass production ones) (see Schuldt 1994). It might also depend on the background of managers (e.g. whether they come from west Germany or foreign countries or whether they are the old directors or new east Germans). It will be one task of the survey analysis later in this book to examine the applicability of these scenarios in the clothing industry.

3.2 Current practice of workplace relations

Having outlined the institutional context of the transforming workplace relations the discussion now turns to the salient characteristics of the evolving workplace relations. There is a considerable amount of research on the development of works councils, mostly based on expert interviews and/or case studies of specific companies (interviews with management and works councillors) (e.g. Dathe and Schreiber 1993; David 1992; Mickler *et al.* 1992; Röske and Wassermann 1991; SOFI group Göttingen (e.g. Bluhm, Kern and Land, Kirschner, Voßkamp and Wittke); Berlin/Göttingen group and WISOC group, see p. 37). The review that follows focuses on the development and quality of the works council–management relationship (i.e. workplace relations in a narrow sense). Three interrelated questions are posed to structure this discussion. First, can we characterise a typical works council–management relationship in east Germany? Second, how successful or effective is the current works council's interest representation? And related to this, have works councils been successfully 'institutionalised' so that workplace relations have become formalised?

As mentioned at the beginning of the book, it is commonly assumed that the formal transfer of the works council practice has been successful (e.g. Fichter 1996: 2; Kädtler and Kottwitz 1994: 14; Schmid and Blancke 1995: 569; Turner 1992), but the literature is ambivalent about the extent to which the institution is *working properly* (i.e. functioning as in west Germany). However, the literature fails to specify the actual 'functioning' of institutions and how one can measure it.

Depending on how the development of workplace relations in the last few years is interpreted, some authors are more optimistic than others. For example, the WISOC group (e.g. Ermischer and Preusche) declares that in the instances where 'co-management' is practised, it is indeed effective, and thus institutionalised. The Berlin/Göttingen group (e.g. Jander and Lutz) on the other hand is more pessimistic, stating that the works councils are not working effectively at all (due to the problems outlined below) and that they are therefore not properly institutionalised (also Lippold *et al.* 1992: 96).

In an attempt to clarify the definitional problems, this book assumes two main preconditions of *functioning* works councils: co-operative relations with management and effective representation of workers' interests. Neither of these is sufficient on its own. Thus, works councils can only stay effective without being co-operative for a short period of time. Due to the mandatory character of works councils, both sides have to deal with and depend on each other. In the long run therefore, works councils can only represent workers' interests effectively if they co-operate with management. Similarly, works councils will only be able to co-operate with management without being an effective interest institution for a limited period of time. The workforce would not accept such an institution in the long run and hence co-operative workplace relations would be at risk. In sum, the conditions are interrelated and both need to exist for workplace relations to be functioning in the desired way (i.e. as outlined in the legislation).[12] The following section reviews the literature on the current state of workplace relations in east Germany with regard to these issues of 'co-operation' and 'effectiveness'.

Co-operative works councils or 'extended arms of management'?

Research on east German workplace relations commonly distinguishes between the periods before and after privatisation, since privatisation is seen as having a radical impact on the power relations between management and works council in that it lowers the position of the latter and raises the position of the former (e.g. Dathe and Schreiber 1993: 6; Ermischer and Preusche 1992; Hürtgen 1992; Mickler *et al.* 1996: 240).[13]

With regard to the *pre-privatisation period*, one may distinguish two views. Although there is widespread agreement on the existence of co operative attitudes on the part of the newly established works councils in east Germany, the literature is divided over whether the relationship between management and works council is a *real* co-operation, between two more or less equally strong partners,[14] or whether it is one in which the works council is typically sub-servient, and thus incorporated or ignored.

Analysts in the first tradition see the enterprise as being characterised by a co-operative relationship, thus 'co-management' (Ermischer and Preusche 1993) or 'partnership for progress/construction' (*'Aufbaupartnerschaft'*) (Röske and Wassermann 1991), and they offer three main reasons.

First, the legacy of socialisation and 'collective' experiences in socialist work-places (e.g. life-long employment in the same firm, everyone knowing each other, and with no extreme social status differences between management and workers) is said to enhance co-operation (e.g. Liebold 1996: 217). Second, there is said to have been a particular interdependence between management and works councils: both parties had an equal status in the beginning, or it was even that management was sometimes in a weaker situation since it had to earn/regain legitimacy from the workforce (i.e. unclarified power relations or 'power vacuum') (e.g. Kirschner 1992: 85). Consequently, it is claimed that management was dependent on the works council to get the support of the workforce for any restructuring. It is argued that this worked as a force for co-operative relations in order to have at least one stabilising factor during the difficult survival process. According to Ermischer and Preusche (1995: 55) 'the co-operation enhanced the plant level process of transformation and helped to compensate for the lack of experience of both management and the works council with the strange economic and legal system'. One should also note that the common 'enemy', the Treuhand (the state privatisation agency), arguably induced 'survival pacts' (*Notgemeinschaften*). Third, there was the par-ticularly unifying aim of preparing the enterprise for the market economy (e.g. Dathe and Schreiber 1993: 9), and of dismantling the political structures, thus 'de-ideologisation' of the work structure and organisation (e.g. getting rid of the 'red socks'). Some even argue that there has been an additional unifying aim: the development of more employee involvement (Ermischer and Preusche 1992: 2).

In sum, these authors conclude that co-management generally emerged in their case-study companies because of the specific internal situations after the '*Wende*' (turn-round). For example, Ermischer and Preusche's (1993: 185) empirical investigation (interviews in 34 companies, mostly in the metal industry, in Saxony from 1991 onwards) concludes that in the majority of cases the management and works council saw their relationship as a positive, co-operative relationship with the aim of achieving consensus.

It is a weakness of these studies, however, that we are not told which interview questions were asked, nor are important terms like 'co-operation' clearly defined. For example, the perception of 'shared goals' does not necessarily lead to an effective co-determination. It is also possible that if a works council shares the same goals as management, it does not see the need to become pro-active.

This view is supported by the other school of thought on these issues which proposes that co-operative works councils in east Germany are 'extended arms of management' rather than 'independent' and effective worker institutions (e.g. Jander and Lutz 1993a; Kädtler *et al.* 1997: 22; Mahnkopf 1991: 275, 1993: 17). In such a scenario, the works councils' willingness to compromise is seen as an indication of its weak bargaining power (e.g. Röbenack 1996: 204).

Jander and Lutz (1991b: 411) found that cases of pro-active works councils were the exception rather than the rule, and they speculate that these were likely to have been concentrated around Leipzig and Dresden (the home of the civic movement in 1989). They also found that even in the beginning, when works councils formally attended management meetings, they did not participate greatly in the decision-making, but basically agreed to decisions which sounded economically rational. For example, there was no works council in their sample which had developed alternatives to management's concept of reconstruction. In general, works councillors were found to be very open to economic arguments because of their belief that economic irrationality led the former system into ruin. Therefore, economic rationality and especially technological progress were often seen as panaceas (also Dathe and Schreiber 1993: 42; David 1992: 132–4). This is further supported by the fact that a large majority of east German works councillors are from the technical professions (in contrast to the west where works councillors are usually recruited from the skilled core of blue-collar workers) (e.g. Artus *et al.* 1996).

Mickler *et al.*'s case study (1992: 16, 1996) of the new Volkswagen car factory in Saxony gives an impressive account of the works council's agreement to the introduction of lean production without any restrictions whatsoever. Moreover, according to Jander and Lutz (1991b), east German works councils generally did not (and still do not) mobilise against staff reductions, because they are recognised as unavoidable. They also avoid any politicisation of labour relations, since this is seen as a core reason for the former mismanagement. Consequently, as Kädtler and Kottwitz (1994: 27) argue, the 'works council as a partner/arm of management' is often believed by works councillors themselves to be the ideal type (see Kotthoff's typology below). Accordingly, as the authors conclude, the relationship between management and works council is not seen by the councillors as the expression of any fundamental conflict of interest but as a 'functional complementary relationship'. Similarly, their study found that works councils, having realised that their scope for action is very limited, were persuaded that co-operation is the best posture. The authors (1994: 28) mention that 'it is not the announcement of a third or fourth redundancy round which causes a "hardening of the fronts" but instead the times when management violates the rights of the works council or is guilty of negligence'. Thus, only when informal norms were violated, did the works council become 'aggressive'.[15]

Jander and Lutz also remark that the early attendance of the worker council at board meetings in some firms could easily be seen more as a management strategy to get the workers to accept organisational changes than as an indicator of co-management. In addition, Kädtler and Kottwitz (1992: 8–10) cannot find any evidence to suggest that there were conflicts in the early period (Winter 1989) in those enterprises which had quite extensive rights for their worker councils, over the introduction of the more restrictive German works councils law. He goes so far as to argue that even if the broader participation rights had been kept, the outcome of 'co-management' would have been the same, largely due to the particular economic and political context.

With regard to the *post-privatisation period* both groups observe changes but this does not radically shift their point of view. There is ample case-study evidence that the ongoing difficult economic situation of most firms and changing power relations after privatisation reduces the task of works councils to that of administrating redundancies instead of 'co-managing' the ongoing reorganisation (e.g. Röbenack 1996: 190). For example, Mickler *et al.*'s study (1992, 1996) of Volkswagen in Saxony showed that the informal 'survival pacts' which existed in 1990 were starting to fall apart by 1992. Here, management wanted more productivity and the workforce wanted to keep their traditional piece rates and customs. According to the authors (1992: 21), it is not 'the democratisation of workplace relations, but company survival, massive redundancies and the securing of a minimum social standard [which] determines the daily work of the councils'.

However, the data are interpreted in the literature in different ways. The WISOC group for example argues that workforce, works council and management no longer jointly face the Treuhand in safeguarding the interests of the enterprise and thus the '*Notgemeinschaft*' (survival pact) is threatened (Ermischer and Preusche 1995: 59; Lungwitz and Preusche 1994, 1996). Management strengthens its position (e.g. legitimised by new owners or by a management buy-out) and frequently reinforces Taylorist control and disciplinary methods (also Bluhm 1992; Lippold *et al.* 1992; Voskamp and Wittke 1991b). Yet, according to Lungwitz and Preusche (1996), although the relationship becomes more conflictual it remains essentially co-operative (also Ermischer and Preusche 1995: 60). Unfortunately, this is a rather vague statement, especially since they fail to specify whether works councils can be characterised as more conflictual (e.g. more 'militant', aggressive), co-operative, ignored or isolated. Other analysts are more specific in arguing that privatisation neither led to a more conflictual relationship nor to a complete isolation of the works council but instead to an even 'stronger form of co-operation' between unequally powerful partners with strong managers and weak, dependent works councils. Artus *et al.* (1996: 298) describe it as the development from 'survival pacts' to 'productivity bargaining pacts' or 'workplace loyalty pacts' (also Kädtler *et al.* 1997). Another example is Röbenack (1996: 206) who found widespread co-operative attitudes and a tendency to pragmatic, rational compromises among her case studies. She concludes by hoping that this constellation will stay on 'despite the increasingly asymmetrical power relations and increasing formalisation and functionalisation of workplace relations [seen as opposed to a politicisation of workplace negotiations]'. In a nutshell, these analysts describe the works councils as 'enterprise-focused, rational, functional, professional, pragmatic, instrumental, or a-political' (e.g. Röbenack 1996: 204; Kädtler *et al.* 1997: 267). Heidenreich (1996: 144) describes a development from 'company communities' (*Betriebsgemeinschaft*) to 'instrumental communities' (*Zweckgemeinschaft*). What is emphasised here is the fact that it is remarkable that managers did not terminate the co-operative partnership of the early transitional years but kept a co-operative attitude towards the works council (e.g. Artus *et al.* 1996: 299). Moreover, the initial possibility of works councils shaping the restructuring process as a joint partner of management has now been drastically reduced to an administrative function to safeguard workers' interests in the rationalisation and redundancy processes. Yet, this development is seen by some analysts as having the potential to foster a re-orientation of works councils to defend workers' interests rather than being co-managers of the management (e.g. Röbenack 1996: 190). Thus, it is assumed that on the one hand privatisation diminishes works councils' power position as a co-manager but on the other leads to a clearer distribution of roles between management and works councils. The latter could lead to a formalisation of their relationship (e.g. Aderhold *et al.* 1994; Förster and Röbenack 1996; Röbenack 1996). However, these positions are hypothetical predictions rather than empirical findings.

Although most agree that workplace relations did not become conflictual nor were works councils ignored or isolated, there are voices that emphasise that the co-operation in the east is different from the western norm. They argue that it is not a real co-operation between 'equal' partners but rather one of weak, subservient works councils whose tasks are reduced to a social cushioning of the restructuring processes. For example, Mickler *et al.* (1996: 240) mention that in many of their car industry case studies, works councils' power has been weakened and they have no real alternative but to be defensive and subservient to management's wishes. Liebold (1996: 213) refers to 'highly co-operative and consensual' relations which emphasise the complementarity of the interests of capital and labour rather than the differences and are seen as genuinely different from west German habits (also Bergmann 1996: 282). Kädtler *et al.* (1997: 256) call their relationship to management a 'functional co-operation rather than an institutionalised class conflict'. Artus *et al.* (1996: 304) point to the negative impact of the works councils' 'plant-egoism' and their pragmatic, apolitical, non-ideological understanding of their roles with respect to the unions which will be weakened by such works councils' policies. Moreover, the 'dual system' of interest representation will lose its capacity of being a 'functional differentation of conflict regulation' for which the German model is known (also Altvater and Mahnkopf 1993: 185). Finally, Hyman (1996: 627) speaks explicitly of 'incorporation' rather than 'co-operation' and argues that the logic of such 'incorporation into a unitary management team' is that the scope for independent representation of separate employee interests disappears.

Broadly, one might tentatively classify the above viewpoints into two ideal-typical camps, a positive/optimistic one that emphasises the continuing co-operation between management and works councils (despite increasing difficulties), and a negative/pessimistic one that stresses the weakened position of works councils as well as the difference from the western counterpart.

One general problem of the literature is that it fails to provide reasons to support the different interpretations. Why, for example, as Lungwitz and Preusche (1996: 133) argue, would managers increasingly want to isolate the works council and stop integrating it into strategic decision-making when it appeared to have been a beneficial arrangement for both sides? On the other hand, why would works councils permit themselves to become subservient and incorporated into management when they had had a relatively strong position in pre-privatisation days?

A further related problem is definitional, with lack of clarity for concepts such as 'co-operation' and 'co-management'. For example, what exactly does Liebold mean by 'highly co-operative' (*hochkooperativ*)? Is this still co-operation between equal partners or already incorporation? And how can a works council be co-operative in principle but increasingly conflictual as Lungwitz and Preusche argue? Moreover, why should pragmatic negotiations between works council and management be genuinely different from western habits as Röbenack argues? Was this 'ideal-type' of a political, class-conscious works council ever typical in west Germany, particularly in times of economic recession? Kotthoff's findings (see below) suggest a different reality where pragmatic, co-operative works councils are the norm in west Germany. Moreover, how can one assume a unique east German type of works council without any comparative research with the west?

Thus, a major problem is that the analysts seem unable to clarify what they mean by these terms, nor are they specific as to how these terms should be operationalised. In addition, more representative data seem clearly necessary to substantiate either of these interpretative streams.

Effective works councils?

Related to the question of co-operation is whether or not works councils effectively manage to represent workers' interests. There is little (west) German research evaluating the quality of workplace relations, particularly the examination of the interrelation between the two actors in terms of effective interest representation, that is effective from the view of the workforce. Works councils in general have only gained academic interest in recent years (e.g. Hoffmann *et al.* 1987; Trinczek 1987, 1989, 1993; Promberger 1991; Weinert 1984), and most studies thus far have concentrated on the contextual changes and challenges (e.g. new technology, lean production). The only major study which focuses on the quality of interest representation is Kotthoff's longitudinal case-study analysis of sixty-four companies (1981, 1994),[16] which created a useful typology of effective and ineffective works councils and distinguished between the categories as follows: (i) deficient forms of interest representation: 'the ignored works council', 'the isolated works council', 'the works council as an extended arm of management'; and (ii) effective forms of (autonomous) interest representation: 'the respected, co-operative works council', 'the respected, steadfast works council', and 'the works council as a co-operative hostile power'.

Unfortunately, there is no corresponding east German research on this issue[17] which is partly explained by the fact that it is especially hard to measure the effectiveness of interest representation during times of transformation. However, there is some discussion on the related question as to what extent the new works councils have managed to formalise the workplace relations. In other words, whether the earlier informal negotiations (or the mixture of formal and informal relations) have been substituted by formal interest representation through the works council. There is overall agreement that the traditional behavioural patterns and rules have been lost. For example, Kern and Land (1991)[18] argue on the basis of their case study that the former informal networks and 'plan fulfilment pact' (see Chapter 2) have been destroyed, and that the workforce is happy to get rid of the informal networks, since they are seen as illegal and part of the old, inefficient system (also Kirschner 1991; Lippold *et al.* 1992). Yet, opinions are split about what has been established instead. Kern and Land do not make any judgements, but others are more optimistic in that they see the formalisation taking place. Kirschner (1991: 1041),[19] for example, interprets the new formalised regulations (e.g. labour law) as the new basis of working together, which both sides (management and workforce) accept and legitimise. Lippold *et al.* (1992: 76) observed that works councils are currently determined to make formal written agreements and stick to the law in a pedantic way (also Alt *et al.* 1993: 20). Furthermore, Kirschner (1992: 87) argues that the works councils may even become the only actor for interest representation. In such a scenario the workforce retires from any direct interest representation and the works council itself becomes more and more distant from the workforce (p. 88).

Others are more cautious and argue that even if formalisation has taken place so far, an increasingly disappointed workforce might also threaten it. Gut *et al.* (1993: 52)[20] stress the danger (but without giving evidence) that the perceived ineffectiveness of the works council will encourage the old informal, company-specific practices to return, which could erode the formal regulations. Senghaas-Knobloch (1992) found evidence in her study[21] that people increasingly bemoan the loss of the former 'cushy' informal system and the related solidarity. This, however, does not necessarily mean that they will react by forming new informal relations. In sum, these studies which provide rather impressionistic data and speculative observations clearly do not allow a final judgement about the extent to which the institutionalisation and formalisation of workplace relations has really taken place.

On the other hand the literature outlines problems which works councils are currently facing and asserts (rather than analyses) that these problems hinder the proper functioning of works councils. There are various problems mentioned in the literature (more by the Berlin/Göttingen group than by WISOC) and it is difficult to disentangle them. The following appear to be the broad categories: (i) the intensified classical dilemma of works councils in which the interests of company and workforce are opposed; (ii) the unsuitability of the west German industrial relations system in the east German context; (iii) problems due to the newness of the institution; (iv) the problematic union-works council relationship; and (v) the low image of the works council. In the following, these five problems will be briefly outlined.

The intensified classical dilemma: opposing interests

Jander and Lutz (1991a: 2) state that interest representation in east Germany has to deal with a fundamental dilemma: on the one hand enterprises are confronted with global competition which makes modernisation and reorganisation (including the reduction of staff overheads) necessary and which leaves little room for negotiation or alternative ideas; on the other hand the works council wants to fulfil its task of representing the immediate social interests of the workforce (also Kädtler and Kottwitz 1994: 19; Kädtler *et al.* 1997; Liebold 1996: 215; Mickler *et al.* 1996: 212). Thus, they are caught between the logics of competitive efficiency and social responsibility and increasingly face new management with a hard-nosed commitment to the former (Ermischer and Preusche 1995: 59; Kottwitz 1991: 417). The result at best has often been a kind of social damage limitation (Röbenack 1992: 197).

One might wonder, however, whether west German works councils do not also face severe economic constraints and do not also have to deal with Jander and Lutz's 'fundamental dilemma'. As Hyman (1996: 629) rightly concludes one should not compare existing east German reality with an idealised stereotype of independent and strong works councils in the west. Reality in the west is differentiated, particularly amongst smaller firms or during economic difficulties. An additional question is why this situation should prevent works councils from functioning properly, and thus from representing workers' interests effectively under the given conditions. Obviously this depends on one's definition of effective representation, either in a ideal-typical way or in a relative way taking the given situation into account.

The unsuitability of the west German industrial relations system in the east German context

A related argument refers to the non-existence of economically prosperous firms in east Germany, especially since such firms are assumed to be a necessary precondition for the successful functioning of the west German industrial relations system (Kädtler and Kottwitz 1994: 19, 1992: 3; Kädtler *et al.* 1997). Yet, the authors leave the consequences of this conjecture open. Does this mean that the western industrial relations system is intrinsically unsuitable for the east? Jander and Lutz (1993a: 16) are more specific in arguing that the institutions are overstrained and cannot cope with the vast problems of privatisation and de-industrialisation, and that this indicates that these institutions (e.g. works councils) are not made for managing the transformation from planned to market economy. Matthies *et al.* (1994: 32) argue that in the west institutions of collective interest representation became consolidated within the framework of a 'social market' which provided employment security for most individual workers. In the absence of this 'normal employment relationship', they continue, it has been impossible for these institutions to function effectively in the east. This thesis has been taken on by other authors as well (see Gut *et al.* 1993; Jacoby 1994: 24; Mahnkopf 1992), who go on to speculate that this presumed inability to cope with the economic problems could jeopardise the much needed social integration of eastern society and could in the long term hinder the successful institutionalisation of industrial relations.

A related argument is made by Kädtler (1993: 3) who states that the right of the works council to be informed about any plans of management which will affect the employment situation of the firm (e.g. privatisation, acquisition) was repealed during the privatisation process so that all Treuhandanstalt negotiations took place without the works councillors and sometimes also without management. Thus, crucial decisions took place outside the realm of the firm and thereby outside the domain of co-determination (also Dathe and Schreiber 1993: 13). Yet, one can argue that these exceptional measures were taken in order to adapt the western regulations to the specific east German situation, exactly what the authors demand.

However, we are not provided with a convincing argument as to why all these problems should evoke a dysfunctioning of the works councils and thus also prove the unsuitability of the west German industrial relations system. The authors do not give evidence as to why the east German works councils should act in a significantly different way from that of their western counterparts. Furthermore, without wanting to go into the debate as to how far the situation in the east today is comparable with that of west Germany after 1945 (see Jacoby 1994), it seems a dubious assertion that the west German industrial relations system only 'works' in prosperous economic situations. The system seems to have survived various recessions during the last few decades in west Germany.

Problems due to the novelty of the institution

The third problem said to hinder the proper functioning of the works councils is the novelty of the institution; works councillors still have to gain experience and learn their trade. One might object that management also needs time to adjust to the new situation. Additionally, other sources have stated that the lack of information, for example on western labour law, was quickly addressed by the east German works councils (Gut *et al.* 1993: 48).

A related point refers to the different background of east German councillors which makes them behave differently from their western colleagues. For example, Mahnkopf (1991: 275) and Jander and Lutz (1993a) argue that the 'tacit skills' necessary for the effective articulation and representation of interests are lacking. They can only be learned with time and experience. However, these authors do not specify such skills.

Additionally, Mahnkopf (1991: 281) speculates that works councils' avoidance of conflictual struggles with management not only results from their inexperience and their uncertainty about legal rights, but also from the fact that they often actually 'hide' behind the legislation, trying to legitimise their passivity and unwillingness to become active. Thus, references to the authority of the law are used as an excuse for inaction. This argument assumes that the former east German 'socialisation' process provoked the avoidance of individual responsibility and 'pro-action'. However, the author does not provide any evidence to support this assertion.

Finally, works councils frequently lack the vision to generate forces from within the enterprise in order to influence higher-level industrial relations or politics – except in the case of rescuing a single, insolvent firm when the liquidator is the government or Treuhandanstalt (e.g. the famous Bischofferode's hunger strike was initiated by the works council). According to the Berlin/Göttingen group there is also a strict differentation to be made between the works council's work and its councillors' private political engagement (also David 1992: 134). Whilst in west Germany these areas are often interconnected, east Germans dismiss this because of past experience (e.g. Fichter 1997a: 100; Kädtler and Kottwitz 1994: 29; Kädtler *et al.* 1997: 262). This observation has been questioned in other studies which have instead found highly political works councils (e.g. Dathe and Schreiber 1993: 21).[22] All these statements, however, come from a small empirical base.

Problematic union–works council relationship

There is also an argument that works council–union relations are not at their best in east Germany. Unions have a conflictual relationship with east German works councils because of the rising 'plant-level egoism', which is assumed to be more pronounced than that in west Germany (Artus *et al.* 1996; Kädtler *et al.* 1997: 259; Lippold *et al.* 1992;[23] Mahnkopf 1991: 282, 1993: 17). Furthermore, the sporadic attempts in the early years after the turn-round of some east German works councils to establish regional associations were seen by the unions as dangerous competition (see Jander and Lutz 1993b on the 'works council conference'). It is also emphasised that a growing number of firms have no unionised works council (i.e. works councillors who are not union members), or even no works council at all (Mahnkopf 1993). Although no reliable statistics on the coverage of works councils in either part of Germany are available, most researchers estimate that this is significantly lower in the east than the west (Hyman 1996: 626). Other sources report instead a high 'unionisation' of works councils (David 1992: 131). However, works councils which have merely a formal relationship with the union, but neither expect nor desire union advice, have also been observed. Also, union stewards are virtually non-existent in east German firms (as all studies confirm). Thus, Mahnkopf (1993:

18) concludes that the relationship between east German works councils and unions is much looser than that in the west (where plant-level representatives and the union movement are comparatively well integrated) (also Fichter 1997a: 99). In addition, unions themselves are said not to be very successful in east Germany yet: density is generally declining, and there is an argument that unions face severe difficulties in mobilising their members (Fichter 1997b; Mahnkopf 1991, 1992). Besides, several authors suggest that unions have difficulty in establishing regional industrial policies which, as mentioned above, some authors regard as necessary to tackle the problems of unemployment efficiently (and which would require an uncommon collaboration of single unions at regional and local level) (Jander and Voß 1991; Kädtler and Kottwitz 1994: 32; Lohr 1992).

In sum, the problems unions face impede their services for works councils at a time when works councils are especially dependent on powerful and helpful unions. Rosenbaum and Weinert (1991: 19) therefore conjecture that workplace interest representation will only become fully accepted and effective if the dual system of workplace and industrial interest representation work well together (as they do in west Germany), and where unions have the key role to play.

The poor image of the works council

Finally, there is the assertion that the current problems works councils face (and which account for their apparent poor performance) make the workforce perceive them as ineffective. This in turn weakens the power of works councils (see Jander and Lutz 1992). Hyman (1996: 626) refers to a vicious circle of powerlessness: most works councils lack a perspective of activating and aggregating the workplace potential for collective action, and most workers lack a perspective of engaging spontaneously in such action.

An additional problem mentioned by Jander and Lutz (1991a) is that workers' interests in firms are highly heterogeneous (e.g. the different group interests of short-term workers, workers in retraining, workers in 'employment programmes' (*ABMler*), part-timers and full-timers), and that it is difficult for any council to reconcile these interests. However, this task seems to be an inherent characteristic of any works council (and indeed union), whether in the east or the west.

In short, although most authors do not explicitly refer to the question of the effectiveness of works councils, they conclude that the problems discussed above do in fact constrain their functioning. Kädtler (1993: 4) concludes that the deficiencies in workplace relations have implications for the institutionalisation (functioning) of the whole industrial relations system. According to Jander and Lutz (1993a) there is the paradox that although the west German industrial relations system was transferred without any adjustments to the particular east German situation, east Germany could very well end up not practising the same industrial relations as the west, especially because of the ineffective works councils (see also Jacoby 1994). The likely scenario, therefore, is of a few

Table 3.2 Classification of two ideal-typical positions in the literature of workplace relations in east Germany

	Main reason for emergence of works councils	*Management style*	*Works council–management relations*	*Effectiveness of works council*	*Successful institutionalisation of works council*
'Optimists'	industrial democracy	employee involvement	functional co-operation	yes (implicitly)	no comment
'Pessimists'	reconstruction of the enterprise, 'consumer revolution'	'Taylorism'	incorporation (works council as extended arm of management)	not effectively working due to various problems	no successful institutionalisation

companies with 'good' workplace relations surrounded by a majority of companies with poor co-determination practices (see also Mahnkopf 1991).

However, listing possible reasons why works councils might not be effective is not an entirely satisfactory exercise. The authors do not provide evidence as to why these problems render works councils ineffective, nor do they analyse whether these problems are short-term (due to the novelty of the institutions) or long-term (due to the structural unsuitability of western regulations in the east). In addition, there are other points which are not discussed. For example, we are not told how the problems interact with each other and whether they are valid for all or most councils. Also, there have been no tests as to how far these problems, rather than, for example, uncooperative management, account for the works council's ineffectiveness. Finally, to reiterate, these studies are based almost entirely on interviews with works councillors (and sometimes with management and union officials). Very few come from more comprehensive case studies and none includes workers' attitudes and behaviour towards the new institutions, which would seem to be a straightforward measurement of institutional effectiveness.

3.3 Conclusion

It might be useful to summarise (Table 3.2) the literature on workplace relations into two alternative, 'ideal-typical' positions (in Max Weber's sense), which reflect the discussed items of workplace relations. The classification into 'optimists' and 'pessimists' reflects the actual academic division in the debate on the entire industrial relations transformation in the east and indeed on the future of the 'Rhine' model of industrial relations. Famous protagonists here are Lowell Turner, the 'optimist' (e.g. 1997), and Wolfgang Streeck, the 'pessimist' (e.g. 1995). Clearly, this rather crude classification does not provide great help in understanding the possible reasons for the two extreme positions. However, it highlights the significance of the normative assumptions of the reviewed literature.

The polarity might also emerge from a different (implicit) weighting of the three major general concepts guiding the current analysis of the transformation in post-socialist societies. 'Path dependencies' (i.e. socialist legacies) (Ekiert 1998; Hausner *et al.* 1995; Stark 1992), 'structural conditions' (i.e. new institutions) (e.g. Reißig 1993; Zapf 1991), and 'social actors' (strategic choice) (e.g. Offe 1994; Sztompka 1994; Wiesenthal 1993, 1994) are seen as the major alternative factors shaping the post-socialist transformation processes.

For example, optimists and pessimists acknowledge the dependency of the socialist past but refer to different legacies. Whereas WISOC emphasises the co-operative, 'humanistic' legacy of managers and managers' and workers' joint experience of co-operative workplace relations in the past, Berlin/Göttingen and others highlight the legacy of passive, instrumental actors not able to create the necessary cultural conditions of the new interest institutions. Why do researchers refer to different legacies? No answer is provided. One might be inclined to suspect that people pick and choose from the socialist past whatever best suits their hypotheses. Furthermore, both groups differ in their approach to the dichotomy of 'structure' and 'actor'. Whereas WISOC refers to external circumstances for the deterioration of workplace relations in privatised firms, Berlin/Göttingen points to the lack of actors on the labour side. In this case the works councillors are to blame because they are not real independent actors but incorporated in the management system.

To conclude, this chapter discussed the various approaches to understanding the take-over of the socialist unions, the changes in personnel management styles, the establishment of works councils and their subsequent problems. Questions arose as to whether the works council has been institutionalised and is effectively working in terms of interest representation. Whether the works council is institutionalised by now, thus whether workplace relations are formalised, becomes a crucial issue especially with regard to the informal networks as discussed in the previous chapter. However, as we have seen, these issues have not yet been conceptualised and tested to any satisfactory extent. In addition, most of the reviewed empirical studies on the development of works councils are based on interviews with the councillors only and do not include workers' attitudes and behaviour towards the new institutions. This is also true for the discussion of the functioning and institutionalisation of the west German unions in east Germany. The next chapter introduces the first part of the empirical research on works council–management relations in the clothing industry, focusing on workplace co-operation. In doing so, it will rectify the outlined deficiencies in the current literature on transformation.

4 Social partnership in the east German clothing industry

This chapter examines the transformation of industrial relations actors by focusing upon the east German clothing sector. It also analyses the extent of workplace co-operation by looking at works councillors' perceptions of their relations with management in selected firms in east and west Germany. The purpose for such a comparison is to test the applicability of some of the findings and hypotheses of the studies reviewed in the previous chapter in the context of a specific industry. The core question is to what extent we can speak of a successful institutionalisation of the new labour institutions in this, a declining industrial sector. Finally, the chapter provides background information for the union membership surveys to be discussed in Part III.

4.1 The clothing industry in decline

Unification exposed east German industry overnight to west European and international competition as well as effectively eliminating the traditional east European markets. The clothing industry was particularly hard-hit since 50 per cent of workplaces depended on those traditional markets. A rapid collapse of the economy followed. During the first half of 1990 (i.e. before the 'currency union'), east German industrial production fell to 93 per cent of its 1989 level and matters worsened dramatically with the introduction of the Deutsche Mark at a 1:1 conversion rate on 1 July 1990. From July to December 1990, the economy-wide 'net production' (value of production minus input costs) dropped by almost 50 per cent (Buechtemann and Schupp 1992: 95). Between 1989 and 1994, overall employment decreased by around 3 million to 6.3 million employees (Nolte and Sitte 1995: 302); 1.1 million people were officially unemployed; and the other 2 million were short-term contract workers in 'public job-creation programmes' (*Arbeitsbeschaffungsmaßnahmen*), in retraining courses, in early retirement schemes or in the reserve labour force. Employment in the east German industrial sectors decreased by 63 per cent from 3.4 million to 1.3 million during the same period (see IWH 1994). Although subsequently there were some signs of recovery (e.g. 9 per cent increase of GDP in east Germany in 1994, Kittner 1995: 201) all expectations of equalising the economic strengths of the two regions before the end of the century evaporated. East Germany looks likely to remain for a long time a 'dependence and transfer economy' (see also Nolte and Sitte 1995: 300).

The transfer to a market economy and the collapse of the eastern European markets was especially hard for the clothing and textile industry.[1] In only three years (1990–3) the eastern European market share of this industry fell from around 50 per cent to 3 per cent. Already in 1993 more than half of the east German garment production was produced for the west German market (source: DIW 1995).

Historically, this industry had major economic importance in east Germany, primarily because the centre of German clothing manufacturing before the Second World War was in Saxony (e.g. Breitenacher *et al.* 1997: 13). The industry's share of east German industrial production was 7 per cent in 1989, and its share of east German employment was 8 per cent[2] compared with 3 per cent in west Germany (Küchle and Volkmann 1993).

Between 1990 and 1993 the clothing and textile industry lost 72 per cent of its net production (Statistisches Bundesamt 1994). Taking for example 1992, the year with the most drastic employment reduction, the net production of the clothing industry dropped by 25.3 per cent (2.6 per cent below the average of all industrial sectors) (Küchle and Volkmann 1993: 5). Labour productivity (output per employee) remains around a third of that in the west German clothing sector (Küchle and Volkmann 1993: 4).

In terms of employment, the overall picture is equally depressing. However, the precise figures are unfortunately not very reliable since different sources produce different data. For example, one source argues that there were 220,000 clothing and textile employees in 1989 in east Germany (67 per cent of employees were female, Rasche 1993). Another source speaks of 320,000 (GTB data, interview January 1995) and the *Neue Zeitung* even claims there were 380,000 people working in this industry in 1989 (5 August 1993).

According to Schmidt (1996: 231) the entire east German workforce in this industry declined by 90 per cent between 1989 and 1994. The employers' association speaks of a 90 per cent decrease between 1989 and 1992 (Jahresbericht 1992 des Verbandes der Nord-Ostdeutschen Textilindustrie). The *Frankfurter Allgemeine Zeitung* (18 October 1993) speaks of a drop from 220,000 to 27,766 employees in 1993.

For the clothing sector alone employment figures are equally confusing. Gebbert and Gebbert (1993: 220) talk of a drop from 72,000 to 11,000 within one year after unification (between 1990 and 1991). The GTB, however, speaks of a drop from 110,000 clothing employees in 1989 to 11,000 in 1994.

Whatever the correct number, it is nonetheless clear that the drop in employment in the clothing and textile sector is significantly larger than in other industries. The overall employment in the industrial sectors (Verarbeitendes Gewerbe/Energie/Bergbau) decreased on average by 70 per cent. Thus, in 1993 the industrial sector employed a third of the original workforce in this sector (Lutz *et al.* 1996: 71).

In Chemnitz (formerly Karl-Marx-Stadt) and the surrounding areas (the centre of the clothing and textile industry in Saxony and the location of the case study), the unemployment rate in the clothing and textile industry was 20 per cent for women and 10 per cent for men in August 1993. According to figures from the regional clothing employers' association, employment in their associated firms fell from 20,670 to 8,260 employees during 1992 alone.

It comes as no surprise that the state privatisation agency, Treuhandanstalt, has been criticised for its relatively low success rate in privatising this industrial sector. For example, by 1993 the Treuhandanstalt had only privatised two-thirds (200) of the clothing firms still in operation, with 100 firms still Treuhandanstalt-owned at that time (*Handelsblatt* no. 14, 21 January 1993). The rest were liquidated. Yet, this reduction process has also to be understood in the context of the ongoing structural adaptation which occurred in the west German clothing industry especially during the 1970s and 1980s. Over the last 40 years clothing has been a declining industry in the west with a 40 per cent fall in employment (from 406,000 to 164,000) between 1966 and 1990, and a 65 per cent decrease (from 5,781 to 2,074) in the number of enterprises (Gebbert and Gebbert 1993).[3]

4.2 Establishing industrial relations actors

Employers' association

In the beginning of 1990 the west German industrial association, BDI (Bundesverband der Deutschen Industrie) gave the go-ahead for the establishment of the three industrial organisations in the eastern regions (industry and trade councils, employers' associations (BDA) and industry associations (BDI)) (see Bluhm 1996 or Henneberger 1993 for the different roles of these bodies). In most industries the west German associations organised the establishment of regional associations in the east (see Bluhm 1996: 150). The establishment of the employers' association in the clothing and textile industry was slightly different in that it was organised by east German employers on their own initiative. Five out of the nine original clothing and textile combines (i.e. company holdings in the GDR) established their own independent employers' associations in 1990. The largest of these associations, 'VTI' (Verband der Baumwollindustrie Sachsen und Thüringen) managed in due course to acquire the other four and was then accepted a year later by the west German clothing and textile employers' association, Gesamttextil, as their official regional representative. The VTI managed to keep its east German executive and administrative staff whereas in most other associations west German officials were transferred to the east.

Since its foundation, the clothing and textile employers' association has faced a constant decrease in membership, due to both liquidations and firms dropping out. The latter is surprising given the favourable sectoral collective agreements for the employers (e.g. an agreement of a 40-hour working week from 1991 which was still in operation in 1996, a relatively slow wage adaptation to the western standard, and an 'opening clause' already established in 1991, see below).

One explanation for the high drop-out rate is, according to the employers' association, the significant decrease in average company size in the clothing industry after privatisation. This reduces the willingness of employers to comply with sectoral collective bargaining (interview with officials at the employers' association branch, Chemnitz, October 1993). In fact, most clothing and textile firms today employ only between 20 and 100 people.

The drop-out rate is clearly a major problem for the employers' association, though it is not unique to the clothing industry, but signifies a general trend in east Germany (see Bluhm 1996).

As one initiative to stop the trend of membership decline, the employers' association created a sub-association ('Förderverein für die Textil- und Konfektionsindustrie e.V.') in 1993 for employers who are interested in using the association's consultation services but do not want to be included in the sectoral collective arrangements. This sub-association gives them the usual membership benefits without the compulsory acceptance of bargaining agreements ('*verbindliche Tarifbindung*'). The clothing and textile association was, together with that in the metal industry, one of the first associations to implement such a strategy (see Bluhm 1996: 145). This exceptional practice is, however, not entirely new in German industrial relations but its appearance in the east is notable in its extent and strategic implications for the regional associations. One hundred and ten clothing and textile firms were members in the main association and the same number of firms were in the sub-association in 1996 (Bluhm 1996).

Thus, this tactic succeeded in keeping a relatively high overall firm density of 'both' associations at 60 per cent. Together they organised 80 per cent of the total east German workforce in this industry.

Overall, it is too early to evaluate the long-term implications of these two categories of membership and of the potential challenges of the overall decline in sectoral bargaining for the German industrial relations system. Some commentators argue that it shows a trend of decentralisation of collective bargaining (e.g. Mahnkopf 1993); others argue that the importance of these problems has been exaggerated by the high level of public awareness (Schroeder in Kittner 1994: 635), and yet others point to potential positive side-effects. Bluhm (1996), for example, stresses that the decline of sectoral collective bargaining must not necessarily mean a decrease in the power of employers' associations. She foresees a simultaneous trend towards decentralisation and towards an increasing importance of the regional employers' associations in relation to their national bodies.

Clothing and textile trade union

The socialist FDGB 'textile, clothing, leather' (TeBeLe) union had 570,000 members in 1989 (Wilke and Müller 1991: 258),[4] two-thirds of them female. There were two west German equivalents, the GTB (Gewerkschaft Textil

Bekleidung) which was the tenth largest DGB union (out of 16) with 250,783 members in 1990 (which equals 3.2 per cent of DGB membership) and the small 'leather' union with 44,583 members (the second smallest DGB union).

During 1990 the TeBeLe dissolved voluntarily (officially on 31 December 1990) after trying to reform itself, and its members were acquired by the west German GTB. However, the GTB differed from other western unions (especially IG Metall) and was similar to the clothing and textile employers' association in that it tried to retain the staff of the socialist union, provided they had the support of the members and had no 'Stasi' affiliation, and hence did not rely on the transfer of west German officials. Thus, all fifteen full-time officials in the east German union district in 1993 were east Germans (amongst them eight females) and many had union positions in the former FDGB clothing branch.

The GTB did not expect enormous membership increases, and even reduced its west German headquarters personnel at that time. However, out of 570,000 former FDGB clothing members (including the leather section plus all the retired members) around 104,837 transferred to the GTB in 1990/91 (see Table 4.1). This was an increase of 30.1 per cent in the overall membership level compared for example to IG Metall with a 27.3 per cent increase and the DGB average of 35.2 per cent (Löhrlein in Kittner 1993: 101). However, in the following years membership constantly declined. For example, in 1992 alone the total membership fell by 17 per cent (44 per cent in the east and 6 per cent in the west) to 288,198.

Tables 4.1 and 4.2 present figures for the union district in east Germany, 'GTB south-east', the district where the fieldwork took place. These membership figures, however, do not include all members in east Germany. There are east German members who are organised by the neighbouring west German union branches (e.g. in Thüringen and Mecklenburg-Vorpommern).

In sum, the clothing and textile union shares the common experience of German unions of immense membership losses in the east from 1990 onwards

Table 4.1 Membership figures of GTB

31 December	GTB total	GTB district south-east	% of south-east of total	GTB total density	West density %	South-east density %
1989	250,783	—	—	—	47.0	—
1990	249,880	98,215*	39.3*	n.a.	46.4	80.0*
1991	348.095	69,484	20.0	n.a.	46.2	70.0*
1992	288,198	39,100	13.6	n.a.	45.9	68.0*
1993	255,708	30,132	11.8	45.9	45.0	56.5
1994	234,240	25,859	11.0	43.1	42.7	48.2
1995	216,288	22,240	10.3	n.a.	n.a.	42.6*

Notes: * = approximately; ** = November 1995; n.a. = not available
Sources: GTB information 1995, 1996; Kittner 1993, 1994, 1995

Table 4.2 Figures of the GTB south-east district (clothing and textile firms)

31 December	Total of clothing and textile firms*	Firms with a works council	Employed people**	Total union members	Female members (% of total)*** (see Table 4.1)	Employed union members	Rest: unemployed, retired, apprentices
1991	675	635	138,280	69,484	52,251 (75)	58,525	10,959
1992	448	n.a.	37,500	39,100	29,766 (76)	23,438	15,662
1993	379	n.a.	29,141	30,132	23,230 (77)	15,075	15,057
1994	385	207	28,070	25,859	19,912 (77)	12,330	17,520
1995	(164^)	205	n.a.	22,240	17,138 (77)	9,449	12,990

Notes: * = data from Statistisches Bundesamt quoted in Schmidt 1996: 225 (which only registers firms with over 20 employees), GTB data provide slightly different, higher figures; ** = approximately, different data from different sources; *** = the percentage of female members in the east compares with around 57 per cent in the western districts and a 60 per cent female rate of the total German membership; ^ = restricted comparability because of statistical adaptations to EU standards; n.a. = not available
Sources: GTB south-east district documents, Statistisches Bundesamt, own calculations

(see Fichter 1997a). Thus, union density rapidly adapted to the lower western level but it is not yet predictable whether it will stagnate at this level or decrease further.

In 1996 the GTB merged with the IG Metall. This decision was clearly influenced by the GTB's continuing membership problems in the east as well as in the west, but should be also seen in the context of a general trend among the DGB unions towards restructuring and merging processes in the 1990s.

Developing sectoral collective bargaining: social partnership under constraint

The development of collective bargaining in the clothing and textile industry in the east reveals a typical pattern. In the first period there was considerable ambiguity over role definitions on the part of both unions and employers. However, economic constraints quickly forced them to get accustomed to their new roles, as they were pushed into more difficult bargaining rounds.

In more detail, according to the employers' association the first collective bargaining rounds were characterised by uncertain and unorthodox behaviour, and 'muddling through' on both sides. Employers' officials' roles were not yet clearly 'understood', thus employers had to remind themselves that 'they were no longer responsible for the "social functions" of the firms' (interview, employers' association branch, TMO Chemnitz, October 1993). For example, at the first collective bargaining negotiation in August 1990 the employers' association was still affiliated with the industrial association and this resulted in the, quite unusual for west Germany, combining of pay politics with industrial policies.

In the following years bargaining typically became progressively more difficult and conflictual according to both parties. For example, already in 1991 the GTB, for the first time in its history (and as the first union in the east), had to agree to 'opening clauses' (*Öffnungsklausel*) for twenty-eight firms (19 per cent of firms). These allow firms in economic difficulty not to comply with the negotiated pay agreement but nevertheless to stay in the employers' association.[5] However, in such instances the union has to agree that the firm is indeed in economic difficulty.

A year later collective bargaining coincided with a parliamentary debate on industrial policies for the east German clothing industry which evoked a protest demonstration in Bonn, organised by the GTB and supported by the employers' association. Since the particular bargaining results were in force at the time of the fieldwork for this book, they deserve to be outlined in more detail. The result was a 5.6 per cent pay increase from May 1993 to April 1994, and an additional 3.3 per cent from January 1994 until April 1994. By the end of 1993 the pay level for blue-collar workers in the east German clothing industry was 66.3 per cent of the average pay level in the west (for white-collar workers it was 55.4 per cent).[6] For workers in the textile industry it was slightly more with 69.9 per cent for blue-collar workers and 55.4 per cent for white-collar workers (WSI Tarifarchiv, 1993). If one includes extra payments (such as holiday pay, '13th month' bonus, government bonuses (*'vermögenswirksame Leistungen'*), the overall average wage in the clothing industry was then only around 63 per cent of the level in the west.[7] One has also to take into account that in west Germany the actual pay normally exceeds the negotiated basic pay (except in the public sector), while the actual pay levels in east Germany largely correspond to the official wage settlements (Mahnkopf 1993: 16). Overall, the west/east pay ratio of the clothing industry was in the fifth lowest group of all 20 bargaining sectors in 1994 (e.g. metal workers earned 80 per cent of their western colleagues' pay) (Bispinck in Kittner 1995: 161; WSI Tarifarchiv, 31 December 1994). Moreover, compared to other industrial sectors historically the clothing (and textile) industry pays less, as is also the case in west Germany and was the situation in the former GDR.

Finally, the collectively agreed working week in the east was 40 hours compared to 37.5 hours in the west (1993). Moreover, the east had 27 days' holiday compared to 30 days in the west, and holiday pay was not given in the east (the west got 758 DM extra holiday pay) (WSI Tarifarchiv, 31 December 1993).

In 1994, bargaining was very complicated and, as the chief official of the union noted, it was 'the beginning of the end' (*'Einstieg in den Ausstieg'*). There was also industrial action for the first time: over 200 members demonstrated in front of the building where the bargaining took place. The subsequent wage agreement resulted in the pay level for the clothing sector increasing to 72 per cent of the average pay in the west, which was nonetheless still lower than in most industries (for example, the metal industry with 87 per cent east/west pay ratio). In 1995, bargaining was even worse according to the union officials. After months of negotiations an agreement for the clothing sector was only reached thanks to token strikes organised in seven sites (involving 4,000 people) and a collection of signatures of union members. This was the first time people had gone on strike in the clothing industry in east Germany. The result was a sequence of pay increases which totalled 8.75 per cent over the next twelve months.

In sum, the increasingly difficult bargaining rounds for the union clearly manifested growing economic pressures and employers' interest in keeping labour costs competitive. However, this did not lead to a total breakdown of negotiations. Interview data with union leaders and employer officials revealed that both sides declared a strong willingness to maintain co-operative working relations. This is perhaps best seen by considering the attitudes and behaviour of the chief union official.

Overall, the chief union official, who was a former middle-rank union official and elected (still by the FDGB) to become the chief official in 1989, was seen as a highly energetic, hard-working, down-to-earth woman with strong support and admiration from her colleagues, and known in the sector to be a hard but fair negotiator. She revealed a pragmatic, co-operative attitude towards the employers and was explicitly in favour of social partnership to achieve union goals: 'we are all sitting in the same boat', 'I know of no employer who puts the profits in his/her own pockets'. If she negotiates an 'enterprise contract' (*Haustarif*), for example, she takes the economic situation of that firm into account, although she is not sure whether the (west) German headquarters of the GTB likes this. She stated that she is the 'favourite enemy' of the chief official on the employers' side, that they have frequent informal contacts and that both seem to be aware of their common interests. On several occasions both together visited companies which wanted to leave the employers' association in order to persuade the management to reconsider this idea. Such a working relationship is, as she argued, often criticised by the works councillors, whom she considers to be sometimes more 'opportunistic' and not always co-operative in their approach to management.

She prefers objective discussions instead of using rituals and ideologies during collective bargaining and is not happy that collective bargaining became increasingly conflictual. Her general aim is to make the union an even better service institution for members and the works councils. Yet, if it is necessary she also uses collective action. Although she stated in 1994 that she is not in favour of strikes – 'there is no benefit to it in this economic situation, and firms are too small' – only a year later she initiated token strikes which brought the collective bargaining rounds to a positive end. She firmly believed that without this instrument they would not have achieved an agreement. In addition, she argued that this strike was 'good for the people in that they experienced for the first time the strength of collective action'. However, this does not mean a reversal of the unions' overall non-militant, co-operative strategies.

To conclude, this section has highlighted the pressures on employers and union following the industry's dramatic decline and described the quick learning process on both sides (union and employers' association) as they attempted to define their new roles and interests after unification. However, it is interesting to note the mutual agreement to pursue a co-operative rather than antagonistic strategy in such a depressed economic situation. Both social partners were aware of their common interest in keeping sectoral collective bargaining alive, since the existence of both organisations depends on it. To what extent this 'social partnership' strategy has evolved as a result of the west German industrial relations regulations and the influence of the west German headquarters, or the actors' own beliefs and strategies, is obviously hard to tell. Yet, as mentioned above, the chief union official seemed to act quite independently from her head-quarters. Thus, one might speculate that these actors have created their own strategies, which might be influenced partly by the structural conditions of the industrial relations system and partly by their own (socialist) background and experiences.

4.3 Partners at shopfloor level: east and west Germany compared

How do the institutional changes discussed above influence workplace relations? Did east German works councillors adapt the co-operative partnership model that west German companies are known for or are east German works councils more likely to be incorporated into management? In an attempt to answer these questions, a comparative attitudinal survey of works councils of east and west German clothing firms was administered.

The survey, conducted in 1994, looked at 53 clothing firms (with over twenty employees) across the bargaining region of the south-east branch of the GTB. The south-east branch comprised, at the time of the fieldwork, 207 clothing and textile firms (with a works council) with 28,070 employees, of whom 12,330 were union members. This results in a union density of 44 per cent (GTB information 1994). One hundred clothing firms were approached and 53 returned the questionnaire (a 53 per cent response rate).

A year later the survey was repeated in 76 clothing firms across two west German districts of the GTB: Westfalen/Osnabrück which is the largest district and Nordrhein which is of average size. Overall, Westfalen/Osnabrück comprised 379 clothing and textile firms (with a works council) in 1995 with 52,118 employees, of whom 25,599 were union members. This results in a union density of 49.1 per cent. Nordrhein comprised 222 clothing and textile firms (with a works council) in 1995 with 25,145 employees, of whom 12,433 were union members. This results in a union density of 49.5 per cent. The overall union density in all (west and east) districts of the GTB was 43 per cent in 1995.

The sample comprised 123 clothing firms in Westfalen/Osnabrück and 53 firms in Nordrhein (with more than twenty employees and with a works council). Only 36 firms of the former district returned their questionnaire (a response rate of 30 per cent), whereas in Nordrhein 40 firms returned the questionnaire (a rate of 76 per cent). However, much of this difference might simply reflect the different level of enthusiasm of the district union officials in conducting the survey. The combined response rate in west Germany adds up to 43 per cent.

In total, the German clothing industry comprised 9,850 companies in 1994, half of these with less than twenty employees (Branchen special, Volksbanken/Raiffeisenbanken, Nr. 32, January 1998). There is unfortunately no classification into east and west German firms.

The surveys were distributed by branch union officials. The questionnaire consisted of two parts (twenty-six questions in total plus a few additional questions in the east), one dealing with background company information, the other dealing with a set of Likert-scale attitudinal questions on the workplace climate. These were adopted from Dastmalchian *et al.* (1991), Angle and Perry (1986) and Allen and Stephenson (1983).

Background company information

In the east most firms in the sample had been privatised (only seven were still owned by the Treuhandanstalt) and belonged to west German or foreign companies or in some cases, via management buy-out, to east German managers. Changes in management had occurred in most sites, yet there was a mixed picture regarding old/new managers. Twenty-two (out of fifty-three) firms had either kept all or most former managers and thirty firms kept no or only very few former managers. At the supervisory level, nothing really had changed, with forty-one firms having kept the former supervisors. No significant differences between private and state ownership with regard to changes in management were revealed by *t*-tests. Thus, privately owned firms did not necessarily have more 'new' managers than did Treuhandanstalt firms.

With regard to changes in the work organisation, a majority of firms in the east invested in new machinery and restructured the production process. A majority of forty-nine east German works councils perceived the work pace on the shop-floor to have increased enormously since 1989. The data provide no detailed information on any new production methods such as lean production. According to the union, however, no such innovation has been introduced with the emphasis being instead on improving the existing assembly-style, Tayloristic production line. In the west, most firms had invested in improved machinery and technology but had not changed the production process itself.

In terms of staff reductions, the size of the firms in the east decreased considerably, supporting earlier claims of this east German industry-wide trend. In 1994, 72 per cent of firms (in total thirty-eight firms) comprised less than 100 employees and 28 per cent had over 100 (and less than 800) employees. In 1989, 42 per cent had less than 100 employees and 58 per cent had more than 100 employees (including 17 per cent with over 1,000 employees). Thus, most firms reduced their staff by at least 50 per cent, which was also not uncommon in other east German industries (e.g. Nolte and Sitte 1995). According to the union officials, this size distribution is roughly representative of the east German clothing industry (interview, GTB south-east, September 1994).

The female dominance in the eastern workforce remained high in 1994: in only three firms was the female rate less than 50 per cent of the total workforce, and in sixteen firms it was higher than 90 per cent.

In the west companies were on average larger than in the east. In 1995, 22 per cent comprised less than 100 employees and 78 per cent more than 100 employees (including 19 per cent of over 500 employees). In 1990, the picture was similar with 20 per cent having less than 100 and 80 per cent more than 100 employees. This distribution is strongly biased towards larger firms. In the total district, Westfalen-Osnabrück, 42 per cent of firms (with a works council) had more than 100 employees (162 firms out of 382) in 1994 and in Nordrhein this figure was 39 per cent (92 firms out of 235) (source: GTB, works council election data 1995). This over-representation of large firms was a result of the explicit wish of the district officials to select predominantly large firms with over 100 employees for this survey.

When asked about the medium-term prospects of their firms, the east respondents were split: twenty-two were sceptical and twenty were more optimistic. Privately owned firms were more optimistic than Treuhandanstalt firms, and firms with new management felt more secure than those with former managers staying.[8] In the west, 60 per cent of the firms had experienced layoffs during the last few years and a third expected more staff reductions in the following twelve months. Over half of the works councils were, however, confident about the medium-term prospects of their firms.

Union density was high in both samples: in eleven east firms it was over 80 per cent and in twenty firms it was between 30 and 79 per cent (which is roughly in line with the 48 per cent union density of the district). It was revealed by t-tests that the density was stronger in firms with former managers and where medium-term perspectives were less optimistic, but not necessarily stronger in Treuhandanstalt firms compared to private ones. Union density was not correlated with the size of the workforce, though it was correlated with the female share in the workforce (the more females the stronger union density). Thus, one might speculate that female workers were more inclined to join this union than their male colleagues (perhaps because their jobs were more at risk). In the west, union density was at a similar high level: over three-quarters of the firms had a union density of more than 50 per cent. In eight firms it was even over 80 per cent.

There were only three incidences (out of fifty-three) of industrial unrest (e.g. walkout) in the east so far, but slightly more in the west: a quarter had experienced industrial unrest. However, both sets of data support the idea of the clothing industry as a non-militant sector.

Finally, over half of the east German works councillors who responded have been in position since 1990–1, and forty-five west German works councillors (nearly 70 per cent) have been in this position for more than seven years. All were members of the GTB. In the east, sixteen councillors had been officials

Table 4.3 Level of items of works councillors' perceptions of workplace relations (as percentage), their means (1 = strongly disagree, 5 = strongly agree) and significance levels (* = p ≤ 0.05, ** = p ≤ 0.01) in east and west Germany (N = sample size)

		Strongly disagree	Disagree	No view	Agree	Strongly agree	Means significance level	N
Works councillors' general perceptions of their relationship with management								
1. In general, relations between the works council and management in our company are good.	east	7.5	15.1	1.9	54.7	20.8	3.66	53
	west	12.0	9.3	0.0	54.7	24.0	3.69	75
2. Management is a trustworthy bargaining partner.	east	9.6	23.1	11.5	40.4	15.4	3.23	52
	west	12.2	20.3	6.8	41.9	18.9	3.35	74
3. Management tries to foster a trustworthy relationship with the workforce.	east	7.5	26.4	5.7	41.5	18.9	3.38	53
	west	16.0	25.3	8.0	34.7	16.0	3.09	75
4. Management tries constantly to strenghten their power position.	east	3.8	13.2	5.7	41.5	35.8	3.93 *	53
	west	17.3	17.3	4.0	32.0	29.3	3.39	75
Works councillors' understanding of their role								
5. Works council can only be successful if it harmoniously works together with management.	east	7.5	11.3	3.8	32.1	45.3	3.96	53
	west	3.9	7.9	0.0	34.2	53.9	4.26	76

6. We regard ourselves primarily as a connecting link between management and workforce.	east	3.9	3.9	5.8	26.9	59.6	4.26	52
	west	5.3	6.6	1.3	25.0	61.8	4.32	76
7. We try to do the best for the firm even if this sometimes contradicts union policies.	east	7.5	9.4	7.5	37.7	37.7	3.89	53
	west	15.8	11.8	6.6	31.6	34.2	3.57	76
8. The works council here is strongly supported by the workforce.	east	13.2	20.8	13.2	41.5	11.3	3.17	53
	west	14.9	12.2	2.7	45.9	24.3	3.53	74
9. Unions and employers have opposed interests.	east	5.7	11.3	5.7	54.7	22.6	3.77	53
	west	8.0	13.3	6.7	49.3	22.7	3.65	75
Works councillors' perceptions of day-to-day work relations with management								
10. We often solve problems with management informally.	east	7.8	13.7	5.9	51.0	21.6	3.51	51
	west	12.2	18.9	4.1	55.4	9.5	3.31	74
11. Management often involves the works council in strategic planning.	east	24.5	32.1	1.9	26.4	15.1	2.76	53
	west	25.0	30.3	3.9	36.8	3.9	2.65	76
12. We are never sufficiently informed by management.	east	3.8	11.3	1.9	45.3	37.7	4.02*	53
	west	13.5	13.5	4.1	45.9	23.0	3.51	74

of the former state union, FDGB, and thirty-four had not. This is in contrast to some suggestions in the literature (e.g. Artus *et al.* 1996; Martens 1992) that former unionists are a majority in east German works councils.

To conclude, although there was some variation among the companies in both samples, interviews with the officials at the employers' association and the union emphasised that overall the companies represented typical firms of the industry in the east and west. Unfortunately, there are no comparable representative official figures for the clothing industry available.

The major difference between the two samples is clearly firm size (around 70 per cent of east German firms have less than 100 employees as compared with around 70 per cent of west German firms having more than 100 employees). The fact that east German firms are relatively smaller than their western counterparts adds a critical factor to the comparative nature of this analysis. Based on the economic argument that small firms are more likely to boost more harmonious (less militant) workplace relations than large firms and that works councils are more likely to be incorporated into management in smaller firms (e.g. Kotthoff 1994), one would expect east German firms to have more co-operative or even incorporated works councils than their larger west German counterparts. In other words, the difference in size should support the null hypothesis that east German works councils are more likely to be incorporated into management than those in the west.

Co-operative workplace relations in the east and west

In order to examine the quality of workplace relations (i.e. workplace climate) and to establish the extent to which workplace relations in the east are significantly more co-operative (from the works councillors' point of view) than in the west, a set of previously tested questions was introduced. It is obvious that this small-scale survey cannot provide a complete picture of the workplace situation nor can it differentiate between the various detailed types of works councils in Kotthoff's categorisation (see Chapter 3). However, the survey should be seen as a first approach to investigating the prevailing assumptions that works councils are powerless and merely an 'extended arm of management'. Moreover, placing this comparison in a declining industry (which arguably induces less militant industrial relations) and having very different size distributions of east and west German firms makes this comparative study into a critical case study.

The first four items of Table 4.3 define the general quality of works council–management relations; the following five items discuss councillors' understanding of their role; and the last three items tackle more practical issues of their daily relationship with management. As a second step, a few selected hypotheses prevalent in the literature were tested to assess whether east German works councils are likely to be more co-operative. Overall, three-quarters of the respondents in each sample agreed on most issues, and there were virtually no missing answers. In terms of the councillors' general perceptions, both samples revealed a highly co-operative attitude towards management and workplace relations. For example, more than three-quarters of the east and west German councillors agreed that the workplace relations in their enterprise were generally good and over a half saw management as a trustworthy bargaining partner. Management was also seen to pursue a trusting relationship with the workforce. However, at the same time more than 60 per cent of the councillors in both samples saw management trying to strengthen their power position. This was the only item that evoked significantly different answers in the west and east. East Germans perceived their management to be stronger and more concerned with increasing their power than did their western colleagues.

With regard to the works councillors' perceptions of their role, over 70 per cent in both samples were convinced of the benefits and necessity of harmonious relations with management to fulfil their tasks successfully. They also described themselves primarily as connecting links between management and workforce, and not as a pure interest-representation group. The well-being of the firm was seen as of prime importance – even more important than pursuing union policies. In addition, the workforce was seen as strongly supporting the works council. However, councillors' role definition as an 'intermediary' organisation did not prevent them from perceiving opposing interests between employers and unions. There were no significant differences between the west and east in this aspect.

On a practical level, the works councillors seemed to be rather sceptical about management's co-operative attitude. Although workplace problems were often solved informally with management (i.e. without formal meetings and agreements), councillors in east and west felt insufficiently involved in strategic planning and insufficiently informed by management. In particular, east Germans felt significantly less informed. This is surprising when we take into consideration that east Germans felt slightly more involved in strategic planning (although not at a significant level), and that there were slightly more informal arrangements on the east German shopfloor than in the west. One possible explanation could be that councillors in the east have greater expectations regarding management's co-operative behaviour because of their former socialist experience where information on essential strategic issues (i.e. 'plan fulfilment') was widely available (information was not a power source for directors *vis-à-vis* the workforce).

In sum, the general picture presents works councillors who were in favour of co-operative relations with management and seemed to do their part, yet without being too subservient or antagonistic towards management. Works councillors in both samples seemed to be well aware of the other side's interests and strategies. Furthermore, works councillors in east and west Germany did not significantly differ in most of their attitudes towards management or in their workplace relations. The absence of any grave difference contrasts strongly with the literature's proposition of qualitatively different east German works councils which are weaker and potentially more 'subservient' than their western counterparts. If anything the data indicate slightly more problematic workplace relations in the east and works councillors who are definitely not subservient but rather cautious about their bargaining partners' strategies.

Determinants of co-operation in the east

Finally, three prevalent arguments in the literature, discussed in the previous chapter, about why eastern works councils are 'too co-operative' are examined further in a preliminary test of the east sample. Ordinary least-squares regression was used to estimate the effects of the following independent variables on east German councillors' perception of co-operative workplace relations ('good general relations between the works council and management') (Table 4.4).

First, there is the argument that the legacy of former co-operative workplace relations on the socialist shopfloor leads to strong co-operation today. This was tested by asking whether east German firms (i) which are still under Treuhandanstalt control, (ii) which kept former directors, or (iii) whose works councillors are former unionists, were more co-operative than privatised firms, in other words firms with new actors. Second, a related assumption is (iv) that the longer works councillors are in their job, the more likely is co-operation to evolve (they have learnt the necessary tacit skills etc.). The third explanation is that (v) the more insecure the firms' economic situation, the more both actors might depend on each other.

In addition, a few general antecedents were tested: the size of the firm (the smaller the firm the more co-operative are workplace relations) (vi); union density (a high union density might put a strain on workplace relations) (vii); the perception of councillors' role as being a co-operative partner should have an impact on the perception of workplace relations (viii–x); the strength of workers' support for the works council should have a positive effect on workplace relations (xi); and finally the perception of strong differences between unions and employers should have a negative impact (xii).

From the table, one can see that the characteristics of management (former or new directors) had an impact on councillors' perception of their workplace relations. Firms employing new directors were more likely to have 'good' workplace relations than firms that kept mainly former communist directors, as suggested in some literature. Yet, ownership (Treuhandanstalt or private) did not make a difference. In addition, works councillors who were not formerly involved in the union were more likely to perceive positive relations than councillors who were former union officials, in contrast to the hypothesis. Yet, the seniority of works councillors had no impact, which is in contrast to the proposition. Furthermore, the thesis that the economic insecurity of the firm influences perceptions of workplace relations cannot be supported. Works councils of insecure firms were also not more plant-oriented as opposed to union-oriented as compared with their colleagues in secure firms. Finally, size did not matter, clearly challenging the argument that industrial relations in smaller firms are significantly different (more harmonious) from those in larger ones. This adds

Table 4.4 Determinants of co-operation ('good general relations between the works council and management') in the east: standardized regression coefficients of 12 independent items

Independent items	Beta	Sig. T
i Current owner of firm (1 = Treuhandanstalt, 2 = private)	−0.169	
ii Current board of directors (1 = mainly former directors, 2 = mainly new directors)	0.278	*
iii Councillor being former union official (1 = yes, 2 = no)	0.284	*
iv Seniority of works councillor	0.012	
v Perceived long-term prospects of firm (1 = secure, 5 = insecure)	0.115	
vi Size: number in workforce (1994)	0.161	
vii Union density	0.052	
viii 'Works council can only be successful if it harmoniously works together with management.'	0.406	**
ix 'The works council here is strongly supported by workforce.'	0.015	
x 'We try to do the best for the firm even if this sometimes contradicts GTB's policies.'	0.089	
xi 'We regard ourselves primarily as a connecting link between management and workforce.'	0.078	
xii 'Unions and employers have opposed interests.'	−0.060	

Notes: * = $p \leqslant 0.10$; ** = $p \leqslant 0.05$; R^2 (adj.) 0.15601; standard error = 1.09509; residual = 40; $F = 1.80104$ (sig. $F = 0.0814$)

support to the previous finding that east German works councils are not different from west German works councils due to their company size.

The major determinant of 'co-operative perceptions' was the councillor's role definition: if works councillors saw it as their duty to work harmoniously with management then they were also more likely to perceive the actual workplace relations in a positive light. In other words, the role definition (which is to a certain extent given by the co-determination law) has a crucial impact on actors' perceptions. None of the other general determinants significantly influenced councillors' workplace perception. Particularly surprising is that the perception of union–employer differences did not influence councillors' perceptions of workplace relations.

It is obvious that this is a very preliminary and rather crude test that cannot stand on its own. Nonetheless, it should be seen as a useful complement to the overall impression derived from the frequency discussion.

Finally, two arguments of the literature outlined in Chapter 3 as to why east German works councils are not an effective interest representative were further examined. First, the 'plant-level egoism' (i.e. priority being given to company concerns rather than industry-wide concerns) of works councils should be stronger in the east than in the west and put a heavy burden on the union–works council relationship (e.g. Lippold *et al.* 1992; Mahnkopf 1991: 282, 1993: 17). In this clothing sample, more works councillors in the west than in the east regarded themselves as connecting links between workforce and management. However, more works councillors in the east than in the west took the firm's interests as their priority. Neither difference was significant, indicating that there was no stronger plant-level egoism in the east than in the west. Thus, the data cannot add support to the argument in the literature that 'plant-level egoism' predominates in east German works councils.

Second, east German works councils are said not to be effective interest representatives because of the low image of works councils which should evoke low support among the workforce. Indeed, the data showed that west Germans thought they were more supported by their workforce than east Germans, though at an insignificant level only. This is further substantiated in the analysis of union members' perceptions of their works councils in Part III.

In sum, these two arguments of works councils' presumed ineffectiveness are rejected in this data set.

4.4 Conclusion

This chapter outlined the transformation of industrial and workplace relations in the east German clothing industry. It can be characterised by heightened economic uncertainty, companies experiencing tremendous organisational changes, an employers' association struggling to keep its members, and a union which is neither dogmatic nor militant but co-operative, although not necessarily 'weak' with regard to the bargaining outcomes. The workplace climate was characterised as harmonious overall from the works councillors' point of view.

In a nutshell, the works councillors presented co-operative attitudes towards management without significant differences between the west and east or between large and small firms. The data add support to the argument of 'co-management' on east German shopfloors (e.g. Ermischer and Preusche 1992). However, they challenge the literature's view that east German works councillors are more co-operative than their western colleagues. The councillors were instead rather cautious in trusting management and were critical about management's willingness to co-operate. Also they did not perceive themselves as extended arms of management.

Moreover, the findings challenge the suggestions that co-management in east German workplaces is at risk in firms after privatisation (e.g. Ermischer and

Preusche 1995: 59), and that privatisation is likely to cause a polarisation between the two sides (e.g. Kern and Land 1991). In contrast, the data revealed that co-operation was more likely where there were 'new' managers and 'new' works councillors. This result is surprising in that it turns the literature's (e.g. Ermischer and Preusche 1992) hypothesis on its head. It suggests that the old socialist networks between directors and union officials are more obstructive than helpful in creating co-operative workplace relations in the new privatised firms. Privatisation enabled 'fresh blood' to make a new start.

Finally, the findings also oppose the view of some researchers (especially the Berlin/Göttingen group) that east German works councils have become incorporated and powerless 'extended arms of management'. Although the councillors in this sample are obviously not 'conflictual, class-conscious works councils' and thus strongly antagonistic (see Kotthoff's typology (Kotthoff 1981)), they were very aware of the different interests of capital and labour and also of the power balance within the firm and did not necessarily trust management. Thus, they certainly did not represent Kotthoff's 'deficient' types of works councils (isolated, ignored, extended arm of management), but more his 'effective' types, in particular the 'respected, co-operative' works council (which was also the major category in his west German study). In other words, the data support more the hypothesis of co-operative relationships than that of a one-sided acquiescence on the part of the works councils. This finding might stir up first doubts about the conclusion of some authors (e.g. Mense-Petermann 1996) that qualitatively different workplace relations are becoming established in east Germany (compared to the west). Broadly speaking, the findings provide an initial support for the successful implementation of a western industrial-relations institution in a post-socialist setting and this in a declining, struggling industry with small firms which would be predicated to experience serious industrial problems. This result strongly contrasts with that of studies which emphasise the lack of east German workers' support for works councils as well as those that postulate that works councils have not yet been successfully institutionalised (e.g. Jander and Lutz 1993a; Mahnkopf 1991: 280; Lippold *et al.* 1992: 92; Spangenberg 1993: 20). Part III of the book develops this discussion by focusing on the 'represented people' and their views on the institutions' effectiveness. Before that, the next chapter offers a detailed narrative of the changes of workplace relations in one particular major clothing company during the transformation. This case study analyses the actual development and functioning of workplace co-operation and adds thereby a different, qualitative dimension to the survey data.

5 Transformation at enterprise level

The case of Bodywear

This chapter presents an in-depth analysis of a successful organisational transformation of one major clothing company in Saxony after privatisation. After a brief outline of its restructuring success and personnel management changes, the discussion focuses on the changing workplace relations as seen from a management and a works council's point of view. Finally, the workplace climate of this company is further analysed by discussing four specific workplace problems that occurred during the fieldwork and how they were dealt with. The purpose of this case study is to complement the survey findings with a detailed insight into the quality and functioning of workplace relations in one particular setting.

The company (henceforth referred to as 'Bodywear') was visited on a regular basis during two years (1993–4) and a final follow-up visit was made in 1995. The fieldwork included a study of the company documents (collective agreements etc.); participatory observation at shopfloor and middle-management level for a month; structured interviews (one hour or longer) with the two full-time works councillors and with all six members of the management (director, three plant managers, two personnel managers) and various follow-up discussions with each of them; and structured interviews with eight supervisors in the three plants. The pilot study of the membership questionnaires was also conducted in this company in 1993 (see Chapter 7).

5.1 Organisational transformation

Chronology of the organisational restructuring

Bodywear[1] is a producer of underwear and belongs to the knitting sector of the clothing industry. The company was selected because it was the largest company in the GTB south-east district, was a full member of the employers' association (thus under sectoral bargaining), was privatised very quickly, and since then has experienced a thorough and financially 'successful' transformation.

Situated in Saxony, Bodywear was formerly the main GDR producer of underwear. Prior to privatisation, it was called VEB Trikotwear and it belonged to one of the large clothing combines, which employed about 52,000 people in fifty-two enterprises. Bodywear was bought in 1991 by a west German/Swiss company (a major underwear producer in the up-market sector) and is now a fully owned subsidiary, but legally an autonomous shareholding firm. Trikotwear was already a subcontractor for this western firm in the 1980s and soon after the turn-round in 1989 negotiations started closer co-operation. The German/ Swiss decided to buy the company in mid-1991 with a debt obligation of 4.1 million Deutsche Mark. It ran at a loss (which was mainly due to high depreciation rates) for the next two years, then in 1993 for the first time had a surplus and a turnover of 38 million Deutsche Mark.

The company reorganised itself soon after Autumn 1989, even before it was privatised. The old company director established an 'action programme' to get all workers involved in the aim of increasing performance and productivity. Special workgroups were created, not dissimilar to quality circles, with the major workgroup consisting of the director, the BGL, the Party secretary and shopfloor workgroup leaders (Aktionsprogramm document, 17 November 1989). However, the director was not seen as competent enough and was soon fired in December 1989. In his place the board of the combine appointed a trained engineer who had worked in the planning department of the combine. He introduced a new strategy to find a western investor as quickly as possible and meanwhile continued with the reorganisation.

The reconstruction process initially involved plant decentralisation. Trikotwear was already decentralised geographically (e.g. 25 production cells in 1980).[2] The firm now managed to privatise/reprivatise or liquidate the majority of the smaller units and non-production-related workshops (such as tool shops, kindergarten, etc.). The main surviving production plants were reorganised and modernised with the three major departments (knitting, dyeing and sewing) becoming independent profit centres. The company then embarked upon a capital investment programme with the major investment going into new dyeing-plant premises (now the most modern in Europe and with the latest environmental technology). A total of 36 million Deutsche Mark was invested between 1990 and 1992 with a further 20 million planned for the following two years. However, the production process itself was not significantly changed.

The reorganisation of personnel started with the dismissal of pensioners who were still working and the temporary Vietnamese 'guest workers' (who went back to their home country). Moreover, a complete reshuffling of staff took place: first, all jobs were internally advertised (as demanded by the works council) only later going to the external labour market. Although most people applied for their old jobs, middle management and supervisors (*Meister*) were nevertheless frequently substituted by east Germans deemed to be more competent, and given another job.

There were now three major middle managers, each responsible for one production unit (sewing, knitting, dyeing). The most important unit (sewing) was led by a west German (from the west German headquarters), the other two were east Germans (who were former employees but new in this position). At the same time, redundant production workers, especially dyers and knitters, were offered a transfer to the sewing department instead of dismissal. The sewing plant was built up as the major and most labour-intensive production unit. However, around 80 per cent of workers did not take up this offer. Sewing paid less and had a bad image (as before in the former GDR: 'those who sew are dull'). Thus, people preferred to go on the dole, presumably in the belief that they would find a job somewhere else. This naive belief, however, changed rapidly in the following years (director, interview August 1993).

In his first company-wide meeting the director declared that there would be no redundancies without an internal job offer. It soon became clear, however, that he could not keep this promise. Especially in the administrative departments, the reduction of staff was necessary due to the typical GDR employment ratio of 2:1 administration to production workers.[3] Initially, employees who were made redundant received compensation in line with the 'social plan' of the Treuhandanstalt. After privatisation, Bodywear management and the works council negotiated a plan which agreed that redundancies should be made '*sozialverträglich*', in other words taking personal social circumstances into account (a typical bargaining success of the east German works councils at that time). However, this was an informal agreement and was not mentioned in the formal social contract between works council and management (*Sozialplan*). This '*Sozialplan*' primarily regulated the level of compensation (once the Treuhandanstalt was no longer in charge). Although the works council insisted that this arrangement worked, they nevertheless admitted that bad performers were and are dismissed without taking their family circumstances into account.

Altogether, Bodywear reduced its workforce by 72 per cent over a period of five years from 2,232 employees (1,640 blue- and 592 white-collar) in 1989 to 625 employees in August 1994. In 1993 the then 680 employees comprised 490 production workers and 154 administrative staff and 'non-productives' (*Ungewerbliche*). The sewing plant alone employed 379 workers in 1993.

Changes in personnel policies and management style

The organisational restructuring also involved major changes in personnel management policies and practices, including payment systems, training, and working time, and also in the supervisory styles of management.

With regard to the wage policy, the company was one of the few companies in the area that constantly paid according to the sectoral bargaining agreements. The director argued that Bodywear had no intention of leaving the employers' association and would have even considered a company contract with the GTB if regional collective bargaining had fallen apart, which was a real possibility in the 1993 bargaining round. It is not clear whether this attitude derives from conviction (a belief in the need for collective bargaining or unions in general) or whether it comes from following policies set by the headquarters in the west. However, he was convinced of the need for high pay in order to motivate people and as a principle of justice ('we are doing good work here'). On the other hand, he perceived a low wage level as necessary to secure Bodywear's competitiveness in the external as well as in the internal market. For example, the recent acquisition of a clothing company in the Czech Republic meant that Bodywear competed with wages there which were about one-fifth of the east German wages.

The company job classification system was introduced in 1990 by the west German headquarters and was accepted by local management and the works council. Most changes were experienced in the sewing department. In the old system, sewers were paid by piece rate, and also earned a group (brigade) bonus. Bodywear introduced new piece-rate norms,[4] which were more demanding than before. Unsurprisingly, this caused a great deal of trouble amongst the sewers (interview with the sewing director August 1993). Although in the beginning everyone got 100 per cent pay (10.28 Deutsche Mark per hour) (i.e. for fully meeting the newly introduced norm) the average individual performance fell from 120 per cent (of the old norm) to 40 per cent (of the new norm) and the workplace climate became highly conflictual.[5]

Furthermore, the company emphasised from the beginning the importance of their human resources for company performance, and took great interest in quality control, flexibility and in selecting good workers and training them well. Whereas in the beginning Bodywear received only simple garments to produce, they were able to produce more fashionable and more difficult items in subsequent years. Both management and works council were proud of this. In terms of training, all sewers received specific training to learn the approved company sewing methods, which meant that those who had been accustomed to sewing in their own way, often for more than twenty years, had suddenly to learn a different sewing technique. Today a method trainer is linked to each working shift on a constant basis, and teaches the necessary sewing methods each time a new item has to be produced. A probation period of several days (with 100 per cent pay) is given. New recruits get a probation period of four weeks, and a training period of ten days. In the first three months they are paid a minimum wage of 95 per cent of the norm.

The east German managers and supervisors went to the west German main plant for a few months to be trained themselves, and west German supervisors also came to Bodywear (some stayed for nearly a whole year). Sewers were then advised by western trainers to learn the formal sewing methods.

There were also major changes in working time. Formerly workers worked 43.5 hours per week. This figure was reduced to 40 hours, which makes five eight-hour days plus an unpaid break of 30 minutes per day. Part-time work did not exist in the GDR, and still did not later on, although some female employees expressed a desire for it. Shift working was, however, commonplace in the GDR: dyers worked three shifts a day and this arrangement has continued, and knitters continued to work two shifts as before. Only those in the sewing department had never had shift work before. In 1992 two shifts were introduced for all workers and one shift only for single mothers with children under 14 years (or older if the husband works three shifts). Shift working has no appeal for sewers. They truly hate it.

Finally, all social services (e.g. kindergarten) which the socialist enterprise previously provided were abolished, including the benefits for mothers (e.g. a day off a month called 'household day'). Bodywear did, however, keep a company transport service, picking people up from home and bringing them back (since people now live quite far away and public transport is inadequate). They also set up an employee shop where Bodywear products can be bought at a special rate. However, it was frequently noted by personnel managers and works councillors alike that not all social policies of the west German plants had yet been introduced in their plant (e.g. counselling in social/private affairs, '*Sozialberatungsstelle*').

In an attempt to discover what changes in supervisory styles had occurred, a short questionnaire was distributed to 8 supervisors (out of 14) in 1993 (see Appendix A 5.1). The supervisor or *Meister* was responsible for a large workgroup (shift) consisting of around forty workers. The findings suggested that the transformation led to an increase in supervisors' status, and that they felt more respected by managers and workers alike. On the other hand supervisors also felt more pressure at work and said that there was more competition between supervisors. This is a common finding in the literature (e.g. Lungwitz 1994: 305). Regarding supervisors' perceived changes in worker (*Mitarbeiter*[6])– supervisor relations, they declared that the work pace was increasing. However, they thought that 'team spirit' still existed among the workforce. Most did not let workers participate in shopfloor decisions, control was tight, and they retained a 'traditional' view of pay as the major work motivator. These statements confirm the picture of a traditionally organised and managed company. Moreover, they thought that the capitalist system treats the workers in a more equitable manner. In sum, the supervisors seemed to provide support for both scenarios in the literature: the 'Tayloristic' traditional management style (e.g. Mahnkopf 1991) and the 'caring' east German manager-type (e.g. Lungwitz and Preusche 1994).

Summing up the various facets of the internal transformation of Bodywear, one can argue that a rigorous reorganisation took place on all hierarchical levels, which implied rationalisation, new organisational structures (e.g. profit centres) and the adaptation of personnel management to western laws and regulations. This was achieved in a very short period of time and without any direct employee participation or major interference by the works council. Overall, the production standards of the west German plants have been introduced, though these are quite traditional and therefore not linked to any new lean production methods. This is nonetheless a widespread feature not only of the east German clothing industry (e.g. Heidenreich 1991b) but also of west German clothing firms (see Taplin and Winterton 1997). Thus, there was a strong division of labour within the production arena and between decision-making and execution. Production workers have no real discretion over their work. Disciplinary measures are taken seriously and control is thought to be tight. For example, 'performance is crucial, otherwise you are sacked' (production manager S). In particular, the west German managing the sewing plant was a firm believer in 'Tayloristic' leadership styles.

In considering the above comments, one can interpret the production system of Bodywear as a combination of Tayloristic work organisation and control mechanisms and of paternalistic personnel policies. The next section describes the establishment of the works council at Bodywear and outlines both management's and works council's perceptions of their workplace relations.

5.2 Workplace relations at Bodywear

Establishment of the works council at Bodywear

The 'turn-round' of worker representation happened at Trikotwear in spring 1990. A meeting of the shop stewards of the BGL in early 1990, in which an election was organised, became highly conflictual because the BGL resisted the demands of some 'reformers' to introduce a worker council (they got the idea after researching 'what the west has got'). However, the election results supported the reformers who then succeeded in abolishing the BGL. The rights of this worker council resembled those allowed by the west German co-determination law (BetrVG, which had not been enacted at this stage).

The first works councillor (who remained in his post until 1995) was formerly active in the BGL, and his demographic characteristics (male, middle-aged, skilled technician (*Facharbeiter*)) are typical of east German councillors (e.g. Kädtler *et al.* 1997; Kottwitz 1991). Technicians have contact with people in all departments through their work, and being highly skilled workers they were interested in the firm's reconstruction and in the introduction of better technology. The first deputy of the works council, a woman, had not been active in the union before, but was voted in as a new steward in 1990.[7] In July 1990 a new 'proper' works council under the (west) German law had to be formed, which made new elections necessary. The council consisted of seventeen members at that time, including two full-timers (councillor and vice).[8] Thirteen members were blue-collar workers, four were white-collar workers and three-quarters were female. Four years later (in 1994) the two full-time works councillors were re-elected.

Workplace relations from management's perspective

In an attempt to discern management's view of workplace relations, interviews were conducted in 1993–4 with the management representatives. In addition, a questionnaire was given to the head of the personnel department during the 1993 interviews (see Appendix A 5.2; an identical questionnaire was filled out by the works council, see below).

Overall, the general conclusion of all data is that the works council is an accepted partner, and that the relationship with the council is functioning, although differences can and do exist. The works council is definitely not seen as an arm of management. In what follows the positions are outlined in more detail.

The chief executive had no problems in negotiating with the works council, but said that 'we are not friends'. Whereas in the first years he negotiated directly with the works council, at the time of the interview it was the personnel department (sometimes the production managers themselves) who did the job. This was because, according to him, he had too much other work to do since he was now in charge of the Czech acquisition.

The director of the sewing plant, the west German middle manager, recounted a different relationship with the works council. Although he acknowledged the need for a good relationship, he did not seem to care for it much and assumed that it was the works council's responsibility (rather than his) to compromise. He also thought that there were some 'trouble-makers' in the works council, and that a lot of sewers frequently went to the works council and complained (interview August 93). In 1995 he took over the day-to-day management of the whole company, due to the chief executives' main responsibilities in the Czech plant. In the last interview, in October 1995, he still considered the works council more as 'a millstone around his neck' rather than a legitimate institution, and only seemed to negotiate with them 'because it is the law'. Whether works council–management relations were now changing and deteriorating could not be confirmed at this time. However, the major day-to-day bargaining partner of the works council remained the personnel department.

The viewpoints of the (east German) chief personnel manager and her assistant, expressed in the 1993 questionnaire, were more in line with that of the chief executive. They saw the works council as a responsible and fair bargaining partner that cares about the well-being of the firm and does not want to weaken the discipline of the workforce or provoke disputes at every opportunity. Problems are often regulated informally. The council was not seen as a mouthpiece of the union. Management was said to inform the works council extensively. Moreover, the personnel manager acknowledged that the works council has strong support among the workforce, but that the workforce was not very interested in the quality of the relationship between management and council.

A year later, however, in the summer of 1994, at a time of a dispute over Saturday work (see below), the personnel managers revealed more negative views of the works council in the interviews. They argued that management sometimes would prefer not to have a council at all. Moreover, the works council was not perceived as trying to co-operate with management, and it did not, they believed, really understand the problems and worries of management. In general the relations between works council and management were considered as being poor.

Despite these apparent contradictions it seems safe to conclude that generally speaking the personal managers indicated a respectful and functioning relationship with the works council, although differences can and do exist. It reinforces the argument that the works council is definitely not perceived as an arm of management by managers. Both managers repeatedly claimed that despite strong differences in opinion they care about the 'harmonious' relationship with the works council, and prefer 'rational' discussions to ideological fights. They have their offices next to each other, know each other from the old days, and have breakfast together every day. Thus, as the chief councillor also claimed, 'personal relations should not suffer' (interview, August 1994).

In sum, the variation in opinion of the director, the production manager and the personnel managers suggests that the works council at Bodywear is certainly not incorporated into management. On the contrary, it cannot even be said that harmonious relations were always the norm. Moreover, the different views among managers suggest that there is no coherent management strategy towards the works council. It seems to be a dynamic interrelationship where expressed opinions are also influenced by actual workplace incidents.

Finally, management expressed similar attitudes towards the union (interviews August 1993). The director claimed an 'objective' relationship with the GTB chief official ('she is a trade unionist but nevertheless quite serious and rational') and accepted the union as a legitimate collective bargaining partner. In a similar vein, the personnel managers regarded the GTB as a responsible bargaining partner but emphasised the divergent interests of employers and unions. And the west German plant manager took the union and collective bargaining as a 'given fact'.

Workplace relations from the works council's perspective

The works council's viewpoint will be presented mainly on the basis of a questionnaire which incorporates identical questions to the above questionnaire of the personnel manager, and which was filled in by the chief and deputy of the works council during an interview in 1993. The questions are also similar to those of the works council questionnaire of the GTB survey (see Chapter 4).[9]

Overall, the management–works council relationship was seen as co-operative by the two full-time works councillors. Management was seen as a responsible bargaining partner (which is in line with what the personnel manager thought about the works council) and as a co-operative partner (whereas the personnel manager described the council as not co-operative). They also agreed that problems are often solved informally, as did the personnel manager. Furthermore, the councillors agreed that management informs the council sufficiently, and also that management respects the views of the council.

The councillors, however, also expressed critical views about the management. For example, management was accused of exploiting each opportunity to improve their power position (whereas the personnel manager did not think the same of the works council). Moreover, they were unsure whether management understood the problems of the workforce, and whether management would prefer not to have a council.

The negative views were more openly expressed in the unstructured interviews a year later. The chief official explained that he did not want to be elected again in four years' time and chose instead to take retirement in 1995. He is, as he says, 'married' to this enterprise: his grandfather and father both worked here and he has known this company from childhood. However, he is fed up with having fewer and fewer opportunities to improve the social conditions in the firm. 'It isn't fun anymore and it is getting worse every year. Your hands are bound, because the demand is down. . . . The constantly increasing pressures on sewers' performance and the increasing threat to those who want to consult the works council is just capitalism at its worst' (interview, August 1994).

There is a slight divergence between the views expressed by the two full-time councillors and the 'normal' members of the works council. The 'part-time' council members had generally a more negative view of the management–works council relationship (structured group interviews, August 1994). For example, they did not agree that management was informing the works council sufficiently, and they also disagreed that problems were often solved informally with management. This difference from the chief councillors' view might indicate that the chief councillors primarily communicate informally with management without informing their colleagues. Thus, they might have informal communications that are often hidden from their colleagues. This is a phenomenon which Kotthoff frequently observed in his west German study (1994). This is further supported by the fact that the works council leader also sits on the supervisory board of Bodywear (comprising two shareholder representatives and one workforce representative), which gives him access to more information, but not, he argued, really influence.

In terms of their relationship with the union (GTB), both works councillors and the chief union official regarded it as generally close and good (interview, August 1994). Bodywear was the largest unionised firm in the union district and both works councillors were active in union committees. In the beginning (1990) there was much joint activity between union and works council in order to unionise the workforce. Later on, the union officials attended works council meetings but besides this were not very active at Bodywear. In 1993, for the first time, the GTB organised a two-day information desk at Bodywear in order to recruit new members (in the canteen, since management did not allow it to be inside the production hall) and this was on the initiative of the works council.

However, the works councillors did not regard themselves as representing the GTB. For them, company interests have priority, but they acknowledged the union position, albeit primarily as a service organisation. Also the GTB was not regarded as intervening in company concerns. Finally, the works councillors acknowledged divergent interests between the two sides, unions and employers.

Union density at Bodywear was around 32 per cent (the works council had no precise figures) and had not changed significantly over the last four years. However, according to the councillor it would be lower if the union subscription was not deducted at source (1 per cent of pay). The density was below the overall density of 57 per cent (1993) in the union district. No reason was given for this low unionisation of Bodywear. However, one should take into account that the south-east region contains many textile and clothing firms and it is well known that the unionisation of clothing firms is on average lower than that of textile firms (union official interview, July 1994).

In August 1995 an interesting event took place which supports the thesis that the councillors put the interests of the firm before union interests. As mentioned before, the union was organising token strikes in several major companies during the collective bargaining period. Bodywear, being a major company, was asked to organise a similar strike. The works council discussed this at their meeting and the majority of members voted against it. This was a few days before the official workforce assembly took place. Shortly before the assembly started, the chief union official (who usually attends) persuaded the councillors to at least try a 'sit-in' after the assembly had finished. Accordingly, the assembly was officially closed after twenty minutes, and then the GTB official asked the workers to remain (voluntarily) in their seats for ten more minutes in order to strike. Most people (200) indeed stayed. Astonishingly, even the personnel manager, who was attending the assembly, asked whether she could stay on and thus in effect joined the strike! However, according to the works councillor, many workers complained afterwards that they had felt overwhelmed by the union, that it was a lousy strategy of the union and that they had not wanted to strike. The councillor agreed with the workers' view. In the interview, the councillor was convinced that most workers did not really understand what was going on. The fact that the personnel manager stayed on further supports this conjecture. The union official, however, argued that the workers stayed voluntarily and that they had the opportunity to leave. This was in fact the first industrial action in the history of Bodywear.

Finally, management was not seen as having strong support among the workforce, and the councillors thought, in contrast to the personnel manager, that the workforce does indeed have an interest in the quality of the relation between works council and management. However, that does not mean that the works councillors were content with the level of activism and interest among the workforce for works council or union issues. They argued that they sought regular contact with the workforce but that the interest of the workers in the works council's work was decreasing. For example, Bodywear still has no union shop stewards. According to the chief councillor, a major reason for this is that workers in former times went to the BGL and were helped, especially if they were Party members. Also, there was much informal networking and nepotism. In modern, capitalist times the works council cannot help everybody and is therefore sometimes, wrongly he claimed, perceived as part of management.

In sum, despite the sometimes mixed accounts, it seems safe to argue that during these three years the councillors' overall perceptions of management were more positive than the more divergent statements of the personnel manager or the works council. Yet both parties indicated a reasonable working and respectful relationship, although differences between both sides can and do exist. Clearly, both sides supported the interpretation that the works council is independent from management and from the union.

5.3 Four examples of personnel policies at Bodywear

Finally, to illustrate the actual practice of workplace relations at the time of investigation (Summer 1993), four major examples of workplace problems and how management and the work council were dealing with them are reported. In the first two problems (high absenteeism rate and low labour productivity) the works council has no legal co-determination rights, whereas it has legal rights regarding the last two issues (the closure of the knitting department, and the introduction of overtime/Saturday work).

First, *absenteeism* was a serious problem in the sewing plant until 1994. However, this had been a long-standing problem, with current rates similar to the high levels in the former GDR. For example, in 1989, 297 working hours per person out of a total of 2,188 hours per annum were lost to absenteeism. This figure amounted to 15 per cent of total working time. In 1992 the absenteeism rate in the sewing plant was somewhat lower at 13 per cent, which was still above the average company total (all European plants) of 9.8 per cent and in particular above the 7 per cent average of the west German plants.

The director related this problem to the increasing 'private stress' of the employees during these times of societal transformation (e.g. many single mothers or single household earners), and also to the fear of not being able to learn the new sewing methods following the introduction of new items. Accordingly, absenteeism rates rose each time new sewing products were introduced. His strategy was to speak to each individual, explaining to them that they need not fear being sacked, and that it was important for the company's success and for their colleagues that they come to work. In addition, the supervisors were told to make people feel that they were missed if they did not come to work. Since this did not help achieve any sustainable improvement, the director repeated the talks a year later in 1993. He made it very clear that if they did not perform to the best of their ability, their jobs would be at risk due to the increasing Czech competition (two plants had already been closed in west Germany). Thus far (1995) these measures appear to have worked. Interestingly enough, such interventions were not opposed by the works council. The councillors shared the concern of management, but also blamed the increasing work pace and stress at work for absenteeism. However, although they were informed of the management's practice, the councillors stayed very much in the background in these discussions.

Second, a related problem was the lower *labour productivity* of the sewing plant compared to standards in the plants in the west. In 1993, an average of 105 per cent of the standard was achieved, which was an improvement on previous years but was still under the west's average of 125 per cent.[10] Management argued that this was not due to lower skill qualifications, but instead that it was a mental problem (i.e. a lack of 'quality thinking'). The (east German) director claimed in general that, '*these* east Germans only want D-Marks and travel, but not to work. Here a strong man is necessary ('hier muß mal ein starker Mann her'). In west Germany there is too much democracy' (interview, May 1994).

The west German manager agreed that 'workers are lazy here' and added that 'they always stand together in groups and complain about something, whereas in west Germany people stand together and discuss positive things, for example their activities last weekend'. He states that in former times the workers went to the BGL or Party and complained, whereas now they have to approach the supervisor and this creates problems for them. However, he distinguished between two basic groups of workers. One group has adapted well and likes the new flexibility, the other does not like it, since it involves too much thought and too many changes for them. In order to improve productivity, management put a lot of effort into persuading workers to work harder, even threatening sewers that they will lose their jobs if they do not increase their productivity. Apparently this has had an effect, since according to them workers' productivity has risen. The works council shared the concerns of management, but also emphasised the improvements already achieved. However, they did not oppose management's talks with employees, or their efforts to extract greater work effort.

Third, another major event was the *closure of the knitting plant*, which was announced by management in the summer of 1993. The reason given was that contracting-out had become cheaper. From Autumn 1993 onwards, production and labour were to be gradually reduced until final closure came in spring 1995. The knitters were informed with very little notice, and they had to decide within a few days whether or not to take up the offer of a job in the dyeing plant. This was the bargaining achievement of the works council: that all knitters were to be offered a new job. Some knitters, who were selected by different criteria (e.g. who were living close to the dyeing plant, or who were actually present at the time and not on holiday), were told to move right away. Others had to move in the months following. For the knitters, many of whom had worked in this plant for the last 20–30 years, this meant not only a change to completely new work but also less money (dyers get paid less than knitters). In addition, there were also supervisors who now had to start all over again as unskilled workers. However, most people obeyed: 'What can I do? It's good to have a job at least' was the common response. And: 'It was a shock, but what can I gain from running around like a "dog without a bone" all the time?' (dyer, August 1993). Another one: 'I don't know why I was selected to move immediately. They decided.' (dyer, August 1993).

Fourth, there was the constant problem of *Saturday work* in the sewing department. Saturday work was not unknown in the GDR; however, it was voluntary and brought not only overtime pay but also a very high extra bonus just for turning up. In 1993, when the topic arose at Bodywear again, most did not really understand the need for it and argued that it was caused by inadequate company planning. According to personnel management, workers still did not seem to realise that in a market economy 'the firm cannot plan as well as it formerly did in the plan economy' (chief personnel manager, July 1993). A year later (1994) sewers, although no longer blaming poor planning, were still reluctant, largely because performance pressures during the week were perceived as being so high that they preferred their weekend for recreation. Under the labour law the company cannot introduce overtime or Saturday work without the works council's permission. The works council acknowledged the need for overtime in the current situation, yet wanted to agree to additional work on a few Saturdays only on condition that workers worked seven hours and got eight hours' pay. However, the collective bargaining contract that year allowed flexible working hours to be worked without additional payments. Thus, as long as workers got a few days off in the following months to recompense the Saturday work, no overtime had to be paid. This resulted in a major conflict between works council and management. In the end the works council had to drop its objections and support management. They argued that workers should be happy to have additional work. For the winter temporary cuts in working hours (*Kurzarbeit*) had already been planned.

Together, these examples of how workplace problems were handled character-ise Bodywear's workplace practices. Overall, workplace problems were dealt with by management in a highly authoritarian but also paternalistic way. For example, the chief executive found the time to talk to each of the 379 (!) sewers indi-vidually, whereas on the other hand the closure of the dyeing plant was carried out without informing the workforce in advance.

The works council seemed to become active in issues where there are statutory (co-determination) rights for the works council (e.g. plant closure or Saturday work), and they tried hard (and were successful) to achieve a compromise which took the social interests of the workforce into account. However, in issues where they did not have formal rights (e.g. absenteeism, productivity, management interviewing workers), the works councillors remained in the back-ground, supporting in principle management's rationale ('survival of the firm'), because they felt they were powerless to react against the overwhelming forces of the free market. However, they were nevertheless informed by management about these personnel issues and about management's action plans. This sup-ports a previous suggestion by Kirschner (1991) that the east German works councils tend to focus on the narrowly defined areas where they have legal (infor-mation, consultation or co-determination) rights, and thus pursue a rather formalistic, juridical relationship with management. But this does not mean that they are incorporated into management.

5.4 Conclusion

This case study presents a company that successfully managed the transformation to a market economy. Its employee relations are characterised by significant changes in working conditions, in particular increases in work pace and quality. The company is a prototype of privatised east German companies organised in a strictly Tayloristic way. Yet, the 'polarisation' scenario of antagonistic workplace relations, suggested by some authors (e.g. Kern and Land 1991) to result fromthe intensifying 'Taylorisation' cannot be supported. The case study presented a specific mixture, whereby managers optimised a Tayloristic work organisation while introducing more flexibility and higher quality standards, practising some 'paternalistic' personnel policies, accepting sectoral bargaining agreements, and negotiating with the relatively strong works council in a mostly co-operative way.

Thus, as with the works councils in the GTB survey and perhaps even to a slightly larger extent, the Bodywear works council could be characterised as being co-operative, but at the same time not an 'extended arm of management'. It was concerned with keeping the interests of the workforce on the agenda. Yet, the works council saw the need for working together in order to maximise benefits accruing to both the firm and the workforce.

What then are the possible reasons for this co-operation? On the one hand one could trace it back to the personal relationships between the actors on the two sides.[11] However, the retirement of the chief councillor (Autumn 1995) seemed not to have affected workplace relations in any significant way, at least not in the short term, according to the vice councillor who took over the post (interview, October 1995). In addition, it might be not so much the personality of the chief councillor and of the chief executive, but rather a legacy of the co-operative workplace climate of the socialist past which accounts for the current workplace relations. However, the case study does not provide data on the former socialist workplace relations and thus cannot contribute to the discussion in Chapter 2. However, it does provide some limited evidence that workplace relations did not become more conflictual after privatisation, as has been suggested in some studies (see Chapter 3). This might indicate that workplace relations also were 'co-operative' in former times (as the literature suggests). Finally, the co-operative relations at Bodywear could also be due to specific, favourable conditions. Thus, the original worker council at Bodywear was installed in 1989–90 explicitly in order to improve interest representation, thus neither to install self-management of the workers, nor to become a management consultant or administrator of the reorganisation. It could be argued that the specific circumstances in this company supported more independent interest representation. Thus, management did not really need the works council to discipline the workforce in the beginning since the early replacement of the director secured management authority. A good example of this is that privatisation and the take-over negotiations, together with the organisational restructuring process, was made without the works council. This is in contrast to other studies whose findings refer to joint efforts of restructuring in the early years of transformation (e.g. Bergmann 1996: 277; Ermischer and Preusche 1995; Röbenack 1996). Furthermore, the early connections with the western investor and an unproblematic relationship with the Treuhandanstalt prevented the works council from becoming a wholesale management accomplice. Consequently, the works council dealt and deals with far more favourable conditions than those of many other east German clothing firms, and might have an easier time in maintaining its independence from management. Yet, as noted above, it is difficult to pinpoint a single reason for this co-operation, since a mixture of various factors might be the most likely explanation.

Finally, the case study cannot support many of the listed problems inhibiting works councils' effectiveness as outlined in Chapter 3. For example, the workforce is quite homogeneous (no part-timers, short-term workers, '*ABMler*') which makes the works councillors' work that bit easier. With regard to the problem of the lack of experience, the interview material did not provide any indicators to suggest that knowledge or 'tacit' skills necessary for effective interest representation were lacking. Both councillors seemed very knowledgeable with regard to the legal regulations (as also mentioned by Lippold *et al.* 1992 and others). Moreover, the relationship between union and council has been stable and co-operative throughout the last few years, and also the disagreement over the token strike did not seem to have challenged the overall relationship (according to the works councillor and chief union official, interview, October 1995).

So, in this respect the works council should work effectively. One might conclude that the works council seemed to belong to the category of works councils that provided an 'effective' interest representation (see Kotthoff's typology, Chapter 3). It seems that the works council understood itself as a representative of workers' interests, as well as being an '*Ordnungsfaktor*', an institution that guarantees the proper functioning and organisation of the workplace. However, the data do not tell us anything about the workers' views yet. These will be analysed in the following chapters.

A last point: the data provided some basic indicators for the successful institutionalisation of the works council at Bodywear (e.g. management accepts works council, overall co-operative workplace relations, the existence of formal work agreements). However, as said before, 'co-operation' does not necessarily imply that the works council is effective in representing workers' interests. And the findings say nothing about workers' acceptance of the works councils. The institutional approach is thus not appropriate for addressing these issues. As argued in the introductory chapter, they can only be addressed by surveying workers' attitudes and behaviour, which will be done in Part II.

Conclusion to Part I

Part I dealt with the first of the three purposes of this book, to describe the institutional transfer of workplace relations in one particular east German industry. It outlined the formal development of industrial relations institutions after unification, and the current workplace practices and problems faced by the interest institutions as seen in the literature. Chapters 4 and 5 contributed to this literature review by outlining the transformation of the industrial relations actors of the clothing industry, by examining management–works council relations from a works council's point of view in a sample of clothing companies, and by providing an in-depth analysis of the workplace transformation of one specific firm.

In short, Part I pursued two aims: to present the current research issues and findings on the institutional transformation of workplace relations; and to examine these in one specific industry. In particular, it dealt with the central question of whether works councils in this industry are co-operative or incorporated or even in conflict. The survey (and case-study) findings challenge the prevailing position held by other authors on this topic: notably that works councils were found to be co-operative but not incorporated in management decision-making.

Some shortcomings of the institutional approach to workplace relations became evident. The approach neglects the workforce–works council and workforce–union relationships and their possible impact on the transformation of the interest institutions. As outlined before, this book argues that these relationships have to be examined if one truly wants to understand the transformation process. For example, the finding that works councillors claim to have a harmonious work relationship with management does not tell us anything about the extent to which workers actually trust and accept the works council or whether they perceive the works council as being effective in representing their interests. This was assumed to be a necessary precondition and thus an indicator of the effective working of works councils. Thus, asking workers about these issues seems necessary in order to understand the extent to which the union or works council has been institutionalised in practice. This is especially true in the face of the informal networks which existed on the socialist shopfloors and which might interfere today with the formalisation of interest representation (see Chapter 2). In addition, workers' attitudes and behaviour can equally advance our understanding of the institutionalisation of west German unions in east Germany. These issues are part of the larger investigation of union member attitudes (and to what extent they are individualistic or collectivist towards their interest representation) which will be discussed in the following two parts of the book.

Finally, a side issue of the membership investigation involves an assessment of whether the 'harmonious' workplace climate in the companies examined in Chapter 4 had an impact on the workers' relationship to management. Thus, do workers reveal low 'them-and-us' feelings towards management and emphasise instead a unitarist 'we'? Analysing workers' perceptions might also tell us something about the general success of the organisational transformation in terms of workers' acceptance and commitment to the changes.

Part II

The cultural embeddedness of new labour institutions in the east

Part I was devoted to providing an analysis of the transformation of workplace relations by focusing on the institutional actors: works council, union and management. Part II introduces an alternative way of exploring the changing workplace relations and the institutionalisation of labour institutions through examining the perceptions of the workforce. Such an approach is deemed essential if one is to obtain a holistic understanding of the transformation process – something which is lacking in most other studies of this process.

The first chapter reviews the literature on worker attitudes in the post-1989 period and identifies a major hypothesis of the individualisation of the east German workforce. Since this book is interested in workers' individualism and collectivism towards their interest representation, the following investigation was restricted to unionised workers.

The next chapter discusses the concept of 'collective commitment' that is used in this study, and describes the methodology and samples of the membership surveys. The findings of these surveys are then discussed in the last chapter. The core question posed is to what extent east German members are more individualistic, instrumental and passive than their west German colleagues and hence less supportive of their new interest institutions.

6 Workers' attitudes in post-socialist east Germany

This chapter reviews existing studies on workers' attitudes towards the reorganisation of the workplace, works council and union during the transitional period. Overall the literature concludes that workers in east Germany are individualistic, passive and instrumental towards collective activities. The chapter then reviews the various explanations of workers' assumed reluctance to engage in collective activities, thus the reasons for the assumed lack of cultural support for labour institutions that are offered in the literature. The increasing individualisation of east German workers is characterised as one core hypothesis of this literature.

6.1 Review of workers' attitudes post-1989

Workers' attitudes towards organisational restructuring

There is a lack of research on workers' attitudes and behaviour towards the organisational transformation at their workplaces and towards the old or new management. There are four major empirical studies with an explicit focus on workers' perceptions and these will be briefly reviewed. Two of these are qualitative studies. Alt *et al.* (1993, 1994)[1] focused on workers' attitudes to the transformation of workplace relations and companies' social policies[2] and investigated 'individualism' amongst the workforce. Lungwitz (1994)[3] interviewed 130 employees (including 70 blue-collars) on a variety of issues (e.g. attitudes to the market economy or to the former work 'collective'), but did not explicitly look at people's reactions to organisational changes. More useful for this book's research are the two quantitative studies, Andretta *et al.* (1994)[4] and Heering and Schroeder (1992),[5] which will be briefly outlined here and discussed further when we analyse the membership questionnaires in Chapter 8.

Andretta *et al.* retrospectively examined general job satisfaction as compared to former times. They found that 44 per cent of the sample (66 per cent for the privatised firm) were more satisfied after unification, 27 per cent were less satisfied and that for 29 per cent there was no difference. Dissatisfaction with the pay–performance relation was high in all firms investigated (p. 13). Andretta *et al.* further concluded that the majority of workers had great problems in adapting to the changing 'organisational life' and especially to the new work requirements. This is partly because it is difficult to change old work habits and attitudes (e.g. they observed the continued extensive incidence of breaks), and partly because of the new requirements that are perceived as being too high and often contradictory: for example, simultaneous demands for efficiency and quality.

Heering and Schroeder (1992) investigated perceptions of the working conditions, of company restructuring, of work motivation, and of general attitudes towards unification. They found a highly motivated workforce, whose relationship to management was, however, less clear. On the one hand a majority (61 per cent) stated a positive general attitude towards management, but only 40 per cent were persuaded of management's capacity to modernise the firm (p. 75).

In sum, both studies – although investigating slightly different issues – come up with a mixed picture of positive and negative attitudes towards the organisational changes during transformation. A more detailed and representative analysis of job satisfaction would seem necessary to substantiate these results. This will be attempted in this book's survey (see Chapter 10).

Workers' attitudes towards the works council

The major argument of the few existing studies investigating this issue is that workers are disillusioned about the effectiveness of the works council in representing their interests. An obvious example is that of mass redundancies, which the east German works councils typically did not resist. Lippold *et al.* (1992: 88)[6] argue that earlier on (1989–90) workers were easily mobilised into collective action, but that when job reductions started they became disappointed about the limited power of the works councils and their increasingly subservient 'co-management' role. There is also the widespread feeling of being increasingly excluded from management and works-council decision-making, which makes the workforce retreat into individual survival strategies. Similarly, Andretta *et al.* (1994: 13) observed in their sample[7] that workers increasingly perceived their chances of realising their interests in the enterprise as low. Thus, only 12 per cent of their sample totally agreed that 'you can achieve your interests in the company quite well'; nearly the same amount (8 per cent), however, agreed to a similar question that asked about the interest representation in the old socialist firm. They conclude that these new interest institutions have not yet achieved a significant change in people's minds. Mahnkopf (1991: 280) speculates that there is a general feeling that 'co-management' resembles the old 'triumvirate' negotiations which evoke the perception that nothing has changed at all. That is, the works council often tries to be accepted by management as a reliable partner in difficult times instead of trying to gain trust and support among the workforce. It also fails to acknowledge that its power rests on this support, and that without it, management will not continue to accept them. The previously mentioned argument of the Berlin/Göttingen group (e.g. Jander and Lutz 1993a) that works councils, as an imported western institution, have no legitimacy on the shopfloor since they do not derive from any worker-led social movement, is related to this.

Overall, the authors conclude that these problems result in a de-solidarisation within the workforce and a low commitment to the works council (e.g. Lippold *et al.* 1992: 92; Spangenberg 1993: 20). However, other sources report different, more positive, results. For example, Mickler *et al.* (1992: 17; 1996) found in their case studies that works councils got more trust from the workforce than the unions did. They distinguish two categories of workers, 'solidaristic, loyal' supporters and 'passive–distant' prosecutors, but do not say how many of their workers were in each group (1996: 161). Heering and Schroeder (1992: 80) found that the workers in their firms had a similar more positive attitude towards their works council (76 per cent were positive) than towards their union (71 per cent). Furthermore, the large-scale survey, *DGB Trendbarometer* (1994) (which has surveyed a representative sample of the employed and unemployed working population every other year from 1992 in the east and west), on attitudes towards interest representation, shows that a majority of east German employees valued the works councils' work in 1994. This is slightly more than in 1992, although they were still more critical than in the west: in 1994, 32 per cent of east Germans valued the work (46 per cent west Germans), 30 per cent marked it negatively (25 per cent west Germans).

Generally speaking, the different findings of the literature might be partly due to the methodology used, through the use of different questions which make comparisons difficult. In addition, the questions are often too vague to be meaningful. Andretta *et al.* for example asked only the above quoted question on interest representation, which merely says something indirectly about the works council. Furthermore, Lippold *et al.* based their statements on interviews only with the institutional actors, and Heering and Schroeder asked questions that were too vague (e.g. 'positive attitude towards the works council'). Because of these deficiencies, one needs more detailed, representative research on workers' attitudes towards their new interest representation. For example, one might distinguish between workers' attitudes and their behaviour towards the works council. They might evaluate the works council's work critically, but still support it. This will be further explored in this book's empirical study.

Workers' attitudes towards the union

The relationship between the western unions and their members in the east is perceived as problematic and in that respect is similar to the attitudes discussed above. East German union members are declining in numbers and are generally seen as passive, individualistic, apathetic and having little interest in the union (e.g. Gut *et al.* 1993: 50; Eidam and Oswald 1993: 167; Fichter 1996: 16; Zech 1993: 28). As mentioned in the introductory chapter, there are virtually no specific empirical or theoretical studies on union members' attitudes and behaviour in east Germany during the current transformation. However, there are some accounts in the literature which will be briefly reviewed: specifically the theoretical notions as to why east Germans joined the new western unions in 1990, and a few large-scale attitudinal surveys with some questions on participation and other issues of union membership.

Reasons for joining the west German unions

With regard to the reasons for 'joining' the western unions in 1990 most academics argue that people demonstrated a highly instrumental decision-making approach. For example, Mahnkopf (1992: 35) proposes that most members who joined the new unions after 1989 did so because the western unions were seen as highly successful and professional and because of the (selective) incentives, such as strike pay and legal advice (also Fichter 1994: 56). Heidenreich (1991a) adds that western unions were seen as belonging to the 'successful' German model of industrial relations, and were even accepted by the successful western companies, which meant that the future economic prosperity might not be much at risk by having unions. Besides, they also symbolised successful interest representation (also Hildebrandt 1990: 102). Thus, the east German workforce did not want any different development from west Germany but instead to take over that western 'success' system. In addition, Kreißig (1990: 2)[8] argued that the major reason for workers to join the new unions was to achieve security against the arbitrariness of employers and the impending job losses. However, Zech (1993: 28) gave an example of the GEW (Gewerkschaft für Erziehung und Wissenschaft) union for teachers and academics. Here west German union officials working in the east declared that east Germans just joined 'out of habit' and now ask what the union is doing for them, thus indicating the prevalence of a 'consumption-oriented' attitude by leaders towards their membership.

Two points can be concluded: first, it seems that the overwhelming rejection of the FDGB had no bearing on people's acceptance of the new unions; and second, most members joined for instrumental reasons. It has to be emphasised that none of these statements are backed up with direct evidence; if anything they are based on second-hand data (i.e. interviews with union officials rather than with the membership/workforce). Furthermore, even if joining was a conscious instrumental decision, and even if people were also instrumental in their decision to participate in collective action, it does not necessarily lead to 'low participation' in further collective activities. Finally, the authors are not explicit as to what they mean by an 'instrumental approach' and what the alternative would be.

Various issues of union membership

There are various statements about union membership in the discussions of the problems west German unions face in the east. The common argument is, as mentioned before, that union members are passive, individualistic and instrumental and thus reluctant to support collective activities. However, these statements have not been tested explicitly. There are only a few large-scale attitude surveys, comparing the west and east German population, which contain some measurement of union participation and attitudes towards unions. For example, one well-known large-scale study on the east German population, '*Sozialreport*' (Winkler 1992: 288),[9] showed a decreasing willingness to participate in voluntary institutions such as political parties or unions (also Winkler 1993: 27). However, they base this interpretation on declining union membership figures, rather than on any direct measurement of willingness to participate. There are four other surveys (Heering and Schroeder, Weßels, IPOS and the *DGB Trendbarometer*) which incorporate some measurement, and these will be briefly reported. The already mentioned study by Heering and Schroeder (1992) found an acceptance (71 per cent) of the unions in their sample. Unfortunately, the questionnaire design is not published. Weßels (1992: 16) used secondary panel data to compare people's attitudes towards public institutions (political parties, occupational associations, unions, churches, environmental movements, etc.) in west and east Germany. There were two questions on participation in union activities and two broader ones which are reported in Table 6.1.

Table 6.1 People's attitudes towards public institutions: examples from Eurobarometer

(a) How often have you recently joined events (meetings etc.) of unions, religious groups, occupational, industrial, social associations? (highest rank = 1, lowest rank = 5)

 % of participation in union activity: (sometimes or often)
 East Germany: 34% (rank 5 out of 5) (east average of all organisations = 40%)
 West Germany: 26% (rank 4 out of 5) (west average of all organisations = 32%)

(b) Have you recently read publications of your own organisation (e.g. union)?

 % of yes answers:
 East Germany: 61% (rank 3 out of 5) (east average of all organisations = 58%)
 West Germany: 82% (rank 3 out of 5) (west average of all organisations = 82%)

(c) Do the following organisations (whether you are a member or not) represent your interests?

(d) Which of those organisations is the most important for you personally?

	East Germany (%)		West Germany (%)	
	I feel represented	*Most important organisation*	*I feel represented*	*Most important organisation*
Unions	68.4	35.1 (1)	48.1	14.0 (2)
Environmental groups	80.1	12.8 (2)	75.1	27.5 (1)
Protestant church	22.1	5.4 (3)	23.9	2.6 (6)
Civic movement	64.1	4.9 (4)	59.2	4.8 (4)
Women's groups	33.3	2.4 (5)	37.1	4.2 (5)
Catholic church	8.1	1.8 (6)	26.3	9.1 (3)
Employers associations	16.0	1.0 (7)	25.1	1.0 (7)

Sources: Eurobarometer study no. 34; representative sample of adults in west and east, 1990 (Wahlpanel, WZB Berlin/Deutsche Forschungsgemeinschaft), quoted in Weßels (1992: 7)

In sum, participation in union activities got the lowest rank in east Germany (the highest participation rate (68 per cent) was found in occupational organisations, but was slightly higher than in the west). Reading union journals was, however, a less appealing activity in the east than in the west (although this might perhaps be due to fewer publications being distributed in the east). On the other hand, unions represented most people's interests in east Germany (second only to the environmental groups), which is higher than in the west, and were also voted as the most important organisations.

In brief, the picture seems quite favourable for the unions, especially relative to their western counterparts. However, one has to keep in mind that both studies report data from the very early years of the transformation when there were still high expectations among east Germans of the western civil institutions, and unions were seen as a safeguard against the increasing labour-market insecurities.

The Mannheimer Institute for Applied Social Science Research (IPOS) found in their representative population poll that east Germans trust unions (after the judiciary) more than they trust parliament, the police, the media, the government or political parties (*Handelsblatt* no. 22, 2 February 1993, p. 6). However, when comparing the results of 1991 and 1992, the degree of trust was diminishing (Gabriel 1993: 9).

Finally, the *DGB Trendbarometer* (1994) concludes that union commitment and engagement is decreasing in both the west and the east. Four examples are given. First, in 1992, a majority of east Germans did not see their general expectations about unions fulfilled; in 1994 the figures were more positive and there is a growing similarity between the east and the west (the majority are happy). Second, regarding the general evaluation of unions' achievements since the '*Wende*' (turn-round) west and east Germans were more critical in 1994 than in 1992: 49 per cent of the total German membership were critical, 28 per cent were more positive (1992: 42 per cent critical, 36 per cent positive).[10] Third, 54 per cent of east Germans considered leaving their union in 1994, which was more than in the west (42 per cent), but slightly less than two years previously: 59 per cent (41 per cent in west). Finally, there is the question as to whether people saw themselves as active union members: in 1994, 20 per cent of west and east Germans declared themselves active, in 1992 this figure was 27 per cent (more east than west Germans then). This survey provides the most comprehensive data available, yet not all data are available to the public, and questions are sometimes quite vague (e.g. with regard to general expectations of the unions).

In sum, studies basically suggest that workers are disappointed about the works councils' effectiveness in successfully representing workers' interests; workers joined the unions for instrumental reasons; and although they regard the union as an important organisation, their trust in it is diminishing. However, there are methodological problems in some of the studies; findings are rarely explained; and they do not provide a comprehensive picture of workers' views of all major aspects of workplace relations.

Another set of studies approaches this topic in a more analytical way, proposing the existence of significant passive behaviour with regard to collective activities on the part of union members. These studies offer some theoretical explanations but are empirically weak and do not refer to the studies discussed above. However, they merit discussion and will be outlined in the next section.

6.2 Why do union members lack cultural support?

As mentioned in Chapter 1 a central assumption of most studies is that the successful institutionalisation of unions and works councils is partly hindered by the lack of a complementary culture of its actors, particularly workers and especially union members (e.g. Armingeon 1991; Eidam and Oswald 1993: 167; Fichter 1996: 16; Gut *et al.* 1993: 50; Lippold *et al.* 1992; Mahnkopf 1992: 35; Neubauer 1992; Zech 1993: 28). Thus, the null hypothesis of this book is that east German union members are significantly more individualistic, passive and negative about the institutions' instrumentality than their western counterparts. In that case one can conclude that the labour institutions have not yet succeeded in establishing a supportive culture amongst the people they represent.

The literature provides a mixture of explanations for east Germans' assumed lack of commitment, referring either to attitudinal legacies of the socialist past or else to the impact of the structural pressures of transformation. Thus, one argument is that post-socialist societies become more individualistic as they go through a modernisation process (e.g. Pollack 1991; Zapf 1992). In particular, the industrial relations literature refers to such individualism as diminishing workers' commitment to the unions, often resulting in their preferring individual to collective action (e.g. Pollack 1991: 280). Another line of argument is that socio-cultural contexts (and people) are more resistant to change and are apt to persist as a legacy of the past. For example, Stark (1992a) talks of the 'path dependencies' of societal transformation, Sztompka (1993a: 243) and Melich (1997) point to the 'deep cultural legacy' of the 'socialist mentality' and Blanchflower and Freeman (1993) suggest a continuing 'legacy of communist labour relations' in workers' attitudes.

Thus, there are differing judgements of the extent to which the transformation process (democratisation and marketisation) determines workers' attitudes and behaviour and to which old habits and values persist. While the 'individualisation' position argues that people adapt to changing structural conditions, the 'legacy' position assumes that attitudes are not so easily changed and that the communist socialisation still has a visible impact on current attitudes and behaviour.

In the ensuing discussion, the following three arguments of this literature will be analysed. First, union members have no collective identities (Eidam and Oswald 1993: 167; Fichter 1994: 56); second, east Germans are passive union members (Klinzing 1992; Woderich 1992); and third, unions and works councils are not regarded as effective interest institutions (Mahnkopf 1993).

'East German union members have no collective values'

Four main reasons for members' lack of union identity are presented. First, there is the argument that due to the centrality of the workplace in socialist times (see Chapter 2) members still identify strongly with their enterprise and management and therefore do not commit themselves to the union. Gensior (1992), for example, found in her survey that employees had a strong emotional link to their company in 1992 (also Dathe and Schreiber 1993: 10; Ruppert 1994: 284). According to Lippold *et al.* (1992: 95), the high incidence of company identity (i.e. perception of 'we are the owners') is still observable and this fosters, in her opinion, company loyalty and lowers the conflict potential in the workforce. Yet, there are other authors who claim that company identity has not existed in the GDR since the 1970s, due to generational changes and the obvious official neglect of the factories' working conditions (Hofmann and Rink 1993: 33). In fact, if it did exist, it is now decreasing in response to the organisational changes, especially the redundancies. However, these assertions lack evidence. For example, it would be necessary to investigate what kind of organisational identity or commitment did exist in former times (i.e. to the company as such, to the management, department, work collective, see Guest *et al.* 1993). Furthermore, it is not evident why company and union commitment cannot co-exist (see the literature on dual commitment, e.g. Guest and Dewe 1991).

The second and related argument is that union members were not morally affiliated to the FDGB and have insufficient experience of being a member of a truly voluntary organisation, thus a social movement. In former times the union functioned as a department of the state, today the union only functions and has power through the support of its members. Thus, the new union members are not prepared for 'solidaristic actions, open conflicts or for thinking in terms of legally defined rights, demands and duties in the dual system of industrial relations' (Mahnkopf 1991: 279, 1993: 16). They are not familiar with the role of unions and the duties of the members in the west (e.g. Heidenreich 1991a). Another author, Klinzing (1992: 20), relates this to the prevalence of the old consumerist attitude towards the union. Thus, the west German unions might need some time to get members 'morally' and emotionally involved with their organisation. However, the question is whether the assumed instrumental attitudes and union identity can co-exist or whether they are detrimental to each other.

Third, there is the proposition of the wider lack of democratic values and attitudes in the east German population (e.g. Jander and Lutz 1993a). Heidenreich (1991a: 33) takes workers' passivity during the peaceful revolution in 1989 as an indicator of the east Germans' apathetic attitude towards the fate of the labour movement. Also, after the turn-round there was little movement within the firms to establish more democratic work organisation in terms of self-management (see Chapter 3). This attitude is well described in the following quote: 'better to earn 3000 Deutsche Mark per month and be exploited than 800 east Mark and participate' (worker quoted in *Hamburger Abendblatt*, 5 February 1990). The suggestion is that there is no identification with the ideas of the labour movement or with industrial democracy and therefore no interest in collective action. However, it is debatable whether a general belief in the goals of the labour movement is really a necessary precondition for identification with the union or for collective participation.

Fourth, there is the proposal that the rapid societal transformation resulted (inevitably) in a high rate of workers' disorientation and insecurity in dealing with the new situation. This included a sudden and complete loss of formerly secure and stable personal and professional identities, material and social positions, and of norms, values, ideological beliefs and behavioural patterns (especially Marz 1993a; Brähler and Richter 1995; Hofmann and Rink 1993; Holst 1991; Marz 1992a; Senghaas-Knobloch 1992; Trommsdorff 1994; Woderich 1992). It is argued that this situation led to a widespread 'identity crisis' (e.g. Belwe 1992; Maaz 1991; Rottenburg 1992) which resulted in a common individual response of general de-solidarisation (e.g. Andretta *et al.* 1994: 110; Alt *et al.* 1994; Holst 1991; Hofmann and Rink 1993) and consequently diminished workers' commitment to the unions and works councils (e.g. Pollack 1991: 280).

Most of these studies, however, are based on population surveys and not specifically of the workforce or union membership. It is also not specified whether members for example de-solidarise with their colleagues, and/or with their company, and/or with their union. Thus, it is not evident why the supposed 'identity crisis' necessarily leads to individualisation and lack of commitment to union and works council. Moreover, it is not clear whether the two provided reasons are complementary or alternative explanations. Clearly, if members had no union identity in former times they cannot lose it during the transition.

'East German union members are passive with regard to collective activities'

Four major explanations are presented here. First, some authors explain that workers' passivity is due to the current economic recession. This relates to the well-known but overly simple argument that collective action is lower in recession than in boom periods. For example, Augustin and Sprenger (1992: 38) argue that people in general are afraid to make use of their 'freedom of speech' at their workplace, because they fear being sacked (also Kurbjuhn and Fichter 1993: 39; Lippold *et al.* 1992). However, this instrumental approach to collective action is taken for granted and not further discussed. One might ask whether the authors regard this as a universal approach or whether they see it as a specific legacy of the former instrumental attitudes to the FDGB. The latter argument is developed by Klinzing (1992: 20), who proposes that workers had an entirely consumption-oriented, cost–benefit approach to their former trade union, which continues today. Thus, in the light of the current depressed labour-market situation, the perceived costs of participation are just too high. Unfortunately, there is insufficient data on workers' former attitudes to state unions to sustain this assumption.

Another argument, which is sometimes emphasised, is that of company size. Most east German industries now consist of small or medium-sized firms (e.g. Windolf 1997: 4) in which workplace relations could be more paternalistic and company-focused than in large companies, and thus collective action is less dominant (e.g. Lippold *et al.* 1992: 99).

Third, some authors stress that east Germans lack experience in 'voluntary' collective action and therefore cannot perceive it as effective (e.g. Klinzing 1992: 20; Mahnkopf 1991: 278).

Finally, there is a frequent reference to the former socialist socialisation and the attempt to find psychological explanations for the supposed continuing passive behaviour (e.g. Belwe 1992; Hofmann and Rink 1993; Marz 1993a; Pollack 1991; Schöbel 1993; Stratemann 1993; Woderich 1992). In terms of unions, the key thesis is that the socialist system of paternalistic 'caring and social security' ('from the cradle to the grave' or 'custodial state', Henrich 1989) resulted in enterprises exhibiting bureaucratic paternalism (Deppe and Hoß 1989). This had psychological consequences for workers in that it reduced individual activism and involvement, both in former times and also today (e.g. Marz 1993b: 78). For example, Mahnkopf (1991: 278) regards self-confidence, self-responsibility, personal initiative and pro-activity as virtues that the socialist system sanctioned negatively. Kreißig (1990) adds that the common (and official) thinking in former times in terms of the 'community' (which prohibited the classical conflicts of distribution), and the fact that the enterprises belonged to all, and therefore nobody really felt responsible, is a legacy which now hinders union members' mobilisation.

'East German union members do not perceive labour institutions as effective interest institutions'

Three explanations have been put forward for this perception. First, it is suggested that east Germans still expect the trade union to fulfil the holistic caring role of former times and are now disappointed about the limited service which the west German unions provide (e.g. David 1992: 133). For example, they are disappointed about the closure of the former 'help lines' of the union which dealt with complaints and proposals; in the event of legal difficulties or conflicts of interest, the union officials sprang more or less automatically into action with a phone call (Mahnkopf 1993: 17). Mahnkopf argues that east Germans therefore have an even higher expectation of unions as pure service and insurance institutions than their western colleagues. Furthermore, because the (west) German unions provide fewer social services than the former state union did and also maintain a lower profile on the shopfloor (e.g. not a large number of union stewards), wage agreements emerge as the primary and most tangible union 'service' to the east German worker (Mahnkopf 1993: 14). As unions are currently not seen to be doing well in pay bargaining, there is a strong disappointment among their members. Similarly, there is the assertion that the current problems works councils face (e.g. restructuring, insecure financial situation of firms) and which account for their apparent poor performance make the workforce perceive them as ineffective.

Another argument, but one which is somehow contradictory, is that people were highly disappointed by the former 'farce of interest representation' of the socialist unions and so continue to have a sceptical, disillusioned image of unions and works councils (e.g. Eidam and Oswald 1993: 167). For example, Klinzing (1992) proposes that today's union members often elect their works councillors and union stewards in order to relieve themselves of any activity. She interprets this passivity and wait-and-see attitude of members as an alienation from the union, which she believes will take a long time to overcome. But if all FDGB members were indeed highly disappointed then they surely would not have joined the new unions. With the massive numbers of east Germans who joined the new unions during 1990/91 (over 4.1 million new members, see Fichter 1997b) one has to wonder how disappointed these members really could have been.

In sum, the literature concludes that east German union members are individualistic and uncommitted in both attitude and behaviour, and that the causes lie in the individualistic legacies and in certain aspects of the structural transformation. The explanations are sometimes complementary, sometimes contradictory. For example, if it is true that members had no union identity in socialist times, then surely the proposed identity crisis would not make any difference. The literature falls short in defining and differentiating between the two approaches identified and is unsupported by adequate empirical data, and in particular by comparative studies of east and west.

Moreover, the concepts of 'individualisation' and 'passivity' are never properly defined in this literature (with regard to decisions to join, to participate in collective activities, or to act individually?), nor do these studies explain the link between certain attitudes (such as instrumentality) and the passive behaviour. Also they do not examine any possible interrelations between the explanations. Thus, is there any relationship, and if so of what sort, between 'lack of collective values' and 'instrumentality', and 'union identity'? For example, are individualistic workers necessarily instrumental with regard to the union? These issues will be addressed in the following chapters when we analyse the membership surveys.

6.3 Conclusion

This chapter provided an overview of the existing accounts of workers' attitudes and behaviour towards the transformation of industrial and workplace relations. It revealed various shortcomings in the literature, in particular a lack of empirical evidence and theoretical underpinnings. The major hypothesis which emerged is that of the individualisation of the east German workforce, but it lacks empirical substantiation or the evidence is contradictory.

Including Part I of this book, the debate has now identified the two main themes which have to be examined in more detail and this will be done in the membership surveys to follow. The first topic is works council/union-membership relations from the viewpoint of the members. This is one of the major themes and is referred to as the 'institutionalisation of the interest institutions' (see Part I). This discusses the extent to which unions and works councils are becoming institutionalised from the workers' point of view (thus members' attitudes and behaviour which indicate the cultural support of the new institutions).

The second topic is the individualisation of union members and how this corresponds to the above outlined three explanations (i.e. east Germans lack collective values, are passive and perceive institutions as not effective). The key question to be addressed here is whether east German workers have become more passive, individualistic and instrumental regarding collective activities than their western colleagues. As was discussed in the introduction to this book, the two topics are closely interrelated in that individualisation has an impact on the institutionalisation and functioning of the interest representation. Put another way, individualistic workers will be less likely to accept and support collective interest representation.

7 Methodology of the union membership surveys in the east and west German clothing industry

This chapter discusses the union membership survey which was conducted in the east and west German clothing industry. As mentioned earlier the purpose was to provide a more systematic approach to test the 'individualisation hypothesis' by comparing collectivist and individualistic attitudes and behaviour in a sample of union members in the east and west. Thus, the comparative data of west German members are used as a benchmark to evaluate the extent of workers' cultural support of interest institutions in the east. This analysis will also provide us with an evaluation of the works councils' effectiveness in representing workers' interests from the viewpoint of the workforce.

As far as the author is aware there is no specific research that analyses cultural support of functioning labour institutions (i.e. 'functioning' is defined as the effective representation of workers' interests). Moreover, in the political sciences the related concept of a complementary culture for political institutions is only vaguely defined, for example as 'a set of attitudes, beliefs, and feelings about politics current in a nation at a given time' (Almond and Powell 1978: 25), 'interpersonal trust' (Almond and Verba 1963), or 'civic or discourse culture' (Sztompka 1993a). Fuchs and Roller (1994: 17) are more specific, however, and develop three cultural conditions: commitment to democratic values, legitimacy of democracy, and a positive evaluation of institutional performance.

To construct a scale to test the extent of a supportive culture among union members an adaptation of Fuchs and Roller's definition has been used plus a related concept in industrial relations, that of union commitment (e.g. Gordon et al. 1980). As originally formulated, the concept of commitment comprised four elements: union loyalty and a desire to remain a member of the union; a feeling of responsibility towards the union; a willingness to exercise a strong effort on behalf of the union; and a belief in and acceptance of the values and goals of the union and the labour movement as a whole.

Functioning labour institutions are then understood in this context to require three major attitudinal and behavioural attributes on the part of their members, which are summarised in the term 'collective commitment':[1] (i) a commitment to collective values (measured as union and group identity and them-and-us feelings), (ii) a willingness to actively support the institutions (measured as willingness to engage in organised activities and in self-initiated activities), and

Table 7.1 Dimensions of 'collectivism' and 'individualism'

'Collectivism'	*'Individualism'*
union identity	no union identity
workgroup identity	no workgroup identity
them-and-us feelings	no them-and-us feelings
perceived strong instrumentality of interest institutions	perceived low instrumentality of interest institutions
perceived strong instrumentality of collective activities	perceived low instrumentality of collective activities
active behaviour: strong willingness to participate in collective activities	passive behaviour: low willingness to participate in collective activities

(iii) a perceived necessity of the institutions and a positive evaluation of their performance (measured as perceived effectiveness of works council and union and of collective action).

The assumption is that individualistic union members are likely to be more sceptical about the instrumentality (effectiveness) of collective interest institutions and collective activities than their collectivist counterparts. Furthermore, they are not likely to identify with their union (i.e. they are basically union members for instrumental reasons or simply because they were members before) and with their workgroup, and they are unlikely to have strong collectivist values and general attitudes as well as them-and-us feelings towards management. Moreover, 'individualistic' behaviour is characterised by a low willingness to participate in collective activities. The 'strength' of the dimensions of individualism/collectivism is measured by the absolute level of the frequencies (Table 7.1). This differentiation enables one to transcend the very general debate about the rise of individualism and to think much more precisely about different facets of collectivism and individualism. It also enables one to recognise that there may be disjunctures between the different facets of collectivism, so that, for example, the absence of collective activities in a particular workplace in and of itself tells one nothing about the degree of collectivist attitudes or of group identity amongst the workforce. In other words, people might not show strong willingness to participate in collective activities, but might still have strong collectivist values. The latter might be seen as partially leading to the former in the future if conditions change.

In sum, individualistic and collectivist attitudes and behaviour are characterised by a number of dimensions without, however, determining which might be necessary or sufficient dimensions. One has to keep in mind that this is a first attempt to conceptualise union members' supportive culture and not an exhaustive measurement. The primary aim is to have a scale to compare the extent of cultural support in the east and west. *Ipso facto* it is taken for granted that west German union members provide a sufficient level of cultural support for their interest institutions.

7.1 Measurement of variables

The three categories of cultural support, or collective commitment, were measured by multi-item scales. All questions were answered on five-point Likert scales, and factor analysis was used to test the validity of the assumed variables (see Chapter 10). Altogether, the questionnaire comprised seventy-three questions. It covered some additional concepts such as job dissatisfaction and attribution of workplace problems which will be discussed in Part III. In addition, each survey included some specific west or east German questions which did not form part of the comparative study (see Frege 1997).

Collective values

The survey distinguished between union and workgroup identity. Union identity is commonly operationalised as an affective attachment to the union and is denoted by (i) positive attitudes towards the union and its values and goals, (ii) a sense of pride in being a member of the union, and (iii) a desire to maintain one's membership (Guest and Dewe 1991: 213). The survey comprised six questions on union identity based on Kelly and Kelly (1993) and Kelloway *et al.* (1992). There were no questions on identification with the works council, because this concept is not appropriate here (the works council is not a membership organisation).

Measuring workgroup identity focused on eight items of general collectivist values and workgroup identification which were taken from Earley (1993) and Kelly and Kelly (1993, 1994).

The concept of 'them-and-us feelings' towards management was investigated by two items from Grant (1992). In addition, the east German questionnaire included a comparison between former (pre-1989) and current them-and-us feelings.

Collective instrumentality

As Newton and McFarlane Shore (1992) state, there is a lack of adequate research on the determinants of instrumentality and its construct validity. Thus, the instrumentality or cost–benefit concept is diversely defined and operationalised in various studies. Some authors refer to the 'instrumentality of trade unions' (DeCotiis and LeLouarn 1981), or to the 'functionality of union activities' (Spinrad 1960), some use the 'perceived influence of unions' (Glick *et al.* 1977), or the 'perceived value and effectiveness of unions' (Anderson 1978; Kolchin and Hyclak 1984; McShane 1986). A broader concept is that of 'union satisfaction' (Glick *et al.* 1977; Fiorito *et al.* 1988). Most research refers to union instrumentality only, although Klandermans (1984a) focuses on the instrumentality of collective action rather than of the institutions and also includes the personal costs–benefits of participation and the expectations of the behaviour of the other workers.

In addition, there are no recent quantitative studies on works council instrumentality. Furthermore, most research is US-based and examines mainly unionisation/joining rather than more diverse participation decisions, which might require a different measure of instrumentality.

This study measures collective instrumentality as a multi-dimensional concept. The survey distinguishes between people's perceptions of the instrumentality of the works council, of the union and of collective action itself. It is assumed that these variables will be strongly correlated. This study does not differentiate between costs–benefits in terms of the individual and the group (which might in certain circumstances differ) (see Elster 1989; Kelly and Kelly 1993: 5) and utilises only questions referring to perceived 'group' instrumentality.

Moreover, it emphasises the distinction between general perceptions of the works council and the union (e.g. 'do we need works councils at all?') and the evaluation of the institutions' success with regard to specific issues, such as job security, workload and pay (e.g. works-council policies concerning overtime pay). This conceptual distinction, between the general and specific perceptions of collective institutions, was introduced by Deshpande and Fiorito (1989). They found specific beliefs of union instrumentality to be more salient determinants of voting intentions for unionisation in their US sample than general beliefs about the union (p. 894) (also Glick *et al.* 1977: 149).[2]

The survey questions were adapted from Deshpande and Fiorito (1989), Fiorito *et al.* (1988) and Hartley *et al.* (1991) and are applied to the specific context (e.g. works council). The comparative part of the surveys included five questions on works councils, two on the union and two on collective action.

Willingness to participate in collective activities

This study investigates the willingness or intention to participate in collective activities, not the actual participation. There are a few studies that have used the actual behaviour, but the large majority focus on the intention assuming that it will predict behavioural outcomes. This has been subject to considerable critique and debate (e.g. Ajzen and Fishbein 1980; Eiser 1986; Fullagar and Barling 1987: 64; Kelloway *et al.* 1992: 208; Kelly and Kelly 1992: 249; McPhail 1971; Schrager 1986: 858; Wicker 1969: 75). For example, Barling *et al.* (1992: 99) claim that more objective measures of participation (e.g. official records) are needed, so as not to rely completely on subjective self-reports. However, several studies have investigated the relationship between 'attitudes' and 'behaviour' and found a robust correlation, in particular if the attitudes were measured on a more specific level (i.e. not just the attitude to industrial action in general but referring to a specific incident) (e.g. Ajzen and Fishbein 1980; Fishbein 1967; and more specifically for union membership: Fullagar 1986; McShane 1986; Premack and Hunter 1988[3]). In the following the term 'participation' refers to willingness to participate, and the term 'behaviour' refers to attitudes towards behaviour.

There is no common definition or measure of participation in collective activities. Most studies tend to focus on a number of quantifiable indices of union member participation, such as attending meetings, voting in a union election, reading union literature, holding union office and participating in industrial action. There is also no agreement on the differences between union action, industrial action, collective action or collective activities. 'Collective activities' will therefore be used as the generic term to describe all activities initiated by a group of workers, a union or a works council. Collective or industrial action is then just one specific form of more militant activity.

Early research defined 'participation in union activities' relatively narrowly as a holding of office (Kolchin and Hyclak 1984) and treated it as a static and dichotomous phenomenon. Thus individuals were classified as either active or inactive. Barling *et al.* (1992: 26) describe this early research as having an 'inconsistent conceptualisation of participation, and either poor quality or inadequate accounts of empirical evidence, and simplistic and bivariate analyses'. In recent years however, there has been an increasing awareness of the inherent dynamics and multi-dimensionality of the concept. In other words it is realised that union participation varies over time and in degree: most of the time little participation is required, and most members most of the time do not participate actively. For example, van de Vall found that 'just over half of all union members in various countries are completely apathetic, while the rest are occasional participants, members who regularly participate and voluntary officials' (1970: 154). Thus, periods of high activity (e.g. during elections, strikes) are followed by dormant stretches and stability.

In addition, recent research has extended the definition towards a more continuous concept that includes a wider variety of union activities (e.g. Fosh 1981; Hartley 1989; McShane 1986, Nicholson *et al.* 1981). Several authors have suggested that different kinds of union activity have different determinants. For example, McShane (1986) tried to demonstrate empirically the multi-dimensionality of union participation by factor analysis and by showing that different kinds of union activity have different predictors. He identified three major types of union participation: (i) involvement in the administration of the union branch, (ii) union voting participation, and (iii) union meeting attendance (p. 180). Gallagher *et al.* (1987) distinguish between administrative, intermittent and supportive activities, as well as participation in industrial action. Industrial action refers to the participation in organised conflict with management (including not only strikes but all collective grievance procedures, such as stoppages, go-slows, interpersonal conflict with management) (see Fullagar and Barling 1987: 67). Klandermans (1986b) defines union participation as being a member, attending meetings, holding positions, taking part in strikes, and voting for a union list in works council elections. A later specification distinguished between (i) membership without engagement in organisational activities, (ii) active membership with participation in day-to-day activities, and

(iii) participation in collective action initiated by the union (van der Veen and Klandermans 1989). Klandermans' study (1984a) found evidence which justified distinguishing between the willingness to participate in strikes and the willingness to participate in moderate action. More recently he proposed a more complex typology of four forms of participation combining effort and time dimensions (low/high effort v. limited/unlimited duration) (Klandermans 1995: 11). For example, attending union meetings is a form that is limited in time and requires little effort or cost, whereas joining a strike is limited in time but involves considerable efforts. Joining a union on the other hand is an undemanding but indefinite form of participation.

Kelly and Kelly (1993, 1994) found empirical support for their distinction between 'easy' forms of activity (discussing union affairs, taking part in industrial action, attending union meetings, etc.) and 'more difficult' ones (e.g. standing as an elected union official, being a union delegate). And finally, Fullagar and Barling (1989) differentiated between formal and informal activities: formal ones are activities which are necessary for the union to operate effectively and democratically (which are related to Kelly and Kelly's difficult ones), and informal activities reflect support for the union but are not necessary for its survival.

In conclusion, although the concept of multi-dimensionality seems logical, the question as to whether the different forms are really statistically independent and have different antecedents has not yet been sufficiently tested. There are also criticisms on conceptual and statistical grounds. For example, Barling *et al.* (1992: 96) argue that the orthogonal solution McShane imposes on his data (i.e. that McShane's participation items are unrelated to each other) is unrealistic. In addition, the dichotomous nature of McShane's data is said to inhibit the interpretation of factor analysis except for a purely heuristic set of criteria. It is difficult if not impossible, according to Barling *et al.*, to express dichotomous variables within the factor-analytic model. They also emphasise that a far greater proportion of the research on union participation has reported one-dimensional scales (e.g. Fullagar and Barling 1989; Huszczo 1983; Kelloway *et al.* 1992).

The authors might be right in arguing that the different forms of participation could be highly interrelated, which highlights the need for more research on the facets of participation and their possible interrelations (see Fullagar and Barling 1987: 68). However, different antecedents for different forms of participation can also provide evidence for the multi-dimensional nature. For example, it might be that participation in a works council has different predictors from those of participation in union activities. One explanation could be that a person who participates in works-council activities might do so because he or she feels committed to the well-being of the company, without being attracted to the union.

This study uses participation as an indicator of membership involvement in union and works-council activities. The possible multi-dimensionality is tested by factor analysis, as well as by the possible different antecedents for the different types of participation (see McShane 1986: 185). The items include participating in strikes and demonstrations, as well as standing for works-council elections or becoming a union official. The questionnaire comprised eight items that were adopted from Kelly and Kelly (1993, 1994).

To conclude, it should be noted that the discussion of the operationalisation of the theories revealed an embryonic research area that has not yet developed standardised or well-established catalogues of questions. Rather, different studies often use different operationalisations of the same theories which renders comparisons difficult, especially when applied in a different context.

7.2 The membership surveys

As mentioned earlier, the questionnaire was tested in a pilot study of workers in the case study, Bodywear in 1993 (291 returned cases) (see Frege 1996). In addition, loosely structured, open-end interviews with a selection of fifteen Bodywear unionised workers (dyers, sewers and knitters) were conducted in 1993 (all taped) to assist in the design of the questionnaire. The main purpose of these interviews was to get a preliminary feel of 'what is going on' at work-place level and the material gathered was used in designing the questionnaire. It clarified the core questions to be asked regarding the variables that were to be tested. The results of these interviews along with the pilot questionnaire suggested that the above outlined attitudinal questions were required in the questionnaire.

In addition, more structured, in-depth interviews (one to two hours long) with ten unionised sewers were conducted in 1994 after the survey research; all of these were taped. The intention was to explore further questions that the survey had left open or actually raised in order to facilitate the interpretation of the quantitative data. These topics were as follows: (i) workplace relations in former times, especially with regard to workgroup solidarity; (ii) expectations and hopes during the turn-round (Autumn/Winter 1989) with regard to desired changes at the workplace; (iii) current workgroup relations; (iv) current work-place problems and individual reactions; (v) general perceptions of changes in their lives after unification.

In addition, the interviews were used as an indicator of reliability, and thus coherence, of people's attitudes after one year. The interview data of the two years did not show significant differences and this indicates a certain continuity of the attitudes and behavioural patterns of the sample. The interview data of both years are integrated in the discussion of the questionnaires in the following chapter. The west German version of the questionnaire profited from long discussions with west German union leaders at headquarters and branch level. No interviews with union members were conducted.

Finally, it should be emphasised that this survey cannot claim representative-ness for the whole membership or workforce of the German clothing sector. However, by using various qualitative and quantitative methodologies (e.g. expert interviews, cross-firm survey and case study) it was assumed that the survey succeeded in providing a valid characterisation of the union membership in that industry.

The questionnaire was distributed through the union and works councils of the two western districts (Nordrhein and Westfalen-Osnabrück) and of the eastern south-east district in the same firms as participated in the works council survey (Chapter 4). In the west, 4,500 questionnaires were distributed to all seventy-six participating firms in 1995; 1,722 were returned, of which 1,691 were usable, giving a response rate of 34 per cent. Of the respondents, 72 per cent were blue-collar, 47 per cent female and 94 per cent full-time workers; 36 per cent were works council members and 15 per cent union officials. The gender distribution is representative (women constituted 49 per cent of union membership in both districts); members of the works council and union officials were over-represented (presumably because the survey was distributed by the union and works councils).

In the east, members were approached in all fifty-three participating firms. Most firms were privatised and all had a works council. Approximately 1,100 questionnaires were distributed and 440 were returned completed, giving a response rate of approximately 40 per cent. These included 75 per cent blue-collar workers and 70 per cent women; 25 per cent were past or present works councillors, 8 per cent were union officials, while 17 per cent declared themselves formerly active union members. Women were slightly under-represented (in 1992 they constituted 77 per cent of GTB members in the east) while works councillors and union officials were slightly over-represented. The age distribution in the east was slightly older than in the west;[4] however, there is no information on the representativeness of these distributions for German clothing firms.

The east German questionnaire asked for some additional characteristics: seniority, which was similar to the age distribution,[5] and qualification which was homogeneous and at a high level (members were all skilled workers with apprenticeship or a higher professional degree).

Virtually no respondent filled in the company's name, which prevented a correlation of workers' and works councillors' questionnaires from the same company. Finally, *t*-tests revealed for the east German sample that males were more often works council members and were slightly older than females. Older employees had been more active in the former union branch, BGL, and they were more often supervisors than were younger employees. Works council members were more often union officials, and had also been more active in the BGL than non-members. Consequently, former BGL activists were more often union officials and more often works council members than non-activists.

Although the response rates may appear low, they are in line with other union membership surveys (e.g. Fullagar and Barling 1989: 26 per cent; Gensior 1992: 45 per cent; Kelloway *et al.* 1992: 36 per cent; Kelly and Kelly 1994: 39 per cent). Indeed, Etzel and Walker (1974) claim that a 'normal' return rate for mail surveys of union members is between 10 and 30 per cent. It should be noted that most clothing jobs involve piecework, which makes it difficult for workers to complete a questionnaire at the workplace; and many (mostly female) clothing workers have the additional burden of housework, allowing less time to do the surveys at home (an argument the author frequently encountered during interviews).

This does not mean that the survey results are biased. On the one hand, active union members may have been more likely than those less committed to fill in the questionnaire. However, on the other hand, dissatisfied members might have been more inclined to participate to make their views known. In fact the pilot survey of Bodywear, which was distributed and collected by the author in person and achieved a response rate of 73 per cent, revealed no significant differences in the answers (Frege 1996: 178). These factors increase confidence in the validity of the present survey results.

8 Collective commitment in the east and west

This chapter compares the responses in west and east Germany in terms of the three categories of commitment specified above: collective identities, collective instrumentality and collective participation.

In order to control for a possible bias caused by the large share of works councillors and union officials in the west German sample, the following analysis was restricted to rank-and-file members (those without an official works council or union post): 312 members in the east and 995 in the west. A bias might also be caused by the larger share of female members in the east; but since women are generally seen as being less committed than men to their union, this should induce an even more individualistic approach in the east, reinforcing the critical character of this study.

8.1 Collective identities

It is very clear from the data of Table 8.1 that members in both east and west identified strongly with their union. For example, 74 per cent of east Germans and 77 per cent of west Germans shared the aims and goals of their union and even more valued union solidarity (79 per cent in the east and the same in the west). Only the question about whether one would stay in the union if unemployed did not receive a strong majority, particulary not in the east.

Differences were not significant between west and east with the exception that west Germans were less likely to think about leaving the union. However, the 25 per cent of east Germans willing to leave the union was much less than the average in east Germany of 54 per cent as illustrated by the *DGB Trendbarometer* (1994).

Similarly, the data yielded strong collectivist values and workgroup identities in both samples. The percentages used to working in groups were 67 per cent of east Germans and 65 per cent of west Germans, and 82 per cent in both samples accepted group decisions. However, east Germans were more convinced than their western colleagues that only those who depend on themselves get ahead at work. This more individualistic response to life chances might be explained by the fact that people think this is how they should behave in the new capitalist world, thus conforming to new norms, but is not necessarily an indication that they actually will behave like this. This was also supported in the case-study interviews: people had a very precise picture of how they *should* behave for their best advantage, perhaps because they saw those behaving in this way getting on. However, most declared that they had problems conforming with these new norms, attributing this to their different, 'old-fashioned' personality.

More than half of the east and west Germans identified strongly with their workgroup. However, east Germans felt more isolated (though this was not statistically significant), and they reported a greater weakening of group solidarity although their group identification was not significantly lower than that of west Germans. One reason for the perceptions of decreasing solidarity could be that the solidarity in the east is under more pressure. However, rather than interpreting this as a lower group identification in the east than in the west, it seems more reasonable to suggest that it indicates the continuing importance of solidarity in the east. One could argue that it is precisely because they still strongly identify with their workgroups that they feel the loss of solidarity so strongly (i.e. significantly more than in the west). In addition, perceiving a declining solidarity does not mean that workers necessarily behave in more individualistic ways.

These findings support the continuing importance of the work collective in the east and the perception of a decreasing solidarity among workfellows, which are in line with various empirical surveys (see also Becker 1993: 35). For example, the Allensbach representative poll in east Germany (1994, in *FAZ* 13 April 1994) found that 87 per cent of the east German population thought that solidarity among people had decreased since unification. Brähler and Richter (1995: 8), using a sample of 2,025 west and 1,022 east Germans, found that east Germans revealed significantly higher collectivist attitudes than their west German counterparts. Also, the strong group identity and the importance of solidarity adds support to the argument of some authors that the previous work communities in the old GDR had an emotional importance for the workforce (and not just an instrumental one, see Chapter 2: e.g. Diewald 1995; Gensior 1992).

It should be noted that the data give no information on the development of group identity (i.e. it might have decreased compared to former times, although this seems unlikely given the strong degree of identity present today). Some critics might object that the surprisingly strong workgroup identity in the samples is due to the predominantly female workforce. Yet, the theoretical justification (that females have a stronger identification with their workfellows than males) might be more difficult to obtain. More importantly, *t*-tests revealed that there was no difference between males and females concerning their workgroup identity. Women, however, perceived more strongly than men that the workgroup solidarity was decreasing.

Them-and-us feelings were strong in both groups (but significantly more in the east) and indicate a collective approach to management–workforce relations. For example, 83 per cent of the east Germans felt 'exploited' (in contrast to 52 per cent of west Germans). An additional question of the survey (not

Table 8.1 Comparison of collective identities in the east and west: frequencies (%), means and t-tests (* p < 0.05, ** p < 0.01)

		Strongly disagree	Disagree	No view	Agree	Strongly agree	Mean, significance level	N
Union identity								
I share the aims and values of the union.	east	4.8	6.3	14.8	45.9	28.1	3.88	296
	west	3.7	6.8	12.9	51.2	25.4	3.88	981
Union solidarity is very important for me.	east	4.1	4.1	12.6	33.3	45.9	4.14	297
	west	3.0	5.0	13.5	39.1	39.5	4.07	980
I am proud of being a member of the union (GTB).	east	11.4	19.5	15.1	36.4	17.6	3.36	300
	west	9.3	13.9	19.0	36.2	21.7	3.47	981
I feel strong ties with the other union members in my plant.	east	14.5	19.0	24.2	32.0	10.4	3.07	297
	west	14.4	20.7	19.7	27.5	17.7	3.14	981
I seriously think about quitting the GTB in the future.	east	40.4	23.3	11.3	14.9	10.2	2.32 **	303
	west	53.2	15.8	12.6	13.7	4.7	2.01	974

I would remain in the union, even if I were unemployed.	east	27.1	14.7	20.5	15.4	22.3	2.98	300
	west	24.6	10.7	25.4	16.7	22.6	3.02	983
Collectivist values								
I accept group decisions even if I have a different opinion.	east	4.5	6.0	7.5	50.4	31.6	3.99	289
	west	5.0	5.2	8.2	49.4	32.3	3.99	967
I prefer to work in groups rather than alone.	east	14.2	11.6	7.1	25.5	41.6	3.67	292
	west	12.1	12.7	10.1	33.5	31.6	3.60	973
In general problems are better solved in groups than alone.	east	4.5	5.9	6.6	52.1	31.0	3.99	290
	west	5.4	6.8	10.5	34.5	42.8	4.03	974
Only those who depend on themselves at work get ahead.	east	15.0	11.3	7.5	23.9	42.3	3.67	293
	west	23.7	20.4	10.0	30.9	15.1	2.93**	972

Table 8.1 (continued)

		Strongly disagree	Disagree	No view	Agree	Strongly agree	Mean, significance level	N
Workgroup identity								
I increasingly feel isolated in my group.	east	43.4	23.2	9.7	16.1	7.5	2.18	290
	west	45.4	27.7	6.4	15.0	5.4	2.07	973
East: in the old days group solidarity was much better. West: solidarity among colleagues diminishes during a recession.	east	10.8	7.4	3.3	21.6	56.9	4.00 **	294
	west	11.3	11.8	21.9	32.4	22.7	3.43	961
I would like to change my workgroup.	east	62.2	17.9	7.6	7.9	4.5	1.75	291
	west	54.8	23.5	7.5	10.5	3.7	1.85	971
I identify strongly with my group	east	18.5	10.6	19.2	32.5	19.2	3.29	287
	west	12.2	13.2	16.5	33.8	24.3	3.45	964
Them-and-us feelings								
I don't trust my supervisor a great deal.	east	6.4	9.3	11.8	46.1	26.4	3.70 **	307
	west	12.9	21.0	13.7	39.2	13.2	3.19	992
East: today workers are exploited here. West: management constantly tries to reduce the influence of the workforce and the union.	east	5.4	7.1	5.0	27.1	55.4	4.18 **	307
	west	6.7	12.0	29.2	25.0	27.2	3.54	987

published here) revealed that this was seen differently in former times: a majority declared that in the GDR they could trust their supervisors and did not feel exploited (see Frege 1996).

A representative survey of the west and east German population found similar results (Möllner Institut, *FAZ* 21 June 1995). One could conclude that them-and-us feelings (re-)emerged after unification whether through privatisation, thus 'expropriation' of workers' ownership of the means of production in socialist firms, or through the interplay of structural factors and management strategies. Correspondingly, some authors (e.g. Kern and Land 1991; Voigt 1973) (and the interviews at Bodywear) suggest that if them-and-us feelings existed in former times they had a different form from the western concept. Thus, they lacked the confrontational connotations that typically mark them-and-us feelings in western capitalist firms. For example, the interviewees normally accepted the people 'on the top' as persons who got their instructions and 'had to do their jobs as well' (knitter no. 3, September 1994). In addition, there was rarely any personal, close contact between them and the workforce. It was a 'live and let live' attitude. They were seen indifferently, because it was the System that was to be blamed. 'They didn't interest me a lot. What could they do against us? They had their job, we had our jobs. You were safe' (sewer no. 3, September 1994). Thus, it was a them-and-us differentiation between people here and people 'above' but without conflictual or ideological connotations (see also Alt *et al.* 1994). In the end, workers felt that they were in the same boat as the directors.

Today, this is changing. The division between management and workforce becomes more evident. For example, 'they are managers' (sewer no. 9, September 1994); 'you see them driving their big BMWs while you are sitting in your shabby Trabi' (sewer no. 4, September 1994). Now managers seem to have become for the workforce what the System was before: the anonymous power which determines your fate and which you cannot influence. However, the sentiments expressed against management might also be biased by people's increasing frustration with the transformation process itself. As one sewer commented, 'the small man in the street always loses out in each system. This was so before and is also now the case. However, in former times the little man could sometimes open his mouth and complain' (sewer no. 3, September 1994). One should note, however, that the data of this study present retrospective views and it might be that the old GDR is seen in a happier, less realistic, light ('golden age').

The interpretation outlined above is not necessarily shared by everybody. Some authors such as Kreißig (1992) argue that 'ideological', class-based them-and-us feelings also existed in former times.

An additional point which might foster them-and-us feelings today is the way companies are being restructured. For example, one could argue that the intensified 'Tayloristic' production methods adopted in most clothing companies during the early years of transformation did not include a participatory approach to organisational change and that might have impeded the development of 'we-feelings' (low them-and-us feelings). Furthermore, this might have also resulted in a general job dissatisfaction among workers, which was also manifested in this sample (see Chapter 10).

To conclude, the finding of strong social identities in both samples challenges the widespread argument in some studies of an identity crisis and a virtual elimination of social identities in favour of individualistic attitudes in the east (e.g. Belwe 1992; Maaz 1991; Marz 1993a; Rottenburg 1992). The similarity between the two samples gives evidence that the postulated east German identity crisis regarding public institutions has not affected this sample yet. For example, it challenges Fichter's proposition (1997a) that high union identity exists only in conflict situations, or Eidam and Oswald's (1993: 167) assertion that the unions have not yet succeeded in developing a culture of solidarity and commitment.

The findings also challenge the view that workers in the east were not morally affiliated to their former union and had an entirely instrumental approach to their membership (it is hard to believe that such a strong union identity could emerge in the few years since 1989).

8.2 Collective instrumentality

The three factors of perceived collective instrumentality (Table 8.2) in most cases yielded significantly different results. The works council was, however, widely perceived to be a necessary institution (89 per cent in the east and 92 per cent in the west felt that they needed a works council because management was not 'caring' enough). Differences between east and west became more obvious when workers were asked about the effectiveness of the interest institutions in dealing with specific issues. West Germans were mostly satisfied with the works councils' work, whereas the east Germans were more divided. This is in line with similar findings of the large-scale survey *DGB Trendbarometer* (1994) which shows that a majority of east German employees valued the works councils' work slightly more in 1994 than they did in 1992, although they were still more critical than those in the west. For example, in 1994, 32 per cent of east Germans (46 per cent of west Germans) valued the work positively, and 30 per cent (25 per cent of west Germans) marked it negatively. In particular, the data presented here are more positive than the DGB results for the GTB (west and east). These were in 1992 considerably below the DGB German average with only 6 per cent approving the works council's work (no separate data for 1994). However, 59 per cent did not answer this question and the sample consisted of only eighty-three persons, which questions the data's reliability.[1] Finally, the new interest institutions in the east were seen as more effective than the former socialist interest representation. That is in line with various studies that argued that people were highly dissatisfied with the former interest institutions (see Chapter 6).

In sum, the support for works councils does not mean that east Germans now rely exclusively on formal interest representation. But it is safe to say that the informal interest representation is not the major form of representation on today's shopfloors in the clothing industry. A mixture of formal and informal mechanisms (with a predominance of the former) is most probable, as the west German experience also shows (e.g. Morgenroth *et al.* 1994: 90).

Union effectiveness was perceived negatively in both groups (but significantly more so in the east). More than half of the east sample thought that the GTB is not very successful in protecting job security and also fails to secure the wage adaptation to the west German standard. Overall, union effectiveness was thus perceived more negatively than works council effectiveness. This makes sense, however, in the context of the German dual system of industrial relations. West (e.g. Morgenroth *et al.* 1994: 109) and east German studies (e.g. Mickler *et al.* 1992: 17, 1996) revealed similar perceptions of the union's relative unimportance regarding workplace issues such as job security.

Finally, there was no difference between east and west in the acknowledgement that active member support is necessary for the institutions to function. West German union members (87 per cent support) were, however, more positive about the effectiveness of strikes than their eastern colleagues, but the result of the east Germans (75 per cent support) was considerable as well, taking into account that they had no actual strike experience in this industry.

How do these results relate to the existing literature? With regard to works council and union instrumentality one needs to relate the findings (i.e. strong acceptance of the institution, albeit with scepticism about its current effectiveness) to the widespread argument that east German workers are extremely disillusioned over the effectiveness of works councils and unions in representing workers' interests. In this sample, east German members were realistic about works councils' limited resources in the given economic circumstances. This might be disillusioning, but it did not lead people to reject the institution itself. Thus, although the findings do not suggest highly effective and powerful institutions, members conclude that this is related more to the economic conditions than to the design of the institution as such. One should add that this result might be biased by the fact that only union members were asked. However, the pilot study at Bodywear which included unionised and non-unionised workers did not reveal any significant differences between the two groups in this respect (see Frege 1996).

In sum, the data add support to the more positive studies about workers' attitudes towards the works council such as that by Heering and Schroeder (1992) who found that 76 per cent of their sample had a positive attitude towards their works council. However, it challenges the pessimistic studies such as that by Jander *et al.* (1992).

With regard to the instrumentality of collective activities, the argument that east Germans do not perceive it as effective mainly because they lack experience in 'voluntary' collective action cannot be supported by the data. Rather, it seems more likely that workers have learnt over the last few years that their interest representation needs active support, and that strikes can make a change. A good example of the latter is the 'successful' strike of east German members of the metal union, IG Metall, in 1993 which lasted two weeks, and involved

Table 8.2 Comparing collective instrumentality in the east and west: frequencies (%), means and t-tests (* $p < 0.05$, ** $p < 0.01$)

		Strongly disagree	Disagree	No view	Agree	Strongly agree	Mean, significance level	N
Instrumentality of works council								
We don't need a works council as management cares enough for us.	east	68.0	21.0	2.8	6.4	1.8	1.48	308
	west	78.6	13.1	3.6	3.4	1.2	1.36 *	992
I can solve my work problems with my supervisor alone; I don't need the works council for that.	east	50.2	22.2	6.1	16.1	5.4	1.94	306
	west	52.7	20.5	5.3	17.7	3.7	1.99	988
The works council does not oppose management strategies strongly enough [to improve job security].	east	14.2	22.5	10.5	28.4	24.4	3.15 **	304
	west	26.8	22.0	14.3	24.4	12.6	2.74	979
Our works council is not powerful enough to negotiate better working conditions.	east	10.4	18.2	15.4	27.9	28.2	3.38 **	307
	west	30.4	22.5	15.2	23.9	7.9	2.56	986
East: the former BGL represented my interests better than today's interest institutions.	east	26.6	23.1	14.6	26.6	9.1	2.69	308

Instrumentality of union

GTB not putting enough pressure on employers [to secure jobs].	east	8.4	8.0	18.9	24.4	40.4	3.72**	304
	west	12.7	16.4	18.6	31.6	20.7	3.31	981
East: GTB is not doing enough to secure the adjustment of east German wage levels.	east	5.0	9.6	9.6	25.3	50.5	3.94**	308
West: GTB is fighting more for its east German members; we lose out.	west	14.8	20.1	34.1	18.1	12.9	2.94	979

Instrumentality of collective action

Works council and GTB will only be effective if they get active support from the workers.	east	6.1	6.5	6.9	20.9	59.6	4.21	304
	west	5.7	4.3	9.3	27.6	53.1	4.18	988
Strikes are an effective means of strengthening the union during collective bargaining.	east	5.7	8.5	10.3	28.8	46.6	3.98**	308
	west	2.8	4.0	6.6	25.7	60.8	4.38	983

Table 8.3 Comparison of collective participation in the east and west: frequencies (%), means and t-tests (* p < 0.05, ** p < 0.01)

		Strongly disagree	Disagree	No view	Agree	Strongly agree	Mean, significance level	N
Organised participation								
If the GTB were to call a strike I would participate.	east	8.2	8.9	19.9	18.1	44.8	3.82	308
	west	3.8	3.9	9.6	20.0	62.7	4.34 **	985
I would take part in demonstrations/rallies during collective bargaining.	east	7.6	13.8	24.3	28.6	25.7	3.58	303
	west	6.3	6.4	16.4	31.1	39.8	3.92 **	981
I will attend the next works council assembly.	east	7.6	1.4	14.4	5.8	70.9	4.42	305
	west	3.4	1.5	9.3	12.6	73.2	4.51	988
		yes	no	N				
Did you vote in the last works council election?	east	81.2	18.8	309				
	west	88.3	11.7	993				

Self-initiated participation

If asked I would stand for the works council election.	east	31.9	20.4	21.9	12.9	12.9	2.77	306
	west	31.5	17.2	24.0	14.9	12.4	2.60	989
If asked I would serve on a committee for the GTB.	east	45.3	22.3	20.9	7.2	4.3	2.19	305
	west	44.7	15.8	21.8	11.7	6.0	2.18	990
I constantly try to recruit new members to the union.	east	41.3	18.1	21.8	15.1	3.7	2.32	297
	west	30.6	22.5	12.2	23.0	11.7	2.63 **	985
I don't see myself as a union activist.	east	4.8	9.2	8.5	34.9	42.6	3.85	300
	west	8.4	10.9	11.1	36.4	33.2	3.75	980

some 100,000 east German workers, and was the first large-scale strike in the east (see Hyman 1996: 612). One could equally argue that workers might remember the 'informal' group actions on the former socialist shopfloor and continue to regard this kind of collective action as instrumental. Consequently, workers might still prefer to rely on themselves to represent their interests rather than use institutional procedures, and thus the informal interest representation might not yet be substituted by formal institutions. However, this analysis overlooks the fact that group actions seem never to have been the norm in the former clothing plants, and that the interest institutions are overwhelmingly accepted by the workforce. As mentioned before, a continuous interplay of informal (group) and formal interest representation at the shopfloor level might be the most likely scenario.

Finally, with regard to the whole section on collective instrumentality, it should be also noted that the variety of results of these variables adds support to the assumed multi-dimensionality of the concept (see Chapter 7).

8.3 Willingness to participate in collective activities

The items on collective participation (Table 8.3) can be divided into two broad categories: 'organised' and 'self-initiated' forms of collective activities (supported by factor analysis, see Chapter 10). The former comprises activities organised by the union or work council where people 'submissively' join. The latter comprises activities where people deliberately take the initiative to become active.

The frequency distribution in both samples revealed a 'high' level of willingness to join organised forms of participation (such as joining strikes or attending works council elections), and a relatively low inclination to become active on one's own. In other words, the involvement in self-initiated activities was much lower in absolute terms than in organised activities. Overall, eastern members were significantly less involved in organised activities than their western colleagues. For example, east Germans were considerably less willing to join a strike (63 per cent in the east and 84 per cent in the west), which supports similar hypotheses in the literature (e.g. Fichter 1994: 56). But they were similar to their western colleagues with regard to activities organised by the works council. Also there were no significant differences between men and women in the east German sample but men were significantly more active in the west than their female colleagues. One could interpret this as a socialist legacy of a high female employment share and a stronger integration of females into the company. This will be further analysed in Chapter 10.

Moreover, one should note that the west German result of over 80 per cent willing to strike is extremely high compared to that found in other west German studies. For example, Wiedenhofer *et al.* (1979) found 60 per cent willing to strike in his sample in the west German food industry. Krieger *et al.* (1989) found 34 per cent willing to strike and 42 per cent willing to join a demonstration in his representative survey of west German union members.

With regard to self-initiated (more difficult) activities there was only one significant difference between the two samples (west Germans were more likely to recruit new members than east Germans). Most would not, for example, stand for a works council election, either in the west or east.[2] But more east than west Germans would stand for election (although the difference was not significant).

Similarly, west and east Germans were not that different in their self-declared activity (19 per cent in the west and 14 per cent in the east). The complete samples (rank-and-file plus active members) yielded 31 per cent self-declared activists in the west and 21 per cent in the east and are in line with other German studies. For example, Weischer (1992) found 20 per cent and the *Sozial-report* (Winkler 1993: 30) found 23 per cent of active union members in their representative surveys of west German employees. The *DGB Trendbarometer* reported 26 per cent declared activists in the east and only 17 per cent in the west (1994). Furthermore, one should not forget that participation is conditional upon the existence of opportunities (Lawrence 1994: 11), and these might be different in the east and west.

Finally, the question is also an indicator of how far people's own perception of activism correlates with the survey's 'artificial' measurement of participation (Chapter 7). The correlation is significant ($r = -0.30$), which can be interpreted as supporting the question's validity.

In sum, the willingness to engage in collective activities in the east and west depended on the type of activity. Overall, both groups were highly interested in joining organised activities but were less motivated to act on their own initiative. Thus, despite notable structural conditions of this industry (i.e. small-sized firms, economic recession, non-militant union) and certain socialist legacies which should inhibit collective activities, members were not as passive and reluctant to strike as predicted in the literature.[3] In contrast, the mobilisation potential seemed to be rather strong. Thus, members were not so 'individualistic' that they could not appreciate 'collective' activities as is argued in some studies. On a final point, it is remarkable that east Germans were more similar to west Germans in their interest in self-initiated action – the more demanding form of participation – than in their interest in organised activities. This doubly challenges the widespread presumption of the east Germans' legacy of being passive and obliging. In other words, one would have expected them to comply with their union's call for a strike rather than becoming active on their own.

8.4 Discussion and conclusion

A summary of the findings is presented in Table 8.4. Both samples yielded largely similar results and these were in most cases collectivist. In other words, workers were supportive of their new institutions rather than being individualistic (and non-supportive). This challenges the popular assumption in some of the literature that union members in the east are strongly individualistic, instrumental and passive towards collective interest representation.

Table 8.4 Attitudinal and behavioural dimensions and survey results

Dimensions	Results
Union identity	East as collectivist as west
Workgroup identity	East as collectivist as west
Them-and-us feelings	East more collectivist than west
Instrumental value of trade union and works councils	East more negative (individualistic?) than west about effectiveness of institutions with regard to specific issues
Instrumentality of collective action	Mixed: in one respect, east as collectivist as west; in another, east less collectivist than west
Willingness to participate in collective activities	Organised participation: east less active (collectivist) than west
	Self-participation: east as active (collectivist) as west

East Germans' collectivist attitudes were characterised by a strong union and workgroup identity, strong them-and-us feelings, general collectivist attitudes, a mixed perception of the instrumentality of the interest institutions and strongly positive perceptions of the instrumentality of collective activities, and a rather low interest in collective concerns. Thus, the average east German union member is not alienated from collectivist values – on the contrary he or she has a strong sense of solidarity and of them-and-us feelings. Moreover, he or she perceives the interest institutions as important to have, and does not dismiss them as useless just because they are not perceived as highly successful at the moment. These results are particularly remarkable in the case of the clothing industry, where individualistic reactions might have been anticipated.

In a nutshell, judging by most of the dimensions of workers' attitudes and behaviour towards the new institutions, the cultural institutionalisation was successful. As a result, the study's null hypothesis cannot be supported. The study found no evidence for the scenario suggested by some writers (e.g. Mahnkopf 1992) of individualistic, apathetic, alienated union members in the east, who hinder the institutionalisation process of their new interest representation. The expansion of west German interest institutions in the east was accepted and supported by the workforce. In addition, the results also suggest that informal interest representation does not play a major role in these clothing companies; thus the formalisation of interest representation in the west German system did succeed.

There are three wider conclusions to be drawn. First, it is impossible to classify either the west or the east German trade unionists as pure collectivists or pure individualists, since many gave mixed responses when confronted with different issues. Both were clearly on average more collectivist than individualistic. For example, there were mixed degrees of willingness for different categories of collective activity (which adds further support to the hypothesis of participation being a multi-dimensional concept). Reasons for this mixed pattern might be the fact that the parameters of their decisions are often not known, unclear and confusing, that too many factors play a role, or because a fear of job insecurity overshadows all decisions. People seem essentially to muddle through in their new situation. They might react individualistically on one occasion or another (and who can tell that east Germans did not do this in the past?), but many of their values and attitudes are (still) rooted in collectivist ideas. Hence, that people have complex views on interest representation underlines the complexity of workers' attitudes in general and in particular in times of change and also comprises an important methodological point on debates about collectivism, instrumentality and unionism. There are likely to be various dimensions of individualism/collectivism, rather than a simple 'black and white' picture. Indeed, the comparative analysis revealed that the mixed pattern of individualistic and collective attitudes is not an east German phenomenon, but a normal state of affairs. This was also supported by various western studies which have pointed to the co-existence of collectivist and individualistic characteristics among union members (Lind 1996; Waddington and Whitston 1995; Zoll 1979).

For example, Zoll (1979) developed a useful typology comprising three ideal-types of union members in an empirical study on 'strike and worker consciousness' during a large-scale strike by the IG Metall in west Germany. First, there are 'passive members' who show little active support for the union and whose interests are represented by the general union interests. These have a consumption approach to the union (service-oriented) and delegate the representation of their interests to the union machinery. They are generally against industrial action and prefer co-operation and negotiation. Second, there are 'actively committed members' who are conscious of their own interests, participate extensively in union activities ('we are the union'), and reveal a strong identification. Third, there are 'average members' who show a low involvement in 'normal' times but who can be mobilised in critical periods. They see the necessity of interest representation at both company and industry level. They can be critical of the union in certain circumstances but this does not affect their general attitude towards the union. They think that interest representation should adapt to circumstances, and they are for peaceful bargaining but also in favour of strikes if necessary.

Leaving possible criticism of this kind of typology aside, one can conclude that although both of our samples obviously contain members of all three categories, the modal members are of the third type. They have a basic identification with the union and what it stands for, and although they are not too ambitiously active they can probably be mobilised on certain issues or occasions and they are convinced of the possibility of the effectiveness of collective action. Thus, they 'switch on' collectivistic or individualistic characteristics depending on the situation. These findings urge us therefore to recognise the importance of different dimensions of collectivism/individualism and in which circumstances and under which conditions they are switched on rather than assuming a general trend towards a uniform individualised workforce in the east.

The second conclusion stresses the fact that the east Germans' low trust in the effectiveness of their institutions has not (yet) had negative repercussions on their union identity. As discussed in the introductory chapter and in Chapter 3 one essential, necessary condition of the effective functioning of the collective institutions is that the actors involved accept them. The results presented a strong belief by the east German workers that the two labour institutions are necessary and important, although they were realistic with regard to the restricted power of the institutions during difficult economic times. This is a reassuring result that after three or four years the institutional transfer has already settled in people's minds. It also confirms the findings of the works councillor interviews. These gave the impression that, perhaps selectively or whenever possible, management works together with the works councils rather than trying to avoid and obstruct them, and confirms the works councillors' view that the workforce is supporting them (see Chapter 4).

Moreover, these results are also in line with similar findings on east German attitudes to the new political institutions (e.g. Dalton 1991; Fuchs and Roller 1994; Seifert and Rose 1994). For example, in a representative sample of the population in 1992 Fuchs and Roller (p. 42) measured attitudes towards three aspects of civil institutions: their culture, structure and performance. They found a high degree of support for the institutions that constitute the structure of liberal democracy, a high acceptance of democratic cultural values, but less confidence in the performance of these institutions.

The resulting complexity of attitudes might indicate the relatively early stage of cultural transformation, but equally it might characterise the normal complexity of people's attitudes towards representative institutions.

The authors conclude (p. 10) that the evaluation of the institutions provides a feedback that might stabilise or indeed erode collective values and behaviour and people's perception of the institutions' legitimacy. However, their conclusion that a positive feedback is less likely to develop in the coming years is not shared by the current author. Multivariate analysis[4] (see Chapter 10) in both GTB samples revealed that the factors of institutional effectiveness were not major determinants of either union identity, or perceived necessity of the institutions or participation. Thus, for example, respondents who thought unions did not fight hard enough for them were not less likely to identify with their union than colleagues who believed in their unions' effectiveness. One might infer therefore that east Germans' perceptions of the functioning of industrial relations institutions are not likely to have a major backlash on their general support.

Finally, the third concluding remark refers to the fact that this study cannot make any final judgement on the extent to which union members are shaped by their past experiences or by current structural conditions. Its cross-country, point-in-time data do not indicate trends in workers' attitudes over time nor directly suggest possible causes of the existence (or non-existence) of collectivist attitudes. Thus, whether the similarity between capitalist and post-socialist workers is due to recent attitudinal (or behavioural?) changes among the east Germans cannot be entirely excluded. However, an additional question in the pilot study (which was not included in the survey) asked workers to what extent the societal changes after 1989 influenced their behaviour; a strong majority of 57 per cent said 'not at all'. This is similar to the findings of a similar question in the large-scale survey in east Germany in 1991 (ISDA 1992: 246). These results reinforce doubts as to whether people change so quickly following societal transformation (see also Stratemann 1993), but more representative data are clearly necessary to substantiate this point.

On the other hand, one can also not exclude the possibility that some collectivist attitudes indicate a persistence of socialist legacies in people's attitudes and behaviour that is frequently assumed to make these workers significantly different from their western counterparts. However, the data do not support either a uniform trend towards individualism or a uniform persistence of collectivist legacies. The results leave one with the suspicion that neither socialist legacies nor current structural forces can be taken as key determinants of union members' perceptions and reactions during the transformation. Moreover, as noted earlier, since socialist legacies are not precisely defined it is hard to predict exactly which legacies (attitudinal, behavioural or others) have which impact on people's current attitudes and behaviour. For example, should disappointing experiences with past unions make people more attracted to the new western unions or would they – as the literature suggests – result in complete non-involvement? The pilot study of non-unionised and unionised workers at Bodywear revealed that 30 per cent of non-members did not join the new western union because 'the former union disappointed me too much'. However, 21 per cent of the union members declared they joined because 'I have been a union member in the past' (see Frege 1996: 247). Moreover, the comparative evidence shows that east German union members express a willingness to participate in strikes and regard them as effective weapons although they have been socialised to be 'passive', lack experience of such action and have suffered from an ineffective interest representation in the past, and despite being surrounded by unfavourable labour market conditions.

The findings seem to alert us to the fact that despite all legacies and institutional changes, union members are first and foremost independent social actors in their own right. They decided deliberately to support their new representative institutions, thus constituting a stabilising factor for the successful institutionalisation of the new labour organisations. We will come back to this point later on.

Conclusion to Part II

Part II dealt with the descriptive analysis of the union membership surveys. The first chapter summarised the existing hypotheses and results of east German workers' attitudes and behaviour and characterised the individualisation of the workforce as a core hypothesis in the literature. The next chapter introduced the methodology of the surveys that were then discussed in the last chapter.

Whereas the first part of the book discussed the transformation from a viewpoint of the institutional actors, this part was concerned with workers' perspectives of the transforming workplace relations. It was earlier proposed that this perspective is necessary to really understand the transformation process. In a nutshell, discussing workers' commitment to their new labour institutions led to the exploration of three relationships: that between workers and management (e.g. them-and-us feelings), between the workers themselves (e.g. workgroup identity), and between workers and works council/union (e.g. collective identity, collective instrumentality).

Worker–management relations were not harmonious in the east German sample. Management were seen as having worsened the working conditions in virtually all aspects (e.g. through an intensification of work), and were described as distrustful 'exploiters'. Workers felt betrayed, humiliated and not involved in the organisational transformation process. Yet, in terms of workforce relations, this development has not led (yet) to a complete de-solidarisation and increasing competition between the east German workers. Although workers felt a decreasing solidarity among their colleagues, they still identified strongly with their work collectives.

Finally, regarding the relationship between the workforce and the new interest institutions, the result was mixed. Works councils and the union were accepted, but their specific effectiveness was evaluated differently and, on average, more negatively. On the other hand the instrumentality of collective activities was seen slightly more positively and the willingness to participate depended on the form of activity. The comparison with the west German counterparts suggests that the hypotheses of east Germans being more individualistic and less committed to their labour institutions cannot be sustained. This will be further examined in Part III.

Part III

Explaining post-socialist participation in collective activities

This final part of the book takes the descriptive discussion of the membership surveys a step further and analyses the similarities and differences between the two samples in terms of their reasons for participating in collective action. Placing the discussion of workers' attitudes and behaviour in a theoretical framework of explaining collective participation is especially welcomed given the absence of theoretical concepts in most existing discussions of the workplace transformation in post-socialist countries. Investigating people's inclination to collective participation contributes to the discussion of whether east German workers are 'individualistic' with regard to collective interest representation. In other words, a final test of the 'individualisation' hypothesis should be whether east Germans reveal a more instrumental approach to participation than their western colleagues. Thus, is the supposed passivity of post-socialist workers reflected in a highly instrumental decision-making process?

This study also provides the opportunity to contribute to the theoretical discussion on the relative explanatory power of these theories since the four theories have rarely been tested together in previous studies. In addition, it provides a useful ground to test the theories' cross-cultural applicability: the theories of collective action have been developed and primarily tested in a western (advanced capitalist) setting (mainly in Anglo-Saxon countries).

The first chapter introduces the various theories of workers' willingness to participate in collective action and the following chapter discusses the results of the regression analyses: why people participate in collective action and whether there is a difference between east and west Germans.

9 Theories of participation in collective activities

This chapter surveys what has been written on workers' participation in collective activities. It focuses on four social-psychological theories which will subsequently be tested in this study. They are frustration–aggression theory and the theories of rational choice, social identity and attribution. The reviewed theories provide alternative explanations for people's behaviour towards collective activities; in other words who participates and why.

The chapter starts by defining 'participation' and provides an overview of the existing theories of participation. It briefly reviews selected traditional theories, and then focuses on the four social-psychological theories. The chapter finishes by outlining previous empirical tests of the antecedents and theoretical propositions of possible interrelations between them.

9.1 Theories of participation: an overview

Participation in union activities first emerged as a major research topic in the USA in the 1960s (e.g. Spinrad 1960; Tannenbaum 1965; Anderson 1978), and later in the UK (e.g. Nicholson *et al.* 1981). However, there is no such interest in Germany where union research is traditionally biased towards the analysis of institutions. There was a stream of work in the 1960s examining union democracy (e.g. Bayer 1979) and workers' (class) consciousness in sociological and political terms (e.g. Kern and Schumann 1985; Popitz *et al.* 1957), but membership behaviour and the micro structures of the unionisation process were not frequent topics of interest at that time and are still not today. An exception is Nickel's (1972) study of the relationship between unions and blue-collar workers, which comprised several surveys on motives for joining or leaving the union. Even there, the underlying causes of people's decisions were not analysed. There are also a few studies in the 1980s on workers' attitudes towards collective interest representation, with particular emphasis on the effects of the recession (Bertl *et al.* 1989, Feist *et al.* 1989 and Krieger *et al.* 1989; Prott 1993; Wiedenhofer *et al.* 1979; Research group 'metal strike': Zoll 1979, 1981, 1984a, b) and the annual *DGB Trendbarometer* and its interpretations (e.g. Schreiber 1995 on the IG Metall survey). However, none of these studies investigate the reasons for people's willingness to become active. According to Weischer (1993) there exist no other, more recent major studies on union membership in Germany.

The following sections will outline the major approaches in the mainly Anglo-Saxon literature to individual willingness to participate in collective activities. Emphasis will be placed upon those studies that seek to account for variations in this participation.[1] In other words, the following discussion will not be concerned with the process of participation or with mobilisation itself (see Kelly and Nicholson 1980 on the social process of strikes; or Zurcher and Snow 1981).

There is no substantial literature on the participation in works council activities (which is not a research topic in either the German or Anglo-Saxon literature). It shall be presumed, however, that the theories of union participation can also be applied, perhaps with certain amendments, to other collective activities such as those initiated by the works council. It should be remembered that works councils and unions are not competing institutions with regard to workers' commitment, but have their clearly defined and complementary areas of activities. In addition, most works councillors are also active union members.

Theories of antecedents (or predictors[2]) of participation have been classified and discussed in various ways. Barling *et al.* (1992), in a comprehensive review of participation, distinguish between demographic, personality, work-related, union-related, non-work-related and structural predictors. Kelly and Nicholson (1980), in a study on strikes, differentiate between environmental, institutional, sociological and psychological factors. Guest and Dewe's (1988) study on why people stay in a union distinguishes between structural factors, job dissatisfaction, frustration, rational choice theory and solidarity.

Another group of authors focuses more specifically on social-psychological explanations of participation. Hartley (1992) differentiates between personal and occupational characteristics, job attitudes, social and instrumental beliefs (class consciousness and instrumentality of unions), and social networks (socialisation). Klandermans (1986a, b) focuses on psychological factors only and deals with frustration–aggression theory, rational choice theory and social interaction theory. Finally, Kelly and Kelly (1992) separate individual attributes (demographic factors and worker attitudes) and individual decision-making (based on expectancy–value theory and social cognition theory).

In an attempt to summarise the above, a broad classification between 'traditional' and more recent approaches might be useful. The first category comprises macro/structural explanations and demographic accounts, which will be only briefly reviewed (they have been extensively reviewed elsewhere).[3] The second category focuses on social-psychological theories dealing with the individual decision-making process. It is on this second category of theories that this study will mainly focus.

9.2 Traditional theories of participation

Structural approach to participation

This approach emphasises four external or structural conditions which are said to influence the individual's inclination to collective action: (i) the economic situation, (ii) the size of the company, (iii) technology, and (iv) the industrial relations context. The common proposition is that people participate in collective activities not because they are demographically, psychologically or attitudinally compelled to, but because their structural location in the world makes it easier for them to do so (see McAdam *et al.* 1988: 707). In other words, it matters little if one is demographically or psychologically disposed towards participation if one lacks the structural vehicle to pull one into activity.

The standard argument is that the economic situation (as indexed by the state of the labour market) determines union members' behaviour. Thus, in times of economic crisis industrial action (e.g. strike rate) is low, whereas in prosperous times it is high (this could refer to short-term business cycles or long wave theories) (e.g. Ingham 1974; Kelly 1996a: ch. 8; Knowles 1952; Shalev 1983; Shorter and Tilly 1974).

Other authors refer to company size: an increasing size reinforces pro-union attitudes since it fragments the work community. For example, the emerging social isolation in large plants leads to polarisation (the 'size-leftism' hypothesis) (see Barling *et al.* 1992: 116; Dewey *et al.* 1978: 126; George *et al.* 1977; Ingham 1970; Parkin 1967; Prais 1977; Revans 1956).

A related argument refers to the organisation of technology (e.g. division of labour, job interdependencies, work layout) as a crucial determinant of collective action (e.g. Sayles 1958; Kuhn 1961). For example, Sayles relates the organisation of technology to personal interaction, group cohesion and power resources. One hypothesis is that team-work organisations are supportive of collective action, whereas individual piece-rate systems hinder the creation of collective interests and action.

Finally, there is a vast amount of literature on various industrial relations factors and their impact on collective action. Thus, Clegg (1976) argues that whether industrial conflict is manifested in the form of strikes will depend upon the existence and quality of joint regulatory mechanisms at the workplace. In addition, there are factors such as state intervention, trade-union unity, growth of collective bargaining, and changing union and management policies which are invoked to account for the alleged trends in collective activities (see Ross and Hartman 1960; Kochan 1980). A related type of theory deals with the industrial relations climate, i.e. the perceived nature of the relationship between labour and management (e.g. Anderson 1978; Brett 1980; Strauss 1977). The argument is that the climate will influence participation such that under conditions of a more hostile, non-co-operative relationship between management and labour, union participation will be greater (e.g. Kelly and Nicholson 1980; Stagner and Eflal 1982). A group of theories also suggests that characteristics in union officers such as the ability to communicate, accessibility and leadership in times of industrial conflict, enhance members' participation (e.g. Fantasia 1988; Fullagar *et al.* 1992; Hartley 1989; Kotthoff 1994; Nicholson *et al.* 1981). And finally, there is the hypothesis that the power of the union is a pivotal factor in strike causation and also in other forms of participation (Kelly and Nicholson 1980). For example, Dubin (1960) argues that conflict is a curvilinear function of the relative power of the parties, being lowest under conditions of mild disparity.

While these theories help us to identify broad structural conditions for membership growth they nonetheless have a number of deficiencies. For example, they neglect to take other possible predictors and their interrelations into account (e.g. between the economic situation and industrial relations system and political situation, or between size, industrial sector and technology). Moreover, some empirical studies found contradictory evidence,[4] and some concepts such as the leadership of union officials also lack an underlying theory (see Barling *et al.* 1992; Kelly and Nicholson 1980; Klandermans 1984b).

Most importantly, however, structural theories might explain broad trends but do not account for variations in individual participation patterns. These theories do not explain why some people are nevertheless active in such conditions. For example, one could argue that the theories would predict a low level of participation in the east German (clothing) industry with its being characterised by a devastated labour market, small company size, traditional work organisation with piece-rate systems, and the existence of west German industrial relations institutions. However, as we have seen in the previous chapter, this cannot be supported by the presented data.

Clearly, in order to test these theories properly one needs cross-sectional data which are not available in this study. However, the propositions render this sectoral study of the clothing industry a critical case study. As argued earlier, the findings of workplace co-operation and strong membership support in such an industry strengthen their generalisability, and thus the argument that similar patterns can be expected in other sectors.

Demographic variables

Another stream of research has sought to answer the question as to why some people are more engaged than others on the basis of the individual characteristics of movement activists (McAdam *et al.* 1988: 706). Particularly in the 1960s, much research was aimed at establishing whether an active 'trade unionist type' existed. Thus, analysts tried to discover the social and personal characteristics of union activists, such as age, gender, personality, occupation, seniority and wage level. Studies declared that union activists are better educated (McShane 1986; Oliver 1984), have a greater occupational status (Nicholson *et al.* 1981; Spinrad 1960), have been socialised in families whose members were unionised and actively involved (Purcell 1953), enjoy higher salaries (Farber and Saks 1980; Kolchin and Hyclak 1984; Oliver 1984; Spinrad 1960; Strauss 1977) and are full-timers rather than part-timers (Geare *et al.* 1979) and blue-collars more than white-collars (Gallie 1989: 9). The two most popular demographic variables, however, were age and gender.

With regard to age, most research focuses on the relationship between age and joining the union rather than participation. There are three different hypotheses here: younger workers are more likely to join the union than older colleagues,[5] they are less likely,[6] and that younger and older workers are both more likely to join than the middle age group.[7]

It is not clear whether all three interpretations can be easily applied to union activity, and which of the hypotheses is right. However, Kelly and Kelly (1992: 247) note with regard to a largely empiricist literature on age and union militancy that it has produced conflicting results, shows dubious associations and has no body of theory.[8]

In terms of the impact of gender on participation there is widespread evidence that female employees are less likely to be union members than their male counterparts (e.g. Bain and Elias 1985; Bain and Price 1983: 8), are less committed to the union and are less active (Gallie 1989: 15; Gordon and Ladd 1990; Lawrence 1994; Purcell 1979). Several studies trace it back to general gender differences in personality, perceptions and attitudes (e.g. Snyder *et al.* 1986) or to women's lower commitment to their employment (see Lawrence 1994). However, if one controls factors such as employment conditions (part-time/full-time work), occupational mix (e.g. less female employment in male-dominated and traditionally unionised industries), and the degree of concern of unions to recruit such workers, studies find no gender difference in the willingness to join and stay in the union or with regard to female perceptions of union instrumentality (e.g. Bain and Elias 1985; Booth 1986; Fiorito and Greer 1986: 161; Gallie 1989: 17; Kochan 1979; Richardson and Catlin 1979: 379). However, no studies were found which specifically dealt with gender differences in participation.

Overall, most of the demographic studies and their call for a stereotypical union member have either very weak or inconsistent associations with measures of participation, and lack a clear body of theory. Typically they justify their discussions on any grounds other than that they are proxies for more fundamental arguments (e.g. Barling *et al.* 1992: 195; Gallagher and Strauss 1991; Kelly and Kelly 1992: 247; Klandermans 1986b; Kolchin and Hyclak 1984; Nicholson *et al.* 1981).[9] However, since some variables such as gender and age are still commonly in use in most studies, they have also been included in this study. In addition, age is particularly interesting to test the generational effect between the older east German workers (who had been socialised longer under socialism) and their younger counterparts. It could be argued that younger workers have become more individualistic than their older colleagues and are therefore more passive. The gender variable is interesting in this context because of the supposed equalising gender politics of the socialist GDR state (see *Feminist Review* 1991). Thus, gender should then be a less significant determinant of participation than it is in the west.

In summing up the 'traditional' approaches to collective activities, it appears that some variables have explanatory power but they do not offer a satisfactory account of union participation. For example, the structural theories tend to assume that union participation is an unconventional, irrational type of behaviour (e.g. Klandermans 1984b; Schwartz 1976). Moreover, there has been an increasing awareness in the last few years that the dichotomous foci on either micro or macro factors are not helpful and that an integrative model is necessary. The question is then how the approaches can be linked in a theoretically informed and empirically grounded way (Snow *et al.* 1986: 464). There are four distinct recent social-psychological attempts trying to address this issue by focusing on the individual decision-making process: the frustration–aggression theory and the theories of rational choice, social identity and attribution.

9.3 Social psychological theories of participation

Frustration–aggression theories: job dissatisfaction

There is a large literature on workers' attitudes and union membership, of which only the most important concept of job dissatisfaction will be reviewed and tested. Drawing on theories of cognitive consistency (Rokeach 1969), of cognitive balance (Bem 1967: 128), of relative deprivation (e.g. Geschwender 1964; Gurney and Tierney 1982; Walker and Pettigrew 1984), of frustration–aggression (e.g. Dollard *et al.* 1939; Gurr 1970), or dissatisfaction–withdrawal (e.g. Birchall 1975; Hackman and Lawler 1971), the general approach is based on the idea that when people become conscious of a social inconsistency, it is in their psychological self-interest to change the situation.

The most popular version with regard to the union context is the theory of relative deprivation linked with the frustration–aggression hypothesis. This theory holds that it is an unfavourable gap between what people feel entitled to and what, in fact, they are receiving that leads to expressions of discontent in terms of joining the union or becoming actively involved in union activities. In other words, frustration (dissatisfaction) at work encourages activism by the psychological mechanism of tension reduction (Klandermans 1986b: 199).[10]

The empirical nature of the relationship between dissatisfaction and participation is equivocal. Several reviews of the earlier literature conclude that job satisfaction rather than dissatisfaction is positively correlated with union participation (e.g. Perline and Lorenz 1970; Strauss 1977). Compared to their non-active counterparts, active members appear to be more satisfied with their jobs, have a greater interest in work (Tannenbaum and Kahn 1958), and have higher job status (Blyton *et al.* 1981; Sayles and Strauss 1953; van de Vall 1970).

Spinrad (1960) explains these relationships by arguing that union participation enriches the individual's overall job satisfaction and provides a means for greater interpersonal influence, status and meaning. However, the causality remains unclear in that job satisfaction might be a cause of union participation as well as a consequence. In addition, according to Brett and Hammer (1982:

245), there is no research that either confirms or refutes the proposed causal direction.

On the other hand there are recent studies which support the outlined theoretical hypothesis. Job dissatisfaction is in this instance positively correlated with joining or voting decisions and also with participation in union activities (Guest and Dewe 1988; Hamner and Smith 1978; Hills 1985: 245; Kochan 1979; Kolchin and Hyclak 1984; Olson *et al.* 1986).

Finally, there are empirical studies which show only a small positive correlation between job dissatisfaction and union activity (e.g. Flanagan *et al.* 1974; Scott *et al.* 1963). McAdam (1986: 705) even concludes that for all the apparent theoretical sophistication, empirical support for the theories behind this account has generally proved elusive. He claims that although the frustration–aggression hypothesis works in animal studies its application to human studies has been significantly discredited and its explanatory power regarding union participation or strike causation is questionable at best (Hartley 1984) and has not been empirically supported. Also Kelly and Nicholson (1980: 865) argue that the empirical relationship between job dissatisfaction and propensity to strike is neither consistent nor substantial.

In addition to the empirical lack of clarity, there are several theoretical objections. For example, Klandermans (1986b: 199) states that the frustration–aggression paradigm seems of limited significance, since dissatisfaction is neither a necessary nor a sufficient condition for participation. Moreover, the relationship between tension reduction and participation is weak (see Kelly and Nicholson 1980: 865 for a similar argument with regard to aggression and militancy). Also, the theory does not explain how dissatisfied individuals are activated and why they prefer one form of participation to another. Thus, Kelly and Kelly (1992: 249) argue that workers who experience dissatisfaction in their job have a series of options – to raise an individual grievance, to retrain, to press for promotion, to work harder, to quit – of which collective industrial action is but one (also Klandermans 1986b; Zurcher and Snow 1981: 451). Moreover, there may be circumstances where dissatisfaction is not necessary for collective action at all, such as in sympathy strikes.

Finally, Guest and Dewe (1988) highlight a conceptual problem in using job dissatisfaction to explain continued union membership, i.e. ongoing participation as opposed to joining the union. A persistent dissatisfaction presumably means that union membership does not help to eliminate the sources of dissatisfaction, so it is then hard to see why membership is continued. However, studies confirm that union members are not more likely to consider leaving the firm, despite greater dissatisfaction, which gives some support to the argument that the union provides a 'voice' for the expression of discontent (ibid.: 185).

To conclude, despite the empirical and theoretical problems, frustration–aggression theory is still widely in use (also by its critics, such as Klandermans 1995). It was included in this study because workers in east Germany have experienced tremendous changes in their work organisation (see Chapter 5 and 10) and there may be considerable scope for feelings of frustration or dissatisfaction. In such circumstances, therefore, dissatisfaction might be associated with, or help to determine, collective activity.

Theories of rational choice

Rational choice or cost–benefit theory is associated with Olson's theory of collective action (1971). It focuses on the individual worker and proposes that individuals are calculating actors who attempt within the bounds of rationality to judge the potential costs and benefits of various lines of action. Thus, this theory analyses the process by which prospective participants rationally approach the decision to participate: the individual decision-makers approach a choice (of action) by searching the environment for information about outcomes, alternative choices and their personal value. They then select the choice that maximises the probability of favourable outcomes by weighting the anticipated costs and benefits so as to opt for the one which has the greatest ratio of benefit to cost (see Brett and Hammer 1982: 251; Friedman 1983; Kelly 1996a, ch.4: 1; Oberschall 1973: 116). A major consequence is that they will participate in collective action only if they believe that their union (or works council) is instrumental in achieving important work-related outcomes (see Barling *et al.* 1992: 102; Klandermans 1986a).

A more sophisticated version of these basic assumptions is Klandermans' 'value–expectancy' theory (e.g. 1984b, 1988). In general, value–expectancy theories consider the individual's action to be related to the person's expectations and the subjective value of the consequences that are perceived to follow the action (Feather 1982). According to Klandermans (1984a, 1986b), collective action is contingent on anticipated outcomes. Optimism about the outcome of collective action will enhance the probability of participation: when the benefits of union activity are perceived as high, and the costs low, then willingness to participate will be high.

Klandermans tries to overcome the 'free-rider problem' which has been outlined by Olson (1971) and which underlies rational choice theory. Thus, if the costs of participation are seen as extremely high, then many potential recruits are expected to choose another course of action. Olson's contention is that rational calculation would lead few actors to choose collective action as a means of obtaining public goods, since they could expect to obtain those goods whether they were active or not. He believed that he refuted the popular view that individuals with a common interest would act together so as to achieve that interest (except in cases with selective incentives or possible sanctions on non-participants in small groups). However, Klandermans and others (e.g. Gamson 1975; Schwartz 1976) argue that people will participate in activities to produce a collective good precisely because they are aware that the good would never be produced if everyone sat back and waited for someone else to do something. Klandermans (1984b: 585) argues further that the value of a collective good is a function of its instrumentality for social changes which the movement hopes to achieve, and of the value of changes.

Five major objections to the social-psychological theories of rational choice are outlined below: (i) the basic assumption of rational choice, (ii) the neglect of the social character of the decision-making process, (iii) the neglect of the processual character of decision-making, (iv) the causality between rational choice and participation, and (v) empirical support.

(i) Rational choice theory in its basic form assumes that individuals act rationally and have complete information about their situation (i.e. of all possible costs and rewards) (see Kelly 1996a: ch. 4). Yet, Zurcher and Snow (1981: 468) argue that the most obvious shortcoming is this tautological character of the rationality assumption. People are supposed to participate in social movements because it is rewarding to them. Defining participation, rewards and rationality in terms of each other precludes finding negative cases. Thus, the circularity of the argument renders a central component of the rational choice theory unfalsifiable.

Another major problem of all versions of rational choice theory (including value–expectancy theory) is that it is basically an 'optimal' theory. It postulates how people might behave if they had complete information and the ability to process that information in a maximally rational manner. Clearly this is not realistic, and even if all these conditions existed, people would not always behave in a purely rational manner.

(ii) Most rational choice theories, including Klandermans' value–expectancy theory, try to explain the emergence of a collective phenomenon out of individual decisions, but without specifying the social context and processes in which the decisions are made (Kelly 1996a, ch. 5: 20; McAdam 1988: 137). They ignore the generation of expectations on which choice depends and which is a profoundly social process, i.e. shaped by the interaction with other social actors. For example, they do not explain the nature of rewards, nor how they come to have a subjective meaning as rewards. Do they vary from situation to situation? And is it possible to assess the rationality of strategies without assuming that goals of action are well-defined, consensual and relatively stable? Moreover, the theories take interests or preferences as given and although they assume that people operate under constraints they do not offer an explanation for the origins and durability of those constraints on preferences and do not explain where different interests and preferences come from (see Kelly 1996a, ch.4: 9). As Schrager (1986: 859) notes, collective activity might be more than the sum of individual economistic calculations: 'social and ideological factors figure powerfully in people's willingness to act'. In addition, the importance of people's interpretation of events and grievances relevant to participation is also not acknowledged (Snow *et al.* 1986: 465).

A related point is that the theories assume that people are mobilised solely on the basis of instrumental calculations of individual self-interest. As Kelly

(1996a, ch. 5: 20) points out, individuals with a strong sense of social identity may think in terms of group interests and group gains and losses (also Fireman and Gamson 1979), or might be mobilised without thinking through costs and benefits at all (also Jenkins 1983). For example, Kelly and Kelly (1992: 253) illustrate that especially long strikes, where workers often suffer acute financial hardship (e.g. UK miners' strike in 1984/5), cannot be explained by an instrumental motive alone. What is necessary is a consideration of the underlying social processes, i.e. the relationship between management and workers, and hence an awareness that the industrial conflict is an instance of 'inter-group relations' (Kelly and Kelly 1992: 256) or, as they later state, 'what is critical is that individuals identify with the union as an organisation' (Kelly and Kelly 1993: 19). In short, it is the individuals' identification with various groups (e.g. workforce, company) which will affect their perception of inter-group relations and also of the costs and benefits of participation.

In sum, the underlying critique rests on the theories' profound individualism. Klandermans, for example, acknowledges this point and increasingly emphasises the importance of social interaction theory (social motives) in his recent work. He writes that the costs of participation are all socially constructed, 'which is to say defined in social interaction with one's social environment' (1995: 5).

(iii) Another problem concerns the decision-making process. Most rational choice theories see the decision-making rather mechanically and non-processually, thus treating participation (or willingness to participate) as quite a static dependent variable, based on a single, time-bound, rational decision (Snow *et al.* 1986: 465). This overlooks the contextual and activity-based nature of much movement participation. One can argue that just as social movements change over time, there is variation in the individual's stake in participating in new activities. Decisions to participate over time are thus subject to frequent reassessment and re-negotiation. For example, with regard to Klandermans' work, beliefs of expectancies are temporally variable and can be modified during the course of actual participation (Snow *et al.* 1986: 471). To conclude, it is argued that rationales for participation are both collective and ongoing phenomena, and have therefore to be conceptualised and studied as processual phenomena.

(iv) Finally, it has been argued that the theory does not really investigate the causes of behaviour, but instead looks for rationalisations of it. Kelly and Kelly (1992: 254), for example, state that workers' strike calculations may be rationalisations which are designed to justify their decision ('*post hoc* justifications'), just as much as rational reflections which precede their decisions as rational choice theorists sustain. Thus, the causal link between cost–benefit calculations and the willingness to participate is not clarified in this theory (Kelly and Kelly 1992: 254). However, according to Bem (1972), this is true for attitudes in general: attitudes are a justification for, rather than a cause of, behaviour (also Weick 1969).

(v) As Newton and McFarlane Shore (1992) state, there is a lack of adequate research on the determinants and validity of instrumentality. There are several case studies and surveys showing that workers make cost–benefit calculations about industrial action in certain circumstances (e.g. Batstone *et al.* 1978; Cole 1969; Martin 1986; Woolfson and Foster 1988). However, Newton and McFarlane Shore (1992: 279) claim that union instrumentality has been mostly studied in relation to union certification voting in the USA (e.g. DeCotiis and LeLouran 1981; Fiorito and Greer 1982; Heneman and Sandver 1983; Klandermans 1986b; Premack and Hunter 1988; Zalesny 1985), and there has been little investigation of the role of instrumentality after voting decisions.

One might conclude that the major potential weakness of rational choice theory lies in the neglect of the social processes of mobilisation. This is the focus of social identity theory, and therefore it seems a good idea to test both theories together in order to study their compatibility.

Rational choice theory was tested in this study because it might provide a powerful explanation of the behaviour of east German workers. As will be remembered from the discussion in Chapter 6, there are widespread hypotheses in the literature on east Germany that workers perceive the costs of collective activities as too high (in the face of the devastating labour market situation), and/or do not perceive the new interest institutions as effective and therefore remain passive. The question then to be asked is whether east Germans are more likely to take a rational choice approach to participation than their west German colleagues, as is argued in the literature. Yet, rational choice theory could also be applied differently. One could argue that due to their collectivist past people might value collective activities as more effective than individual ones, and they might also perceive the new interest institutions as more instrumental than the old union.

Social identity theory

Social identity theory (e.g. Tajfel 1982; Tajfel and Turner 1986) emphasises the embeddedness of individuals in social groups and the influence on their behaviour of inter-group relations. The focus is on the social processes between individuals within social movements (such as unions). Social identity is defined as the 'individual's awareness that he or she belongs to a certain social group, together with the evaluative and emotional significance of that membership' (Kelly and Kelly 1994: 4). Thus, this group is a (positive) 'reference group' and not merely a 'membership group' as defined by outsiders, i.e. it is not simply a group which one is objectively in, but one which is subjectively important in determining one's actions.

The theory has three fundamental tenets. One is a proposed positive relationship between levels of in-group identification and inter-group differentiation (Hinkle and Brown 1990; Kelly 1993: 60). Thus, individuals want to achieve a positive social identity (since this contributes to positive self-esteem) and this is achieved by demonstrating 'positive in-group distinctiveness' through engaging in social comparisons with out-groups (Kelly and Kelly 1994). In other words, social identification entails social categorisation (the division of the world into manageable social units such as men and women, workers and managers. etc.) which may lead to perceptions of the out-group in a stereotypical manner (them–us). There is evidence that a strong group identification is associated with more conflictual perceptions of 'us' and 'them' (e.g. Kelly 1993: 67). It follows that strong 'them-and-us' feelings will lead to a strong willingness to participate in collective action (e.g. Kelly and Nicholson 1980; Stagner and Eflal 1982).

The other tenet of this theory is that strong group identification facilitates participation in collective action by promoting shared perceptions within the in-group concerning the desirability and possibility of social change (Kelly 1993: 77; also Triandis *et al.* 1988). Applied to the union context, this proposes that the more people identify with their union (social group) the more willing they are to participate in collective activity (cf. the literature on the concept of union commitment, e.g. Fullagar and Barling 1987, 1989; Fukami and Larson 1984; Gordon *et al.* 1980, 1984, 1990).[11]

Finally, as Kelly and Kelly (1994: 5) outline, research on differences in individual orientation (collectivist or individualist) suggests that this factor might also have a direct impact on the willingness to participate in collective action. Thus, individuals with a collectivist orientation are more likely to get involved in collective activities (e.g. Triandis *et al.* 1988; Wheeler *et al.* 1989). This resembles the long-standing argument in industrial relations that collectivist attitudes are related to union activism. For example, Fosh (1981) examined the consequences of strong class consciousness (i.e. collectivist attitudes) and concluded that active members manifest a strong commitment to collectivism in that they have a firm belief in the political and social as well as economic goals of the union rather than an instrumental belief in trade unionism as a means for acquiring individual ends extrinsic to trade unionism (also Huszczo 1983).

One can distinguish two main problems with social identity theory. The first refers to the associations between the variables (union identity, them-and-us feelings and workgroup identity) which are not sufficiently explored in the theory. Social identity theory assumes a correlation between them-and-us feelings and identification with the union which need not always exist. Workers with strong them–us attitudes need not necessarily have a strong union commitment. They may not even be union members (e.g. they can think that the union is too weak or not appropriate for representing their interests) which means that them–us attitudes and union identity can exist without each other, that they are independent although they share a conceptual affinity. One could argue that them-and-us feelings are, though not a sufficient precondition, still a necessary condition for union identity.

Similarly, in a favourable group context (i.e. with a strong degree of collectivism) and where strong group identity and them–us feelings exist, the relationship towards collective action is not entirely clear. Are both factors each independently correlated with participation or are they highly interrelated? And if they are related, has union identity a moderating role between them–us and participation (as Kelly and Kelly suggested) or can them–us also have a moderating role between union identity and participation?

Moreover, the theory does not explore the relationship between workgroup identity and union identity. And, besides, it does not investigate the possible problem of various social identities, i.e. the problem of dual commitment (e.g. Guest and Dewe 1988).[12] Kelly and Kelly (1992: 260) suggest that studies focusing on the impact of group identity have to examine not only the strength but also the meaning of that identity to the individual. However, Brown and Williams (1984) advanced the theory in this direction by arguing that it is necessary to examine the ideological meaning of group identification, as well as to recognise the existence and consequences of the different group memberships and identities of one person.[13]

The second major deficiency refers to the intra-group mechanisms which have been insufficiently dealt with in social identity theory. Thus, the theory is not explicit about how individual group members will behave in a 'disadvantageous' group situation where the group wants to adopt collective strategies to change its situation. There are propositions that relate members' choices (to behave collectively or individually (e.g. leaving the group)) to the presence or absence of cognitive alternatives to the existing situation, and whether the present situation is perceived as legitimate and stable or illegitimate. For example, if a member sees the present situation as legitimate and stable, then that member is unlikely to try to change it through inter-group confrontation or any other means (Taylor *et al.* 1987: 82). Yet, it is not clear where the individual gets his/her perception of legitimacy and stability from, and how one accounts for individual preferences of collective or individualistic strategies. The theory only argues that when one's self-image as a group member is salient, one will behave as a group member (thus collectively). And when personal identity is salient, individual group members are likely to resist group pressure and take individualistic strategies. However, this explanation is potentially tautological and runs the risk of constructing individuals as 'cognitive automatons' (Abrams 1989), entirely constrained by their perceptions of the social field. It leaves no room for individual variation once the social identity is salient; thus it overestimates homogeneity in groups (also Klandermans 1986b: 200).

In sum, these criticisms point to the insufficient empirical work on the associations between the variables, and to the inadequate explanations of intra-group mechanisms. With regard to the latter one could imagine rational choice theory contributing to our understanding of why group members might choose different strategies (e.g. individual or collective action), which gives another reason for testing the theories together.

This study is not primarily interested in the antecedents of social identity, but tests social identity theory because of its potential explanatory power of participation in the east German context. Thus, applied to the east German context, the theory would suggest that low participation arises from weak identification with the union. Thus, people have not yet identified enough with their new union and are therefore less willing to become active, and/or generally they prefer individualistic strategies which overshadow their group identities. However, social identity theory could also argue that people had strong group identities and collectivist attitudes in former times which might continue today and therefore should lead to strong activity. The latter is supported by the data presented (Chapter 8). The question is to what extent east Germans are less guided by social identity than their western colleagues when deciding upon collective action.

Attribution theory

Attribution theory (e.g. Heider 1958; Kelley and Michela 1980; Weiner 1985) is concerned with the ways individuals try to explain the behaviour of people and, more generally, events in their own social environment (Klandermans *et al.* 1991: 52). Attribution is defined as an explanation for an event or action in terms of reason or causes or both (Kelly 1996a, ch. 5: 9). A basic assumption is that in order to make sense of the world people will make judgements about the causes of behaviour or events. It is conventional to classify attributions along three dimensions: personal (internal) versus situational (external) causes, stable versus unstable factors, and controllable versus uncontrollable factors (Hewstone 1989, ch. 3). The theory then argues that each attribution has different consequences for future behaviour. For example, external and controllable attribution of workplace problems leads to mobilisation, i.e. collective action (e.g. Ferree and Miller 1985; McAdam 1988), whereas internal attribution could lead to fatalism or individual action (Kelly 1996a, ch. 5: 9; Klandermans *et al.* 1991: 55).

This theory has rarely been tested in relation to union participation. An exception is the study by van Vuuren *et al.* (1991) who found external attribution to be significant in determining participation.

In the post-socialist context, attribution theory raises the question as to whether workers attribute their problems to themselves (e.g. 'I do not work hard enough therefore I will be dismissed') or to external factors (e.g. controllable ones such as 'the current economic crisis' or uncontrollable ones such as 'unqualified management'). According to Stratemann (1993: 16) external, situational attribution (which also means delegating responsibility to external authorities) has been the prevalent form of attribution in the GDR ('the System' is to be blamed), and it is therefore likely that this will continue to be so for some time. In other words, this theory would consequently expect a rather high level of collective action (as was found in the discussion of the GTB samples, Chapter 8) and would not support the picture of the passive, lethargic east German.

9.4 Interrelations of the theories of collective activities: previous empirical findings and theoretical propositions

Empirical findings

As mentioned before it is rare for 'alternative' theories to be tested together (see also Kelly and Kelly 1993: 7) and the current author is not aware of any recent study testing the four social-psychological theories together. This, plus the previously mentioned problem of different conceptualisations of the variables in the literature (union identity etc.), renders comparisons of the results of this study with previous studies difficult. Furthermore, as mentioned before, there are no comparable (east or west) German studies.

Most recent studies concentrate on either union identity (e.g. Kelly and Kelly 1994) or instrumentality (e.g. Klandermans 1984b) as the major determinant of participation. A few studies, however, have tested a selection of antecedents and come up with mixed results (e.g. Fullagar and Barling 1989; Glick *et al.* 1977; Guest and Dewe 1988; Kelly and Kelly 1993; Klandermans 1986b; Kuruvilla *et al.* 1990; McShane 1986; Martin 1986; van Vuuren *et al.* 1991). Their results will be briefly discussed.

Glick *et al.* (1977) examined predictors of three variables in a sample of members of a US union (185 returned questionnaires): overall satisfaction with the union and two items on participation (willingness to attend union meetings and willingness to represent the union). Six antecedents were used: demographic variables, general beliefs about unionism, perceptions of activities in the union (members' influence, leadership's effectiveness, sense of harmony among union members, etc.), assessments of support to participation given by union leaders and by management, job-related factors (job tenure, job satisfaction, commitment), and individual need patterns. The result was that there were strong positive correlations between measures of individual needs and job-related factors and the two items of participation, and with some measures of 'perceptions of union activities' (e.g. 'members' integration and member influence'); general beliefs about unionism also achieved significance.

Martin (1986) tested the propensity to strike in service sector unions in the USA (141 returned questionnaires; a 33 per cent return rate) against three categories of antecedents: demographic, economic (pay) and political variables (support from significant others, attitudes towards the union and its union officials). He found that political variables were more important than the others. Yet, these variables were general perceptions and did not measure either instrumentality or identity specifically.

McShane (1986) tested three forms of participation (so-called 'administrative' participation, attendance at meetings, voting participation) and nine antecedents in a Canadian union (297 returned questionnaires; 62 per cent return rate): education, seniority, employment status, salary, distance to the union (kilometres between home and union hall), social integration (social attachment to the union branch), value of unions (general attitude towards unionism), interest in union business (interest in day-to-day union affairs), extrinsic job satisfaction, and job involvement. Education, seniority and interest in union business had the most significant positive regression coefficients with administrative participation; salary, distance to the union and extrinsic satisfaction had the most significant regression coefficients with regard to meeting attendance; and employment status was the only significant antecedent with regard to voting participation.

Fullagar and Barling (1989) measured ten antecedents (race, union socialisation, extrinsic and intrinsic job satisfaction, job involvement, life satisfaction, Marxist-related beliefs and work ethic beliefs) with regard to union loyalty and union instrumentality, and then union loyalty and instrumentality with regard to participation in South Africa (453 returned questionnaires with a 38 per cent return rate). They argued that both union loyalty (identity) and instrumentality had a significant impact on participation, yet instrumentality moderated the impact of identity. They found that both variables were equally important predictors of union participation for white manual workers, but found union loyalty was more important than instrumentality for black manual workers (due to limited 'voice' possibilities).

Referring to this study and his own research in the Netherlands, Klandermans (1992) claimed that instrumentality, commitment and social integration (interaction with others) in the union have a 'mutually reinforcing effect on sustained participation' if participation is regarded positively (p. 190). However, he did not investigate this further.

Guest and Dewe (1988) argued that instrumentality is the main correlate for remaining in membership, yet their study (716 returned questionnaires of union members and non-members in three UK plants) suffers from deficient measurements of the two concepts (e.g. union identity is for example operationalised with 'father's occupation', 'vocational education' and 'perceptions of social inequalities in UK'), and its dependent variable is not 'participation' but staying in the union.

Kelly and Kelly (1993) tested Klandermans' expectancy–value theory in a sample of British union members and contrasted it to social identity theory and showed convincingly that union identity is the crucial determinant for participation (350 returned questionnaires; 39 per cent return rate). They also found some moderating effect of union identity for the goal motive alone.

Kuruvilla *et al.* (1990) examined predictors of union participation in Japan (6,600 returned questionnaires; 78 per cent return rate) measuring demographic variables, job-related variables, union attitudes (attitudes towards union leader, identification with local union, perceived value of unionism), social integration in the workplace (similar to group identity), and perception of union–management relations. They found that in general union attitudes variables are better predictors of participation than demographic or job-related variables, and that the union-identity variables scored higher than union-instrumentality variables.

Finally, van Vuuren *et al.* (1991) examined variables of attribution of job insecurity, and cost–benefit perceptions of collective action in a sample of employees who perceive a high level of job insecurity (311 cases in three Dutch companies; 72 per cent return rate). Cost–benefit perceptions were stronger predictors than causal attributions but both were significant and accounted for 43 per cent of the variance in collective action.

Overall, these studies came up with mixed results and are difficult to compare because they use different variables and sometimes operationalise the same variable differently. This is also pointed out by Kuruvilla *et al.* (1990: 375) who argue that diverse orientations coupled with alternative disciplinary orientations have resulted in studies that differ in the participation measures and antecedent or correlate measures used. For example, only the studies by Fullagar and Barling, Kelly and Kelly and Kuruvilla *et al.* have tested two of the major concepts proposed, rational choice and social identity, together. Both concepts were found to be significant in these three studies. Instrumentality was more significant than identity as an antecedent for Fullagar and Barling, but it was less significant than identity for Kelly and Kelly and Kuruvilla *et al.*

Furthermore, most of the above studies did not investigate possible interrelations of these theories (e.g. Kuruvilla *et al.* 1990). Exceptions are Kelly and Kelly (1993) who propose that the link between value–expectancy calculations and participation might be moderated by social identity, and Fullagar and Barling (1989) who suggest that instrumentality moderates the influence of union loyalty (identity) on participation. Thus, union identity may not exist in the absence of positive outcomes or rewards from the union. Both studies found some evidence for their hypotheses. Yet, both studies tested only their *a priori* assumptions, not whether the moderating effect was also possible the other way around. For example, Kelly and Kelly did not investigate whether the perception of instrumentality had any effect on union identity, and Fullagar and Barling did not investigate whether identity had a different effect on instrumentality. However, Fullagar and Barling admitted that despite their longitudinal data a competing causal model could be consistent with their data (1989: 224).[14]

Theoretical propositions

The literature's conceptual treatment of the theories' interrelations is not yet well advanced. There is some interest in the association between the two variables, identity and instrumentality, but most accounts remain rather vague. For example, Etzioni (1975) suggests that 'moral and calculative involvements' may interact with each other, but he does not specify how. More specifically, Guest and Dewe (1988: 179) note that cost–benefit calculations, union identity and also job dissatisfaction are 'competing explanations, but not necessarily mutually exclusive'. Others suggest that instrumentality and 'normative attachments' may arise or exist concurrently (Summers *et al.* 1986; Zalesny 1985).

Some authors outline more detailed theoretical assumptions. For example, Newton and McFarlane Shore (1992: 280) suggest a causal arrow from 'instrumentality-based' membership to 'ideologically based' membership. Thus, they argue that it is unlikely for a strong ideologically based membership to develop unless the newcomer also has strong instrumentality beliefs (p. 293). Instrumental beliefs are a precursor to the development of identity/ideological beliefs but do not ensure this development. This model, however, has not been empirically tested.

Klandermans (e.g. 1989, 1992, 1995) proposes that 'a comprehensive approach' is necessary for the study of theories of participation. As will be remembered, he uses rational choice theory, interactionist theory ('social motives') and frustration–aggression theory which 'each make their own contribution to the social psychology of union participation' (1995: 4). He claims that the empirical data in union studies show that either the 'cost–benefit theory' or the 'commitment theory' are able to explain membership behaviour (e.g. leaving the union in the study by van der Veen and Klandermans 1989: 192). Yet, in explaining the link between the two concepts, he applies Fishbein and Ajzen's (1975) theory of reasoned action as his master frame (Klandermans 1995: 4). He argues that the two theories are not in conflict, but that the concept of commitment (and the theory of frustration–aggression) can be used to complement the cost–benefit theory; thus both influence the motivation to participate but the cost–benefit calculation is the more influential factor. He also acknowledges (which shows a significant extension of his earlier work) that the social environment determines the value of the costs and benefits (being socially constructed) (1995: 5).

In sum, it seems safe to say that the studies either do not deal with possible empirical interrelations at all (e.g. Kuruvilla *et al.*) or the superiority of 'instrumentality' is assumed but not further tested. In contrast, the current study tests the possible interrelations between instrumentality and identity and other independent variables.

The present study predicts that instrumentality and identity are interrelated and mutually reinforce the willingness to participate, and thus does not provide the *a priori* assumption that one variable leads over the other. In other words, it is assumed that workers' perceptions of collective instrumentality are influenced by the degree of their social identities (e.g. union identity), and union identity is influenced by their perceptions of the interest institutions and of collective action. Thus, with regard to the east German context, workers who identify with their new unions (perhaps because they have already identified with the union movement in former times or because they have established in the last five years an increasing loyalty and identification with the union as a new social group) might be seeing the effectiveness of the union and the works council in a more positive light than their colleagues who are not in the union or who are union members only for calculative reasons. At the same time, workers who have good experiences of the interest institutions might increase their emotional affiliation to the union.

9.5 Conclusion

This chapter has principally focused on the four social-psychological theories (frustration–aggression, rational choice, social identity, attribution) which are tested in this study. Most criticisms of these theories refer to the insufficient explanations of the determinants of the concepts and to the fact that most empirical and theoretical work has been confined to developing and testing any one theory while failing to test competing models (see Kelly and Kelly 1993: 19). Consequently, operationalising social-psychological theories requires a rather inventive adaptation of previous sets of items, which is partly due to the lack of well-established sets of items and partly due to the fact that these theories have not yet been tested in a German context.

Furthermore, it should be noted that all these theories assume a causal relationship between their variables (e.g. attitudes) and participation. However, the reservation mentioned with regard to rational choice theory is true for all theories that test attitudes: attitudes might well be justifications for or consequences of behaviour rather than a cause of behaviour (Bem 1972). The present study will continue to assume that attitudes precede behaviour.

Finally, this study's contribution to this literature is to test these theories together, and to test them in a new cultural context. Thus, it deals with the applicability of the theories in a post-socialist context. An underlying fundamental question is whether industrial relations knowledge is generalisable across national boundaries, or whether cultures are so different that any industrial relations theory must be considered culture-specific (see Kuruvilla *et al.* 1990: 374). This becomes interesting especially in the case of post-socialist societies. With regard to east Germany the question is the extent to which forty years of socialism has had a significant impact on workers' attitudes and behaviour towards their union/collective activities. It will be remembered that this is the assumption of a large part of the studies on east Germany.

However, the applicability of theories is difficult to prove and also depends on the scientific methodology used. First, the study can only test each theory's applicability with regard to its sample or population (e.g. east German clothing workers), but might not be generalisable to the whole of east Germany.

Moreover, what are the criteria by which to judge a theory's applicability? A pragmatic approach could be to argue that a theory is applicable if it results in significant determinants of participation. However, since some theories have had varying results in western studies (e.g. frustration–aggression), and others do not yet have a standardised set of variables, it seems unwise to refute a theory merely on the grounds of one empirical test. In addition, which of the existing western studies should be taken as a comparison? Kuruvilla *et al.*'s application of western theories of participation in a Japanese context, for example, is flawed by their lack of matching comparative data for western countries. Thus, a more feasible and valid method is to test these theories in a comparative study, as is done in this book. The task is to examine whether the east German sample yields significantly different results compared to their west German colleagues, and whether the explained variance is similar.

10 Determinants of union membership participation in the east and west

This chapter tests the different approaches to participation in union and works council activities in the east and west German membership samples. Specifically, it investigates whether any of the four social-psychological theories, discussed in the previous chapter, explains participation behaviour in the east German context and to what extent it differs from that in the west. In other words, are east Germans primarily characterised by an instrumental, cost–benefit approach to participation – as the literature predicts – and do their western colleagues approach collective activities differently, for example based on their identification with the union? Following this analysis the chapter assesses the extent to which the findings contribute to the discussion on the explanatory power of theories of collective action, together with the applicability of the theories in a post-socialist context.

The chapter starts with a discussion of the independent (explanatory) variables of members' willingness to participate in collective activities. It then reports the findings of the regression analyses testing the antecedents of participation of east and west German members. The final two sections further analyse the findings in terms of the similarities and differences between members in the east and west, and discuss these findings in the context of previous studies on participation.

10.1 The independent variables of participation

Rational choice theory was operationalised by the 'instrumentality of interest institutions' and 'collective action' variables. Social identity theory used union and workgroup identity, collectivist values and them-and-us feelings. Attribution theory was measured by attribution of workplace problems, and frustration–aggression theory was operationalised by job satisfaction. In addition, gender, age, blue-collar work (only in the east), works council post and union post (only in the west) were the demographic variables used.

The frequencies of the variables of rational choice and social identity theories were discussed as part of 'collective commitment' in Chapter 8 and the demographic variables were introduced in Chapter 7. The remaining frequencies of 'job satisfaction' and 'attribution' will be briefly discussed in the following.

Job satisfaction was measured with four questions: two general and two specific. The questions were selected from the Overall Job Satisfaction scale of Warr *et al.* (1980), developed specifically for use on blue-collar workers. Attribution was measured with regard to three workplace problems: workload, pay and job security, and it asked about internal and external attributions for these problems. Questions were based on Klandermans *et al.* (1991) and also on Zoll (1981: 198). The frequencies are reported in Tables 10.1 and 10.2. The questionnaire was not concerned with the perceived changes in the organisation of work, but with attitudinal reactions only (see Table 10.1). It distinguished between general job satisfaction and satisfaction with specific issues. In most cases east Germans yielded more negative attitudes than their western colleagues. Sixty-five per cent of east Germans preferred the old socialist workplace regime to their new workplaces. Thus, only a third were generally satisfied with their work in contrast to 87 per cent of west Germans. Similar negative data, although not to such an extreme, were reported by Andretta *et al.* (1994). Nevertheless, a majority of east Germans found the capitalist enterprise to be treating their employees more fairly than did the former regime.

For specific job issues, especially those of pay and job insecurity, an overwhelming majority of the east Germans were dissatisfied (significantly more than their western colleagues). The interviews at Bodywear also supported the strong dissatisfaction. Overall, pay was compared with west German levels rather than with their former pay. This is a common finding in the literature (e.g. Andretta *et al.* 1994; Lungwitz 1994: 302). In terms of the increasing work pace, the two German groups did not differ significantly in their disapproval.

In light of the above it seems safe to say that dissatisfaction was a widespread result of the organisational restructuring in east German (clothing) companies after unification. This is in line with empirical studies of other industrial sectors (e.g. Andretta *et al.* 1994). Frustration about work pace, stricter control and supervision overshadowed the improvements in the material working conditions (better machines, working environment/buildings). For example, one person remarked on his/her questionnaire: 'the working life under the capitalists resembles slavery. Working without pay and frequent threats' (anonymous respondent, GTB questionnaire 1994).

However, the existence of job dissatisfaction is not specifically an east German phenomenon. Job dissatisfaction is also a common reaction to organisational changes in western societies. Such dissatisfaction might be due to how organisational change procedures were introduced, thus with or without involving the workforce, and/or due to the content of these changes (e.g. intensification of work). On the other hand, one might argue that dissatisfaction is not a result of the restructuring at all, but a continuation of former job dissatisfaction (see Chapter 2). Yet, the comparative questions on workers' job satisfaction before and after 1989 in the east German survey suggest that people were more satisfied with their jobs in former times.

Table 10.1 Comparison of job satisfaction in the east and west: frequencies (%), means and t-tests ($*p < 0.05$, $**p < 0.01$)

		Strongly disagree	Disagree	No view	Agree	Strongly agree	Mean, significance level	N
East: all in all our work situation is better today than in the former socialist enterprise.	east	33.0	31.7	5.2	26.8	3.3	2.36	306
West: all in all I am satisfied with my work here.	west	3.7	6.3	2.6	51.3	36.1	4.10 **	992
East: 'capitalist' enterprises treat their employees more fairly than did former 'socialist' enterprises.	east	15.3	22.4	10.1	42.5	9.7	3.09	308
West: The working climate between workforce and management is quite good.	west	10.5	21.3	11.4	44.8	12.0	3.26 *	986
I am dissatisfied with the increasing work pace at my job.	east	15.7	18.0	4.3	32.5	29.5	3.42	305
	west	10.8	18.0	6.5	35.5	29.2	3.55	985
I am paid a fair wage.	east	66.7	16.8	3.6	9.4	3.6	1.66 **	309
	west	29.0	22.9	7.6	28.4	12.2	2.72	991
I am constantly worried about losing my job.	east	5.8	7.1	3.9	20.3	62.6	4.31 **	310
	west	14.3	20.5	8.7	27.5	29.0	3.36	991

Finally, as noted in the previous chapter, it is interesting to test the extent to which the strong job dissatisfaction in the east might have an impact on people's willingness to act collectively. As one can see in Table 10.2 there was not much difference between east and west Germans with regard to external attributions. Job losses were affiliated with the competitive market situation rather than with incompetent management (although more so in the west than in the east) but there was a lack of clarity regarding management's role in the increasing work pace. About 80 per cent felt that management had taken advantage of the employment situation with regard to work pace and pay levels. Furthermore, east Germans' concern with work pace was significantly stronger than that of their western colleagues. The same number of people, however, also agreed that it was not so much management's fault as the pressures of the market economy that increased the pace of work. Thus, people might have strong feelings about management's abuse of the devastating employment situation, but when asked whether they thought the latter was due to incompetence or to inevitable market pressures on management, it seems that they preferred to blame the external market pressures. This might reflect the perceived reality in these eastern companies. Another interpretation might be that this attitude arises out of the former experience that directors were merely tools of the System and that this continues today. As one worker argued: 'only the System changed' (knitter no. 4, September 1993).

With regard to internal causes differences between west and east were stronger. Job losses were linked with the lack of solidarity/resistance of workers rather than an inadequate performance of the workforce or too high labour costs. East Germans in particular were keen to blame the absence of worker solidarity and defended their ('high') wage levels. This is in line with the previous finding of the perception of decreasing solidarity in the discussion on workgroup identity (Chapter 8).

One can conclude from the above that external attribution was stronger than internal attribution. As noted in Chapter 6, Stratemann (1993: 16) argues that external, situational attribution has been the prevalent form of attribution in the GDR ('the System is to be blamed'), and these data support the view that this will continue to be so for some time. However, the similarities between the two samples challenge the argument that external attribution is a specific socialist legacy. Nevertheless, it might be interesting to test whether external attribution has an impact on people's willingness to participate collectively.

The discussion of the two variables on workers' perceptions of various facets of the organisational transformation rounds up the picture of workers' attitudes and behaviour outlined in Chapter 8. A major outcome of that discussion was that east German union members are not more individualistic than their western colleagues and are committed union members supporting the institutionalisation of the new interest representation. The data here provided a rather depressing picture of the current working conditions and management–workforce relations in the east. It substantiates the claim made by others that the organisational transformation has left the workers highly dissatisfied and disappointed.

Table 10.2 Comparison of attribution of workplace problems in the east and west: frequencies (%), means and t-tests (* $p < 0.05$, ** $p < 0.01$)

		Strongly disagree	Disagree	No view	Agree	Strongly agree	Mean, significance level	N
External attribution								
Management exploits the labour market situation with regard to the increase of work pace.	east	3.9	6.8	8.5	30.3	50.5	4.17	307
	west	5.6	7.4	13.8	28.9	44.3	3.99 *	992
It is not so much management's fault, as the introduction of a market economy which inevitably increases work pressures.	east	4.2	6.2	9.1	38.1	42.3	4.08	307
	west	4.2	7.9	8.4	34.8	44.6	4.08	990
Employers take advantage of the current labour market situation with regard to pay.	east	6.5	5.2	10.4	19.2	58.3	4.24	307
	west	4.4	5.1	8.3	26.9	55.3	4.24	983
Incompetent management [accounts for job losses].	east	24.4	18.1	25.1	24.7	7.7	2.73	299
	west	22.1	20.9	24.2	21.2	11.7	2.80	973
East: lack of demand for our products [accounts for job losses]. West: low-pay competition from the Third World.	east	19.3	20.3	11.0	25.6	23.9	3.15 **	301
	west	6.5	3.9	7.8	22.8	58.9	4.24	981

Internal attribution

Not enough effort from the workers [accounts for job losses].	east	52.0	19.4	6.6	17.8	4.3	2.03	304
	west	45.6	26.9	10.9	13.6	3.0	2.01	980
Labour costs are too high [therefore job losses].	east	80.7	13.1	2.3	2.0	2.0	1.31	306
	west	33.7	26.8	16.5	16.8	6.2	2.35 **	970
The workforce doesn't show enough solidarity with colleagues made redundant.	east	10.6	22.0	9.5	29.8	21.0	3.36 **	301
	west	13.3	19.4	34.4	18.8	14.1	3.01	973
The workforce does not offer enough resistance to management's strategies [in terms of work pace].	east	5.5	11.4	2.9	30.3	49.8	4.08 **	307
	west	28.4	23.7	16.7	23.0	8.2	2.59	988

In considering the general literature on organisational transformation, particularly that on personnel management in the transformation process (Chapter 3), one could suggest that companies that practise organisational changes without involving their workers and/or have adopted intensified 'Tayloristic' production methods – as most clothing companies did – did not succeed in achieving job satisfaction among that workforce. Instead, such methods conceivably generate future problems in terms of worker motivation and commitment to the company once the threat caused by job insecurity is less predominant. The eastern sample of workers can be characterised as showing 'compliance' but not 'commitment' to their organisation or management (for the difference between these terms see Walton 1985). For example, the east German union members had a more negative view of management and the general workplace climate than did the works councillors. Thus, the question of whether the 'harmonious' workplace relationship between management and works councils (as shown in the councillor questionnaires, see Chapter 4) is also perceived by the workforce can be answered negatively. Together with their 'them-and-us' feelings (Chapter 8) and people's attribution of workplace problems to management, one can argue that these workers in the east yield no 'unitarist' view but rather a 'them-and-us' perception of the workplace relations. To what extent this is caused by the Tayloristic restructuring of the work or by a lack of direct employee involvement is hard to say. As noted earlier, job dissatisfaction and 'them-and-us' feelings are also familiar outcomes of organisational interventions in western companies. Furthermore, it raises the difficult question of how far they are a 'normal' reaction to organisational change rather than a specific reflection of transformation.

To what extent job dissatisfaction and external attribution of workplace problems influence people's union commitment and, respectively, their willingness to engage in collective action will be analysed below.

10.2 Explaining collective participation in the east and west

The predictions of the theories of participation, discussed in the previous chapter, can be summarised in six hypotheses:

(i)   Members who perceive unions/works councils to be effective are more likely to engage in collective activities; and members who perceive collective activities to be an effective means to reach collective goals are more likely to engage in collective activities.
(ii) Members who identify with their union are more likely to engage in collective activities; members who identify with their workgroup and/or have strong collective values are more likely to engage in collective activities.
(iii) Members with a strong job dissatisfaction are more likely to engage in collective activities than satisfied members.

(iv) Members who attribute causes of their workplace problems to external factors are more likely to become collectively active than those who attribute them to internal reasons.

(v) Blue-collar members are more likely to engage in collective activities than white collar members; older members are more likely to engage in collective activities than their younger colleagues; and male members are more likely than females to engage in collective activities.

(vi) East Germans are more likely than west Germans to base their decision to participate on their perceived effectiveness of the institutions and/or of the collective activities as such.

Factor analysis (see Appendix A 10.1) was conducted in both surveys in an attempt to summarise the items (questions) of each (dependent or independent) variable. This provided a check as to whether the indicators are really related to each other (and not to indicators that are supposed to measure other variables). Descriptive statistics (means and standard deviations) were estimated for all variables (see Table 10.3). The antecedents (independent variables) were then put into a (linear) regression analysis (ordinary least squares regression) for the participation factors (dependent variables) of the two surveys (Table 10.4).

In both samples the factor analysis yielded two dependent factors, 'self-initiated' and 'organised' participation (see also Chapter 8). For the independent (explanatory) variables, the factor analysis produced similar factors in both samples:[3] three factors of instrumentality ('negative instrumentality of union/works council', 'no necessity of works council', 'instrumentality of collective activities'); three factors of social identity ('union identity', 'workgroup identity', 'collectivist values'); two factors of attribution ('external attribution to management', 'internal attribution to lacking workers' effort'), and an additional factor for the east ('internal attribution to lacking solidarity of workforce'); one factor of job satisfaction ('general job satisfaction') and an additional factor in the east ('specific job dissatisfaction'); and one factor of them-and-us feelings ('current them–us') and an additional factor in the east ('former trust relations').

Not all factors yielded a high enough alpha reliability (above 0.50). Two regressions were conducted: one substituting the 'unreliable' factors with their single items, the other using all factors (reliable and unreliable ones). The resulting antecedents were mostly identical, and the 'factor-based analysis' was therefore used in the following. Self-initiated and organised participation yielded slightly different antecedents, supporting the earlier claim that the two concepts are distinguished and that participation is a multi-dimensional concept.

For self-initiated participation, there were five significant independent variables in the east sample and eight in the west. However, the major variables were the same in the two samples: high union identifiers, males and works-council/union officials were most likely in the east and west to participate in self-initiated collective activities. Other common but weaker determinants were

Table 10.3 Factors' mean and standard deviation in the east and west

Factors	East mean	East standard deviation	West mean	West standard deviation
Self-initiated participation	2.01	0.90	2.45	1.08
Organised participation	2.82	0.71	2.65	0.48
Negative instrumentality of works council/union	2.57	0.75	1.90	0.70
No necessity for works council	1.32	0.57	2.55	1.37
Instrumentality of collective activities	2.71	0.59	3.39	0.64
Union identity	2.79	0.68	2.89	0.71
Collectivism	2.70	0.65	2.73	0.61
Workgroup identity	2.83	0.73	2.87	0.70
Former trust	2.59	0.84	–	–
Current them–us	3.02	0.61	2.55	0.59
External attribution	3.03	0.56	2.77	0.65
Internal attribution (effort)	1.23	0.60	1.67	0.77
Internal attribution (solidarity)	2.86	0.75	–	–
General job satisfaction	1.82	0.84	2.92	0.70
Specific job dissatisfaction	2.51	0.60	–	–
Gender (1 = female, 2 = male)	1.25	0.43	1.53	0.49
Blue/white-collar (1 = blue, 2 = white)	1.20	0.40	–	–
Works council membership (1 = yes, 2 = no)	1.74	0.44	1.64	0.47
Union official (1 = yes, 2 = no)	–	–	1.85	0.35
Age	2.57	0.96	2.53	1.04

instrumentality of collective action and job (dis)satisfaction (general or specific). Overall, all social-psychological theories were supported in at least one of the four regressions but social identity theory was clearly the major explanatory theory throughout.

To examine whether the general equation was biased due to the slight over-representation of works councillors in the east sample, separate regressions for works council members and non-members were conducted in that sample.[4] The regression for works council members revealed two significant antecedents which were different from the above, works council necessity and general job satisfaction (both with a negative sign). On the other hand, the equation for council non-members produced instrumentality of collective activities and union identity as above, and thus it can be concluded that the councillors did not bias the outcome.[5] Overall, works councillors were driven by a general concern over the deteriorating working conditions and by their belief in the importance of a (strong) works council. Non-members, on the other hand, became engaged because of their affiliation to the union and general belief in collective action, issues not directly related to the works council itself.

In terms of organised participation, there were five significant antecedents in the east and seven in the west. High union identification and a belief in the instrumentality of collective action were both the main explanators in both samples. This is in contrast to self-initiated participation where 'union identity' was the only main predicting theory. Weaker determinants were workgroup identity and external and internal attribution in the east and belief in the necessity of works councils, external attribution, job dissatisfaction, gender and works-council membership in the west. Overall, rational choice theory was the main explanator in the east sample, whereas in the west both social identity and rational choice emerged as the main explanators. The individual antecedents are discussed in more detail below.

In terms of union identity an additional 'item-based' regression (splitting organised participation into its three items, see Appendix A 10.1) came up with an interesting finding. Union identity (in both samples) was significantly related to participation in demonstrations, but not to participation in strikes or assemblies. One could therefore argue that cost–benefit calculations are more difficult to make regarding demonstrations, which renders identification and solidarity more important. Finally, a separate regression analysis revealed that high or low union identifiers were mainly influenced by the same variables.[6]

Workgroup identity yielded a negative beta coefficient (in the east and west sample) which is contrary to the social identity theory, thus the more workers identify with their workgroup the less willing they are to participate. Yet, the item-based analysis characterised 'happiness with the group' as the major item within this factor. The factor might then be explained with the frustration–aggression theory, that people who are dissatisfied with their group are more likely to become active than their satisfied colleagues.

Within the measures of attribution, 'internal attribution' (lack of work effort) revealed a negative impact (i.e. people who do not make internal attributions are more likely to participate) which is equal to the external attribution with a positive sign.

Furthermore, job satisfaction revealed a positive sign in the west sample. Thus, the more satisfied workers were with their working conditions the more likely they were to join organised collective activities. One might explain this phenomenon with the concept of dual commitment (Guest and Dewe 1988). In other words, workers might be committed to the firm and to the works council/ union yet not see this as contradictory but as mutually reinforcing. It is also remarkable that job (dis)satisfaction revealed no significant impact on organised participation (e.g. strikes) in the east German sample as one might have predicted from the strong level of dissatisfaction among the east German workforce.

Interestingly, women were as likely as men to participate in organised activities (where time problems are less severe) in the east but not in the west. This could

Table 10.4 Predicting self-initiated and organised participation in the union and works council in east and west Germany: standardised regression coefficients, hD = hypothesised direction

	hD	East		West	
		Self-initiated participation	Organised participation	Self-initiated participation	Organised participation
Negative instrumentality of works council/union	−	−0.026	0.036	−0.051*	−0.016
No necessity for works council	−	−0.032	−0.029	−0.022	−0.130**
Instrumentality of collective activities	+	0.110*	0.346**	0.045*	0.285**
Union identity	+	0.227**	0.180**	0.403**	0.399**
Collectivism	+	0.057	0.071	0.003	0.035
Workgroup identity	+	−0.032	−0.099*	−0.049*	−0.007
Former trust (only east)	+	0.002	−0.016	—	—
Current them–us	+	−0.054	−0.029	0.004	0.022
External attribution (management)	+	0.086	0.112*	0.043*	0.105**

Internal attribution (lacking work effort)	−	0.006	−0.180**	0.011	−0.031
Internal attribution (lacking solidarity) (only east)	−	−0.016	−0.071	–	–
General job satisfaction	−	0.029	0.015	−0.058**	0.048*
Specific job dissatisfaction (only east)	+	0.133*	0.006	–	–
Gender (1 = female, 2 = male)	+	0.140**	−0.052	0.199**	0.044**
Blue/white-collar (1 = blue, 2 = white) (only east)	−	0.026	−0.032	–	–
Works council (1 = yes, 2 = no)	−	−0.338**	−0.073	−0.224**	−0.106**
Union official (1 = yes, 2 = no) (only west)	−	–	–	−0.131**	0.040*
Age	+	−0.009	−0.016	−0.004	−0.025

Notes: (* $p < 0.05$, ** $p < 0.01$)

East: self-initiated participation: R^2 (adj.) = 0.272, standard error = 0.7641; residual = 322 cases, F = 8.45692 (sig. F = 0.000); organised participation: R^2 (adj.) = 0.26403; standard error = 0.58883; residual = 322 cases, F = 8.15402 (sig. F = 0.000)

West: self-initiated participation: R^2 (adj.) = 0.462, standard error = 0.7901; residual = 1,678 cases, F = 104.678 (sig. F = 0.000); organised participation: R^2 (adj.) = 0.490, standard error = 0.3415; residual = 1,678 cases, F = 117.310 (sig. F = 0.000).

be traced back to the hypothesised 'equal' gender socialisation of the GDR. In contrast, gender was a determinant of self-initiated forms of participation (which are more time-consuming) in both samples.

Finally, a separate regression for works councillors/union officials and the rank-and-file for organised participation (in both samples) revealed that activists were influenced most by their perception of instrumentality of collective activities, whereas rank-and-file workers took other issues into account such as their union identity and degree of external attribution (similar to self-initiated participation). This is different from their approach to self-initiated participation. There, activists had a more cautious, calculative approach to strikes, perhaps because they are more aware of the costs and risks involved.

To conclude, whereas self-initiated participation was mainly explained by social identity theory, organised participation was primarily explained by both social identity and rational choice theory. These differences are most prominent in the east. There one can argue that union identity 'predicts' self-initiated participation (the more 'difficult' form of participation), whereas instrumentality of collective activities is the major factor for 'easier' activities such as strikes and demonstrations.

Overall, although all social-psychological theories became significant in at least one of the regressions, rational choice theory and social identity theory each showed the most significant explanatory power for both forms of participation in both German samples.[7] It follows that the null hypotheses (i) and (ii) can be supported.

The factors of the attribution theory and of the frustration–aggression theory, as well as the demographic factors, did not produce a consistent pattern. Hence, hypotheses (iii), (iv) and (v) cannot be entirely supported. It should be noted, however, that the insignificance of these variables does not necessarily refute their underlying theories (i.e. it might be that the variables did not show enough variation, e.g. general job satisfaction in the east, or that the measures could be criticised for being deficient).

10.3 Are east and west Germans different?

The final hypothesis, (vi) above, which argues that east Germans have a more instrumental approach to collective activities than their western colleagues, cannot be entirely supported either. There is no homogeneous evidence that 'rational choice' (instrumentality variables) was the main approach in the east and 'social identity' in the west. Thus, although east Germans were more instrumental with regard to organised participation than their western colleagues, 'social identity' proved to be the main approach for self-initiated participation in both samples. In sum, a comparison of the regression analyses of the two samples did not reveal that participation in the east was predominantly determined by instrumentality variables. This was further tested with a regression analysis for the merged data set that included a dummy variable ('group') for east and west Germans.

Table 10.5 The merged data set: means and standard deviation, $N = 2,128$

	Mean	Standard deviation
Groups	1.21	0.60
Organised participation	2.55	0.47
Self-initiated participation	2.35	0.75
Negative instrumentality of works council/union	2.09	0.75
No necessity for works council	1.31	0.71
Instrumentality of collective activities	3.32	0.64
Union identity	2.77	0.65
Collectivism	2.79	0.61
Workgroup identity	1.57	0.71
Current them–us	2.50	0.57
External attribution	2.69	0.63
Internal attribution (work effort)	1.57	0.74
General job satisfaction	2.47	0.67
Gender (1 = female, 2 = male)	1.47	0.49
Works council official (1 = yes, 2 = no)	1.70	0.45
Age	2.53	1.02

A factor analysis of the merged data set was conducted which resulted in the same factors as the separate factor analysis of the west German sample. Mean and standard deviation were estimated for all variables (Table 10.5) and they were put into (linear) regression analysis (ordinary least squares regression) (Table 10.6). Overall, similar antecedents as in the separate regressions, particularly in the west German sample, emerged. This provides additional support to the validity of the earlier regression analyses. A minor difference was that of 'age', which revealed no significance in the separate regression analyses, but became a significant determinant of organised participation. A straightforward explanation for this is difficult. In addition, age yielded a negative sign, thus suggesting that younger workers are more willing to participate in organised activities than their older colleagues. This stands in contrast to the individualisation literature that argues that younger generations are more individualistic than older ones. However, it has no strong loading, and thus is not a major explanator of organised participation.

The most important result is that the factor 'group' was not significant with regard to self-participation and had a significant but weak loading for organised participation. In other words, for the more 'difficult' form of participation it did not matter whether you were east or west German. Activists, therefore, were primarily influenced by their level of union identification. On the other

Table 10.6 Predicting self-initiated and organised participation in the merged data set: standardised regression coefficients, hD = hypothesised direction, $N = 2,128$

	hD	East and west self-initiated participation	East and west organised participation
Negative instrumentality of works council/union	−	−0.055**	−0.029
No necessity for works council	−	−0.030	−0.106**
Instrumentality of collective activities	+	0.050**	0.303**
Union identity	+	0.377**	0.291**
Collectivism	+	0.014	0.047**
Workgroup identity	+	0.047**	0.033
Current them–us	+	0.006	0.015
External attribution (management)	+	0.063**	0.137**
Internal attribution (solidarity)	−	0.00	−0.048**
General job satisfaction	−	−0.058**	0.075**
Group (1 = west, 2 = east)	−	0.012	−0.099**
Gender (1 = female, 2 = male)	+	0.189**	0.036*
Works council official (1 = yes, 2 = no)	−	−0.269**	−0.090**
Age	+	0.013	−0.051**

Notes. (* $p < 0.05$, ** $p < 0.01$)
Self-initiated participation: R^2 (adj.) = 0.405, standard error = 0.8038; residual = 2,113 cases, F = 104.486 (sig. F = 0.000); organised participation: R^2 (adj.) = 0.424; standard error = 0.3592; residual = 2,113 cases, F = 112.676 (sig. F = 0.000)

hand participation in strikes, demonstrations or works council assemblies was influenced primarily by the effectiveness of these meetings (and of the works council institution), the degree of union identification and the external attribution of workplace problems to management. Only in a secondary way did it matter whether you came from the east or west. However, that the geographical affiliation ('group') is significant for organised participation comes as no surprise when we look at the frequencies: west German members were significantly more inclined to join organised activities than their east German colleagues.

In sum, these findings add more support to the conclusion of the separate regression analyses. The reasons why people participate in collective activities were similar for the east and west German members of the clothing union. The hypothesis of a divide between instrumental east Germans and solidaristic west Germans therefore cannot be supported here.

10.4 Comparing the findings with previous studies

In the following, the antecedents' results of the two separate regression analyses (east and west) are compared with those of the studies outlined in the previous chapter.

The factor 'instrumentality of collective activities' turned out to be the most important variable of the concept 'collective instrumentality' in the east and west.[8] Moreover, people's perception of collective action was not influenced by their perception of the institutions. This was confirmed when analysing the possible antecedents of the perception of collective action as a dependent variable (all other variables as independent). Overall, this supports the hypothesis of the multi-dimensionality of the collective instrumentality concept. Both instrumentality of institutions and of collective action are in line with previous research, for example by Fullagar and Barling (1989), Glick *et al.* (1977), Klandermans (1986b), Kuruvilla *et al.* (1990) and Martin (1986) who found their measures of instrumentality (of unions) to be associated with union participation.[9]

In terms of social identity theory, union identity was significant for both types of participation in the east and west. Union identity was also found to be the main factor of social identity to determine participation.[10] Overall, this is consistent with Fullagar and Barling (1989) and Kuruvilla *et al.* (1990) who found union identity (loyalty) and participation to be related, as did Kelly and Kelly (1994) with regard to both types of participation (easy and difficult), and McShane (1986: 181) with regard to his variable 'value of unions' and administrative participation.

Work group identity was significant but at a low level for organised participation in the east and for self-initiated participation in the west. Although work-group identity has rarely been examined, Kuruvilla *et al.* (1990) found this variable to be significant regarding union participation. Furthermore, collectivism and 'them-and-us' feelings did not yield any explanatory power. Thus, this is different from Kelly and Kelly's (1994) finding of a significant relation of collectivist values with their variable 'easy' participation (but not with 'difficult' participation) and of 'outgroup stereotyping' with 'easy' participation (but not with 'difficult' participation). On the other hand, our finding is in line with Fullagar and Barling (1989) who found their related variable, 'Marxist beliefs', was not significant for union participation.

Furthermore, three measures of social identity (union identity, workgroup identity, collectivism), but not 'them-and-us' feelings, were inter-correlated.[11] This is in contrast to the hypothesis of the social identity literature which suggests a link between 'them-and-us' and identity (i.e. the stronger the identification with the group the stronger are them-and-us feelings) (e.g. Kelly and Kelly 1992, 1993). 'Them-and-us' feelings might be better understood in this context as a reaction against changing working conditions (i.e. management styles) than as being affiliated with group feelings (e.g. out-group stereotyping).

The interrelations between the three social identity factors[12] were further examined by separate regression analyses (each of the social identity variables

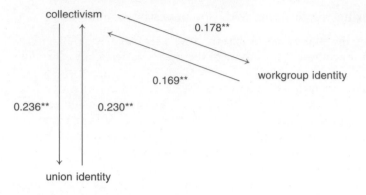

Figure 10.1 Regression coefficients of collectivism, union identity and workgroup identity in the east (** *p* < = 0.01).

being dependent variables and the other two being independent).[13] Union identity and workgroup identity were not correlated with one another, and collectivist attitudes were the pivotal point in the triangle relationship (see Figure 10.1). This finding suggests that collectivist attitudes rather than workgroup identity have an impact on the strength of union identity, and it adds support to a similar finding of Kelly and Kelly (1994: 26) and of Hinkle and Brown (1990, quoted in Kelly and Kelly). Attribution was found to be significantly related to organised and self-initiated participation, though not at a high level. All factors of attribution were inter-correlated and did not show a single main factor. On this theme, there is no known comparable previous study.

Job satisfaction was a significant predictor in both surveys and supports previous studies. For example, McShane (1986) found job dissatisfaction to be related to union meeting attendance (but not to administrative participation in the union); Martin (1986) found dissatisfaction with pay equity to be related to strike attendance; and Fukami and Larson (1984) found it to be related to 'union commitment'. Kuruvilla *et al.* (1990) found extrinsic, but not intrinsic, dissatisfaction to be a significant correlate for participation. Fullagar and Barling (1989) found both to be linked indirectly only to participation (via union loyalty). This contrasts with the argument of Gordon *et al.* (1980, 1984) that job dissatisfaction predicts initial union activity (e.g. joining in studies by Brett 1980 and DeCotiis and LeLouran 1981) but not those which occur later.

However, job (dis)satisfaction did not have a major impact on participation in the present samples, which might be explained by the fact that strikes or demonstrations are not the usual types of reaction to workplace problems in German industrial relations. It also means that the surprisingly strong willingness among east Germans to become collectively active cannot be explained by their strong dissatisfaction with the current working conditions.

Finally, with regard to the demographic variables, gender was found to be an important determinant in most cases, except in organised activities in the east.

That gender did not have a consistent impact on different forms of participation is in line with previous research that is characterised by divergent results. For example, Glick *et al.* (1977) found gender to be associated with the willingness to attend union meetings but Kuruvilla *et al.* (1990) did not find a significant relationship between gender and union participation.

The differences between males and females in the east and west were further analysed. Use of *t*-tests of males and females for all dependent and independent variables (see Appendix A 10.2) confirmed that overall gender differences in the east were much weaker than in the west. Thus, there were significant differences between the genders in the west but not in the east for the following factors: instrumentality of works council/union, necessity of works council, instrumentality of collective activities, and union identity. For example, male and female east German union members had an equally strong union identity and the same (weak) perception of the effectiveness of the new interest institutions. On the other hand, union identification was weaker for female than for male west Germans and females were less convinced of the effectiveness of works councils than their male colleagues. Differences were mixed with regard to self-initiated participation. There were significant differences in all four individual items of self-initiated participation between men and women in the west sample but only in two items for the east.

Differences were less significant for the remaining variables (workgroup identity, them-and-us feelings), and for organised participation in either sample. Thus, in the east and west, women and men had a similar solidarity towards their workgroup, similar feelings towards management and towards participation in strikes etc. To conclude, one could argue that the less pronounced differences between east German men and women provide additional support to the earlier discussion of the regression analyses. These findings might well indicate a legacy of the particular 'equal' gender socialisation of the former GDR. Clearly, only longitudinal studies will be able to tell to what extent women in the east remain more 'emancipated' than their female counterparts in the west, and whether this difference of gender relations in the eastern and western states (*Länder*) will remain a continuing feature in an unified Germany.

Age was not significant in the separate regression analyses and contrasts with previous research such as that by Martin (1986) who found youth to be important for strike participation, or Kuruvilla *et al.* (1990) with regard to union participation. In the east German case this is an interesting outcome, since it challenges the view that older workers who were socialised in former days are more active in the union movement than younger workers.

Works council/union posts was a significant correlate throughout and this comes as no surprise. Finally, contrary to some western findings (e.g. Kuruvilla *et al.* 1990; McShane 1986), job status (blue/white-collar) was not significant.

A final point deserves notice. Throughout the study participation was assumed to be the dependent variable to be explained and collective instrumentality, union identity and others are the explanatory factors. This is obviously a theoretical assumption. Fullagar and Barling (1989: 219) state that the literature is equivocal in terms of the direction of the relationship between union loyalty (identity) and participation in union activities. The ability of cross-sectional data (as used in this study) to prove this assumption, and thus to disentangle cause and effect, is obviously less than if one had employed a longitudinal design. In addition, empirical evidence on whether attitudes such as union identity cause committed behaviour such as participation, or whether enacting behaviour results in committed attitudes remains ambiguous (e.g. Fullagar and Barling 1989: 216; Mowday *et al.* 1982).

In order to test how far the willingness to participate influenced people's union identity and their perception of the instrumentality of collective activities, two further regression analyses were conducted (in the east) using participation as an independent variable.[14] The results will be briefly reported. The instrumentality of collective activities was heavily influenced by organised participation (beta = 0.352**), but not at all by self-initiated participation. Union identity on the other hand was influenced by both types of participation (self-initiated participation beta = 0.203**, organised participation beta = 0.144**). A repeated analysis for the west revealed similar results. In sum, the data showed that the three concepts were highly interrelated and, as explained, cause and effect were impossible to determine. More importantly, the findings provide further support for the results of the above regression analysis. In particular, they confirm the close relationship between organised participation and instrumentality.

10.5 Determinants of the antecedents of participation

As mentioned earlier, the questionnaires did not attempt to explore possible determinants of the independent variables. However, one can examine determinants within the sets of independent variables. As has been noted in the previous chapter, most previous studies have not examined possible interrelations between the antecedents of collective participation in much detail.

A regression analysis was conducted for the determinants of the major variables of the four theories of participation in the east survey: instrumentality of collective activities, union identity, external attribution, and (specific) job dissatisfaction (see Appendix A 10.3). Overall, most of the hypothesised interrelations of the independent variables, as outlined in the previous chapter, were supported.

Union identity and *collective instrumentality* were each other's most important predictor, and their relationship will be discussed in more detail below.

Them-and-us feelings were influenced negatively by internal attribution (i.e. the less workers attribute work problems to their own lack of effort the more likely they perceive a 'them-and-us' climate), and positively by external attribution as has been hypothesised. This is consistent with the earlier assertion that it might not be previous them-and-us feelings which are the cause of the current them-and-us climate but rather the current changes in workplace relations which make workers perceive a them-and-us climate.

Attribution was interrelated with instrumentality, which is an unexpected association, but not with social identity as was hypothesised. Thus, the more people attribute their problems externally the more they perceive collective activities as instrumental (and the other way around).

Specific job dissatisfaction was associated as expected by general job satisfaction.[15] More interestingly, blue-collar workers were more dissatisfied than white-collar workers, and women more than men which might be traced back to the fact that blue-collar jobs and female jobs (sewing) were in general more strongly affected by the organisational transformation than white-collar and male-dominated jobs (e.g. knitting, dyeing). Moreover, external attribution of work problems supported dissatisfaction (as expected), and a strong workgroup identity made workers more satisfied with their working conditions. Thus, the workgroup atmosphere was an important factor of the overall working conditions. Whether this is a general phenomenon or specific to the east German context is hard to tell. However, it is certainly not caused by the female-dominated sample.[16] Finally, dissatisfaction was not linked with them-and-us feelings, in contrast to the proposed association between frustration–aggression theory and them-and-us feelings. It was also not linked with union identity.

In sum, the study found several significant interrelationships between the antecedents of participation, especially between social identity and instrumentality. These correlations might be a major reason why no single antecedent, in either the east or west sample, provided a sufficient explanation on its own. It seems safe to say that the antecedents are more complementary than competitive (i.e. mutually excluding) explanations, as has been sometimes suggested in the literature but not fully tested. Finally, the findings also highlight that the attitudinal dimensions of 'commitment', or indeed of the 'institutionalisation' of interest representation, are not single and independent but strongly interrelated dimensions.

10.6 Relationship between union identity and collective instrumentality

Finally, the strong correlation between the two main antecedents, instrumentality of collective activities and union identity, is further examined. First of all it should be noted that the relationship could simply be due to multi-collinearity, yet according to Bryman and Cramer (1994: 239) this should emerge only by Pearson's *r* exceeding 0.80 (which is not the case). Besides, by using standardised regression coefficients the problem of multi-collinearity is restricted (Bryman and Cramer 1994). It seems therefore more likely to indicate a theoretical affinity.

The interrelationship between the two variables does not yet tell us whether one variable is the leading part. One will remember that this study does not propose *a priori* a master framework for understanding predictors of individuals' decision-making regarding participation, in contrast to Klandermans (1995) and others using rational choice theory as some kind of master frame (also Newton and McFarlane Shore 1992). However, the causality between the two variables is difficult to test with cross-sectional data. Longitudinal research, preferably of a qualitative nature, seems necessary. Gallagher and Strauss (1991: 149) note that the relative scarcity of longitudinal studies in this area makes it difficult to determine the direction of the causal relationship between instrumentality and commitment/identity. However, whether it is possible at all to establish causalities with statistical methods is the subject of a long-standing debate in philosophy (see Howson and Urbach 1990 or Sosa and Tooley 1993). For example, path analysis is not able to confirm or reject hypothetical causalities (Bryman and Cramer 1994: 248).

Even when taking this into account the data can nevertheless tell us something. There are two issues that appear to be particularly pertinent. The first is whether the association between the two variables is a positive or negative relation (Figure 10.2). A negative relation would imply that the more people identify with a social group (union) the more likely it was that they were not calculating a cost–benefit analysis of their participation efforts. This is the relation one would commonly expect. In contrast, the positive relation states that the more people identify with their social group the more they perceive the instrumentality of the group or of collective activities in a positive light. And at the same time, the more a person perceives the instrumentality of this group or of collective activities as positive the more he/she will identify with this group (in order to increase his/her positive self-esteem). Interestingly, the data of the two surveys supported the positive relation (positive beta weights). Thus, the more workers' decisions to become active are influenced by their union identity, the more they are also influenced by their perceptions of instrumentality. This could mean that union members who are not strongly committed to their union also do not care about the costs and benefits of participating, whereas instrumentality issues become important for high identifiers.

Second, the question arises whether there are different determinants of low and high union identifiers' perception of instrumentality of collective activities. Separate regressions were conducted for high and low identifiers (for the merged data set). Collectivism and job dissatisfaction had a major influence on low identifiers' perception of collective activities. Thus, the more they were 'collectivists' and/or are dissatisfied with their jobs, the more they perceived collective activities as worthwhile. The equation for high identifiers was not

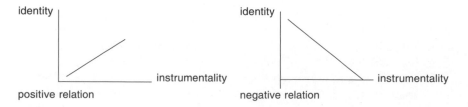

Figure 10.2 Positive and negative relations between instrumentality and identity (for the merged data set).

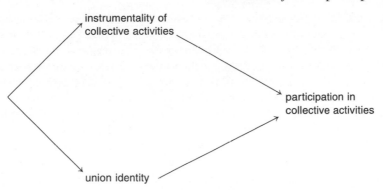
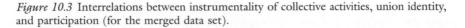

Figure 10.3 Interrelations between instrumentality of collective activities, union identity, and participation (for the merged data set).

significant (they were influenced only by their perception of instrumentality of the union and works council). One might tentatively conclude that low identifiers were less influenced by calculative perceptions than high identifiers, which supports the above result. It also resembles Kelly and Kelly (1993: 16) who found no evidence that a strong social identification with the union reduces the relevance of value–expectancy calculations or that weak identifiers are more likely to weigh up costs and benefits of union participation. Figure 10.3 illustrates the result.

Union identity influences people's perception of collective instrumentality, and at the same time the perceptions have an impact on their identity. What come first remains a 'chicken-and-egg' problem. Yet, it opposes the popular notion of union members (workers) as either 'rational individuals' or 'social beings'. It seems that they might well be both at the same time. In any case, one major implication is that instrumentality is not just a moderator of the link identity–participation, nor is identity just a moderator for instrumentality, as suggested for example by Fullagar and Barling (1989).

10.7 Conclusion

Three major results from the above discussion should be highlighted. First, the data of both surveys (in the east and west) support this study's hypothesis that no single antecedent, and thus no single theory of participation, has encompassing explanatory power for understanding collective activities (see Chapter 9). The antecedents are complementary rather than competing explanations. The fact that east German workers seemed to be guided by both instrumental and collective motives and not exclusively by cost–benefit calculations in a context which makes instrumental approaches to collective activities highly probable (according to several theories), gives particular weight to the argument that the concepts 'social identity' and 'collective instrumentality' are complementary and interrelated.

Second, the similarities between the regression analyses of the two samples support the claim that the theories of participation are applicable to this new cultural context (see Chapter 9). Post-socialist workers participated in collective activities for similar reasons to capitalist workers in west Germany. Thus, it seems possible and fruitful to apply 'western' theories of union participation to a post-socialist context despite the differences between post-socialist societies and western capitalist societies. This point echoes the positive findings of Kuruvilla *et al.* (1990) in applying 'western' theories to Japanese union members.

Finally, the comparison with the west reveals that the east Germans in this sample did not behave in a notably different way from their western colleagues. This reinforces the descriptive analysis of the data (Chapter 8), and thus substantiates the critique of the 'individualisation' thesis. In other words, the finding that east German workers are not exclusively guided by cost–benefit calculations with regard to collective activities suggests that the workforce of the two samples is not yet individualised in this regard.

Conclusion

> Instead of an institutional vacuum, we find routines and practices, organisa-
> tional forms and social ties, that can be assets, resources, and the basis for
> credible commitments and coordinated actions.
>
> (Stark 1992b: 300)

This book has used the insights of a socio-psychological analysis of union membership attitudes and behaviour as a basis to evaluate the successful transfer of
interest institutions and the subsequent transformation of workplace relations
on east German shopfloors. It was argued that the current research on the
post-socialist transformation in east Germany lacks such a micro analysis of the
workplace transformation, which is seen as necessary for a holistic understanding
of the complexities of the transformation process. In particular this book provides insights into the institutionalisation process of the newly transferred interest institutions which neither a macro nor a meso approach can provide on its
own. As an outcome, this micro analysis offers a more optimistic evaluation of
the ongoing transformation of workplace relations in east Germany, which
stands in contrast to the mainstream pessimistic account found in the German
literature (e.g. Mahnkopf 1993).

More specifically, the findings from the clothing industry confirm the conclusion of previous studies of overall harmonious, co-operative relationships
between management and works council on east German shopfloors. However,
the current study challenges the notion that east and west German workplace
relations are significantly different or that the social partnership at east
German workplaces has a different quality from that found in the west (e.g.
Liebold 1996; Mense-Petermann 1996). Specifically, clothing-industry works
councillors were found to be neither incorporated nor co-opted in managerial
strategy or ideology, nor was there any evidence that their 'plant-egoism' was
significantly higher in the east than in the west.

This institutional analysis was supported and enriched by an investigation of
the cultural support by union members for their new interest institutions. The
study found an astonishing level of collectivist attitudes among the east
German membership which was similar to that of their western colleagues.
The expansion of west German interest institutions in the east was apparently

accepted and supported by the workforce. Thus, judged by most of the dimensions of workers' attitudes and behaviour towards the new institutions, one can conclude that unions and works councils were indeed successfully embedded in appropriate social relations at the workplace level. It was concluded that union membership is a stabilising factor within the transformation process of these institutions. In addition, no evidence of excessive individualisation that would impede the institutions' functioning was found amongst the sample of east German workers. This is in marked contrast to the argument in the literature that the persistence of such individualisation is a threat to collective institutions. A certain degree of collectivism remains a necessary condition for successful institutionalisation, and this seems to be present in the data set.

Moreover, it is reassuring to know that it is not mainly east German workers' attitudes and behaviour which are to be blamed for the current unions and works councils problems. These problems appear far more likely to be caused by structural factors (e.g. recession, restructuring of the industry) or by institutional actors' strategies rather than by internal factors or by an unsuccessful institutionalisation of the two organisations.

To conclude, the finding of this book that the workplace relations in this particular sector are developing, in only a very short time period, in essentially similar and parallel ways to those in the west provides important insights into the broader and significant questions of the development of the 'Rhine model'. The data indicate that at the level of co-determination and the firm, the western system already seems to have established itself quite well, which is a remarkable feat in such a short period of time. This conclusion runs counter to current mainstream German pessimistic views. In fact it favours a more optimistic scenario of a continuation of the essentially co-operative features of the German social partnership model. Thus, it fully supports Turner's (1997: 133) claim that 'social partnership has established itself in eastern Germany because of appropriate institutions [transferred in from the west], the flexible adaptation of these institutions to existing historical legacies, and the choices that individuals and organizations have made to support, stretch and work within these given channels'.

To what extent can the findings of this book be generalised? The current study provides only a snapshot and neither the union membership nor the works councillor samples are necessarily representative of the entire east and west German clothing industry. In addition, the limited number of questions and the fact that the investigation was restricted to works councillors and unionised workers (excluding management[1] and non-union worker views) does not allow a final judgement on the quality of works council–management relations in the whole of the German clothing industry. It should also be remembered that the existence of a complementary culture among unionised workers does not *per se* guarantee a successful functioning of the labour institutions. It is a necessary but not a sufficient condition. In addition, such a snapshot of members' commitment is clearly not enough to predict a stable, long-term socialisation in the strict sense that Granovetter's (1985) concept of 'embeddedness' requires.

Longitudinal studies would be necessary to test for the stability of workers' attitudes over time. Nonetheless, the interviews with workers that were conducted, in addition to the surveys over a period of two years, suggest a certain stability in their attitudes. Finally, there might also be doubts about the extent to which the experience in the clothing industry (with its traditional Taylorist production system and distinctive structural problems) can be generalised to other industrial sectors.

Despite the above concerns, it is nonetheless rare to see relatively large samples of works councils and unionised workers in the east and west being examined together, and this in an industrial sector which is normally neglected in such research. Moreover, this industry presents a critical case study because its circumstances could easily point to a very different set of findings. The substantive degree of supportive attitudes and behaviour amongst workers in the east, in a case where one expected to find a rather low degree of a supportive culture, has particular weight and strengthens the argument that similar patterns of cultural support for labour institutions can be found in other sectors of east German industry. Thus, this study's evidence that the social partnership model has been successfully implemented in this particular industry suggests that this is not necessarily a unique case but might be generalised to the whole of east German industry.

There are five broader implications of this study which are briefly summarised under the following headings.

Future of the German model of industrial relations

First, one might ask in what way this study contributes to the general debate on the future of industrial relations in (east) Germany. The literature often outlines two extreme scenarios (Jürgens *et al.* 1993; Reißig 1993: 20; Turner 1992: 12). The 'polarisation scenario' (or arrested transformation, '*abgebrochene Transformation*', Reißig 1993) is the scenario in which the eastern region is exploited for its lower labour costs, with production facilities serving the function of extended assembly lines for western-based mass production (Voskamp and Wittke 1991a). In this scenario east Germany would be at the bottom of a nationally segmented labour market, as a permanently less developed region (a sort of German 'Mezzogiorno') (e.g. Boltho *et al.* 1995; Mahnkopf 1992). German unions would be weakened as employers played the eastern workers off against their counterparts in the west. This scenario would most likely also include the potentially serious destabilisation of the German industrial relations system, and possibly also an increase in industrial conflict.

The alternative is a 'modernisation scenario', which is clearly not dominant in current academic discourse on Germany. In this scenario east German firms would take advantage of eager and flexible workforces and workforce representatives in the east to bring in the latest organisational innovations and new technology. Works councils and unions would be integrated into relations of partnership in the drive towards advanced levels of productivity and flexibility, spurring new growth for Germany as a whole. Unions' influence could expand in this scenario, provided unions adopt bargaining strategies which cater for the innovations in the east, facilitate the transfer of learning in both directions (west–east and east–west), and prevent east–west whipsawing strategies by employers. How do the findings of this book measure against these differing scenarios, recognising the representative limitations acknowledged earlier?

If one takes the findings on the workplace climate of the surveyed companies, they actually support the latter, more positive, scenario rather than the former. Capital–labour relations seemed to be harmonious and trusting rather than antagonistic. In addition, works councils supported most rationalisation decisions. Moreover, at an industry level employers and union were unified in their desire to stabilise collective bargaining. These are surprising outcomes for a declining and struggling industry where one would rather expect employers to use their increased position of power to the detriment of collective industrial relations.

With regard to the workforce data, however, the 'fit' is less decisive. Part of this is due to the absence of information about precisely what kind of workforce these scenarios would require. One might argue that the polarisation scenario would require either highly dissatisfied, militant workers or, if the unions were weakened, workers who are dissatisfied, passive and apathetic. On the other hand the modernisation scenario seems to require workers who are committed to their company and supportive of a trustful, productive relationship between management and works council plus a union which supports the modernisation processes. Yet 'modernisation' might also be thought of as a process which leaves workers and interest representation without any influence.

The study revealed highly dissatisfied members who supported the works council and the union, and who were willing to be mobilised by these institutions. To repeat, there was no evidence for the 'nightmare' scenario of some authors whereby a completely individualistic, alienated, apathetic east German membership let the transformation pass by without any interest, expectations or commitment. Instead the membership became a stabilising factor for the institutions. It might be argued therefore that the members provided the necessary 'software' for a modernisation scenario that includes co-operative workplace relations.

However, it seems clear that the likelihood of this latter scenario becoming a reality for the clothing industry in east Germany will depend largely on other, external factors. There is no doubt that industrial relations, especially at the industry level between employers and unions, are in the process of major change – not only in the east but in the whole of Germany (e.g. Streeck 1997). However, it is too early to judge the extent to which the 'Rhine capitalism' model, with its emphasis on free collective bargaining at industry level and harmonious relations at workplace level, will be maintained and effectively reformed (e.g. Bericht der Kommission Mitbestimmung 1998) or whether its decline is inevitable. Strictly speaking, it remains an open question which way east German actors, including unionists, would react to a significant decentralisation and destabilisation of the institutional network of industrial relations. Yet, there is nothing in the results of this study that suggests that members would behave fatalistically and comply passively with these changes as some people might wish, or indeed fear. Thus, in a nutshell, the micro findings of this book add support to the macro analysis of Turner (1997: 259), who provides a rather positive account in arguing for the basic stability of the social partnership institutions and the capacity of actors in east Germany to adapt to changing requirements of the global challenges.

Institutional transfer

Second, what do these results tell us about the general transferability of the works council institution (as a core feature of the social partnership model) into a different, somewhat foreign context? This question is not only of theoretical but also of practical importance. As is well known, works councils (and their transferability) have attracted growing interest in the international academic and political debate in recent years (e.g. Dunlop commission in the USA; European works council legislation). Moreover, the analysis of a successful transfer of this institution is of prime interest for the current central European applicants to the European Union (which is likely to lead to an extension of the Social Chapter of Maastricht including the European works council legislation to the eastern newcomers).

Granted, east Germany is a specific case: works councils were transferred as part of a whole parcel, together with the other western industrial relations institutions rather than as a single isolated piece. The east German case therefore represents a holistic transfer of an entire industrial relations system. Thus, one might argue that the transferred west German collective bargaining arrangements were an important support for the institutionalisation of workplace interest representation in the east.

What seemed to be another, perhaps even more crucial, factor was, however, the overwhelming support of the east German actors for the installation of the western institutions, as was also shown in this study. This is in line with Jacoby's (1994) proposition that institutional change will be effective and enduring only if it is effected and supported by social actors rather than decreed by policy makers alone. A good comparison is with Hungary, where mandatory works councils were introduced in 1992. They were strongly opposed by the unions in the beginning – with the result that their rights were restricted to an informative and consultative capacity and unions' exclusive bargaining rights were secured at workplace level. Over time, however, these works councils became virtually incorporated into the enterprise unions rather than becoming independent actors (e.g. Tóth 1997). Moreover, there is evidence to suggest that Hungarian workers strongly distrust both works councils and unions (e.g. Frege and Tóth 1999).

It seems sensible to conclude therefore that the holistic approach of system transformation and actors' support makes the east German case an ideal type of institutional transfer. On the other hand, however, the external economic conditions in east Germany were anything but supportive. This book's example of successful workplace relations in a sector that faces devastating economic conditions, which would therefore be predicated to experience serious problems, is quite telling. It suggests that a successful institutional transfer might depend primarily on actors' support and on an encompassing transfer of all industrial relations institutions rather than on favourable economic conditions (contrary to some literature, e.g. Kädtler and Kottwitz 1994). This would indicate the possibility of transforming societies to overcome Offe's (1991) 'dilemma of simultaneity', that is, the simultaneous democratisation and marketisation process. Simply put, the argument is that the establishment of new democratic political institutions is impeded by the economic and social costs of the transformation and on the other hand that the economic transformation is impeded by a democratic political system. However, it seems possible to gain the support of actors under certain circumstances even if economic returns are problematic.

Thus, a crucial finding of this book is the fact that workers seem to have welcomed the western institutions with much goodwill and trust rather than with resistance to change. Thus, it is a remarkable indication of the stability and successful institutionalisation of the German social partnership model that union members in the declining clothing industry in east Germany revealed such a considerable support and trust for their new labour institutions. And this after such a short period of time and despite the institutions' limited scope for action in a depressed labour market. The likelihood of a vicious circle of disappointed members and absence of support resulting in a backlash on the institutional performance is therefore less probable at this stage. Thus, for east Germany one can certainly support what Stark (1992b) suggested (see above) with regard to post-socialist societies in general. There is no institutional vacuum on east German shopfloors, but rather supportive practices and collectivist norms in favour of the interest institutions.

Finally, a necessary proportion of goodwill is clearly something which is difficult to plan or predict when designing institutional transfer, but which is seen as essential for the functioning of these new institutions (e.g. Mishler and Rose 1997). Assuming that the socio-cultural context can have either a positive or a negative impact on the institutionalisation process of new labour institutions, a task of future research should be to examine the structural conditions under which trust and goodwill towards new institutions can be expected to develop and prosper.

The overwhelming support by union members might be partly explained by the fact that there was no real alternative at hand and anything was better compared to their past experience (i.e. no real interest representation by the former socialist unions). However, if that was true then members' support of their interest institutions should be equally strong in other post-socialist economies. That is, however, not the case. Studies in central and eastern Europe continuously reveal the strong distrust and abiding cynicism among workers towards their (reformed or new) unions. For example, the New Democracies Barometer in central and eastern Europe (Paul Lazarsfeld Society Vienna 1994) found in 1994 that unions were actually the institutions least trusted (91 per cent of their multi-country sample were sceptical or distrusted them completely).

Thus, a more promising possible explanation coming out of this study is that the institutional structure of interest representation, specifically the dual system of unions and works councils, and the mandatory character of the works councils and their co-determination rights facilitate the creation of trust and commitment among members. One might argue then – and this is a hypothesis which needs to be substantiated in further research – that the mandatory works council facili-tates the creation of commitment and trust in collective representation among workers even in times when the union is not perceived as powerful enough to satisfactorily represent its members' interests. In other words, workers know that management cannot abolish the works council institution and that the works council maintains a minimum standard of interest representation through its legal rights even in times when management opposes employee participation. This knowledge, it is argued, makes it easier for people to trust their new collec-tive representatives. In contrast, the situation in Hungary for example, where works councils have no co-determination rights and thus cannot safeguard a minimum level of interest representation in difficult times (i.e. weak power posi-tion), does not provide an institutional support for workers' trust in their new institutions. Simply put, the hypothesis is that co-determination rights (the actual participation rights) are incremental to the establishment of commitment and trust in the new works councils. In other words, the mandatory character of co-determination actually helps them to become institutionalised, and thus to gain actors' support. In other words, the legislation helps the institutionalisation of works councils. Taking this thought further one could argue that works councils also facilitate union commitment among workers and hence support the revival of the labour movement in these transforming societies. Works coun-cils would then be seen as a major stabilising factor for the reconstitution of interest representation (and the labour movement) in transforming economies. This is in strong contrast to the argument of several authors that east German works councils are essentially a millstone around unions' necks. It also counters theoretical accounts of the potential danger of social partnership arrangements for the labour movement (e.g. Kelly 1998: 131).

Individualism/collectivism and socialist legacies

Third, the book's findings on members' perceptions of and reactions towards the transforming workplace relations did not conform to the widespread hypothesis that east German workers are becoming clearly individualistic. In many cases members revealed strong collectivist attitudes and behaviour towards manage-ment, colleagues or interest institutions. This conclusion runs counter to the current pessimism of mainstream German analysis. There was no evidence for the scenario of individualistic, apathetic, alienated union members in the east, who survive the transformation without having any interests, expectations or commitment. Thus, the study cannot support the scenario of 'social schizo-phrenia' resulting from socialist collectivist legacies (Blanchflower and Freeman 1993: 13). Instead it suggests a more optimistic scenario for the future of German unions and works councils, at least as far as union members' solidarity is concerned.

However, the data also revealed the complex and dynamic nature of workers' attitudes and behaviour, especially in times of transformation. As said before, it is impossible to classify either west or east Germans as pure collectivists or pure individualists, since many gave mixed responses when confronted with different issues, but both were clearly on average more collectivist than individualistic. Thus, the results clearly cannot support a general individualisation thesis. Yet, a rejection of the individualisation thesis does not mean that people did not change over time. It will be remembered that the study did not investigate the development of workers' attitudes and behaviour over time. Whether the similarity of post-socialist and capitalist workers' attitudes and behaviour is due to changes (increasing individualism) in the east Germans therefore cannot be entirely excluded. On the other hand we can also not exclude the possibility that some collective attitudes indicate a persistence of socialist legacies in people's attitudes and behaviour. However, the results suggest that a supportive culture existed in former times which the west German institutions were able to draw upon. It is unlikely that such a strong identification with the union, as was seen among these clothing workers, would appear in such a short period of time as a couple of years.

Moreover, the findings challenge the argument that east German workers are different from their western colleagues because of their socialist socialisation. The comparative analysis could not find any evidence to support this hypothesis. This cannot refute the claim that socialist legacies influence people's current attitudes and behaviour since the study could not test to what extent socialist legacies or current structural constraints determine actors' behaviour. However, even if socialist legacies still have a major impact, it is not leading to different attitudes or behaviour from those of their western colleagues.

Theories of collective action

Fourth, a major purpose of this study was also to gauge the general applicability of theories of collective activities to east Germany, and to test the comparative validity of different social-psychological theories. The fact that the theories were applicable (in terms of the criteria used) and that most results (e.g. with regard to the level of participation) were similar to the west German results, adds support to the 'structuralist view' in comparative industrial relations. Thus, the evidence presented here suggests that it seems possible and fruitful to apply 'western' theories of union participation to a post-socialist context. Thus, the determinants of union participation have some universality and can, for example, also be extended to emerging market economies, and not only to union but also to works council activities.

In addition, testing the set of theories simultaneously resulted in two major antecedents (union identity, collective instrumentality) which were strongly interrelated. The study emphasises that no theory is sufficient on its own and that the theories are complementary rather than competitive explanators. It also confirms the importance of collective and instrumental motives. However, these seem to have a mutually reinforcing effect on participation rather than one being pre-eminent as has been suggested in some previous research (e.g. Newton and McFarlane Shore 1992). Union identity might influence people's perceptions of collective instrumentality, and at the same time those perceptions might have an impact on their identity. This reasoning therefore rejects the popular notion of union members as either 'rational individuals' or 'social beings': they might well be both at the same time.

Methodological implications for future research

Finally, since this study addressed a complex set of questions, highly specific recommendations cannot be easily made. However, there are two broad methodological suggestions for future research. The study highlights an important methodological point on debates about collectivism, instrumentality and unionism. Future research should acknowledge the complexity and multi-dimensionality of workers' attitudes and behaviour. For example, more emphasis might be put on the different dimensions of collectivism/individualism, and the circumstances and conditions under which they are activated, rather than assuming a general trend towards a uniform, individualised workforce. This also includes a more detailed (preferably qualitative) investigation of the relation-ship between the significant antecedents of participation, especially between social identity and rational choice. The well-known ambivalence about the 'symbolic' and the 'material' dimensions of collective organisation and activities should be acknowledged as a continuing, important feature of industrial relations research (see for example Kelly 1998).

The other area highlighted, one of the notoriously under-researched areas in comparative industrial relations, is the interrelationship between institutions and actors (partly because in countries with a highly institutionalised industrial rela-tions system academics tend to devalue the relevance of the actors). It is hoped that this book's investigation of the newly established interest institutions from the viewpoint of a specific group of actors (workers) has added some new insights to the understanding of the east German institutional transformation, and thus supported the relevance of micro-level research. Future research on workers' per-ceptions and reactions could, for example, compare workers in different situa-tions (e.g. in companies with formalised interest institutions and in companies without) to address the question as to how far specific external conditions deter-mine people's perceptions. For example, do different forms of interest represen-tation affect people's perceptions and reactions differently and if so in what ways?

It would also be interesting to compare east German workers' attitudes and behaviour with those of workers in other post-socialist societies who experience similar organisational changes without such legalised and strong interest institutions at workplace level. For example, what is the impact of different forms of workplace relations on unions' strength in transforming societies? Indeed, comparative studies of different transformation processes and outcomes in central and eastern Europe might be a useful tool for learning more about the causes of and conditions for successful transformation processes in industrial relations. It would also contribute to the relevance of our discipline within the social sciences in helping to understand and evaluate the ongoing transformation processes from socialist to capitalist regimes. There can be no doubt that industrial relations stands at the forefront of any democratic and economic development in post-socialist countries as both political scientists (e.g. Ost and Weinstein forthcoming) and economists (e.g. Freeman 1993) acknowledge. However, the discipline of industrial relations has so far not been very helpful in either contributing to a theoretical understanding of the collapse of the socialist economy (i.e. to what extent did the socialist industrial relations system contribute to the collapse of or prolong the survival of the socialist planned economy) or in the recent attempts among the social sciences to develop a theory of transformation (e.g. Mayntz 1994; Reißig 1996: 256). Moreover, observing the societal regime change should be at the heart of industrial relations research – whether one defines industrial relations radically as the unequal and exploitative exchange (e.g. Kelly 1998: 132) or whether one puts the emphasis on the institutional and normative regulation of employment relationships. It would be a shame to pass up this opportunity to stimulate mainstream industrial relations research by new insights into the theoretical foundations of industrial relations institutions and their power relations.

Appendix

A 5.1 Supervisor questionnaire at Bodywear, summer 1993

Table A 5.1 Items of supervisors' perceptions on transforming workplace relations

	Strongly disagree	Disagree	No view	Agree	Strongly agree
Perceptions of changes in the supervision job					
The company expects more commitment from us than in former times					
The supervisor is more respected today than in former times					
Supervisors are primarily responsible to their superior, not to their workers					
In former times I had more influence over when and how we worked in the brigade					
In former times our main duty was to organise the raw materials, today the main task is to organise and control the work process					
In former times there was more collegiality among the supervisors, today there is more competition					

*Perceptions of current working
conditions*

There is more work to do today
and the pressure to perform is
higher

Those who do not perform well are
dismisse

In former times the brigade
(*Meisterei*) was a real community,
today there is not a great deal of
team spirit

In former times workers also
enjoyed their work, today they only
work for money

Workers here are as qualified as in
the main plant in west Germany

We were better trained in the GDR
compared to the west German
supervisors

In former times more workers
came to me with grievances than
today

A capitalist firm treats its employees
more fairly, because performance
criteria count and not personal or
partial ones

Human beings are lazy by nature,
and have to be forced to work

Workers are primarily motivated by
pay

More participation of workers is in
theory desirable, but practically not
possible

I give my workers a lot of
discretion, I am only interested in
their output

I treat my workers more strictly
than before

A great problem in former times
was that you did not have any real
power over employees

A 5.2 Questionnaire of the personnel managers at Bodywear

Table A 5.2 Items of personnel managers' perceptions of workplace relations at Bodywear

	Strongly disagree	Disagree	No view	Agree	Strongly agree
The works council is a responsible and fair bargaining partner					
The council is as concerned as management about the well-being of the firm					
The works council weakens the discipline of the workforce					
The works council never misses the chance to pick a quarrel with management					
We often clarify differences of opinion informally					
The council does not understand the problems and worries of the management					
The council is simply a mouthpiece of the GTB					
The council pursues union politics intensively					
The management informs the council extensively about the economic situation of the firm					
Management respects the views of the council					
Management would prefer not to have a council					
The council tries to co-operate with management					
In general relations between the council and management are good					
The council has strong support among the workforce					

The council should obtain more
co-determination rights in
economic decisions

The workforce is not very
interested in the quality of the
relationship between the council
and management

Unions and employers have in
principle divergent positions

The GTB is a responsible collective
bargaining partner

Human beings are lazy by nature
and have to be forced to work

Employees are primarily motivated
by pay

A 10.1 Factor analyses

Factor analysis of the east German survey

1. Factor analysis of participation items

All seven questions on participation were put into the factor analysis. Two factors
emerged.

Table A 10.1.1 Factors of participation in the east

	Self-initiated participation	*Organised participation*
I would take part in demonstrations during collective bargaining	0.27	0.79
If the GTB goes on strike I will join	−0.06	0.84
I will definitely visit the next works council assembly	0.16	0.54
If asked I would stand for the works council election	0.80	0.17
If asked I would stand for union office	0.86	0.16
I constantly try to recruit new members	0.71	0.06

KMO (Kaiser–Meyer Olkin Criterium) = 0.67; cumulated percentage of variance: 61.1
Self-initiated participation: eigenvalue = 2.41960 (pct of variance = 40.3), alpha = 0.7257
(standardised alpha = 0.7311)
Organised participation: eigenvalue = 1.24642 (pct of variance = 20.8), alpha = 0.5909,
standardised alpha = 0.5871)

2. Factor analysis of perceptions of collective instrumentality

All nine questions on collective instrumentality were put into factor analysis.

Table A 10.1.2 Factors of collective instrumentality in the east

	Negative instrumentality of union/works	No necessity of works council	Instrumentality of collective action
I don't need works council, management cares enough for workers	−0.06	0.83	0.08
I can solve problems alone, don't need a works council	0.08	0.74	−0.30
BGL was better than works council/union	0.20	0.50	0.25
Works council and union are only as strong as they are actively supported by workers	−0.13	0.03	0.76
Strikes are a useful means to strenghten the union during collective bargaining	0.10	−0.12	0.55
Works council is too weak to oppose management	0.83	0.00	−0.22
GTB provides not enough pressure on employers	0.79	−0.06	0.23
Works councils are not powerful enough to negotiate better agreements	0.69	0.16	−0.22
GTB doesn't do enough for wage adaptation with west Germany	0.64	0.13	0.24

KMO = 0.62; cumulated pct of variance = 56.3
Negative instrumentality of union/works council: eigenvalue = 2.34748 (pct of variance = 26.1), alpha = 0.7314, standardised alpha = 0.7299
No necessity of works council: eigenvalue = 1.59963 (pct of variance = 17.8), alpha = 0.4774, standardised alpha = 0.5084
Instrumentality of collective action: eigenvalue = 1.11591 (pct of variance = 12.4), alpha = 0.2303, standardised alpha = 0.2313

3. Factor analysis of union identity

Four items of the questionnaire were put into factor analysis.

Table A 10.1.3 Factors of union identity in the east

	Union identity
I feel closely related to the other union members in my firm	0.74
I share aims/values of the union	0.82
Union solidarity is important for me	0.82
I am proud to belong to the GTB	0.65

KMO = 0.72, no rotation
Union identity: eigenvalue = 2.32296 (pct of variance = 58.1), alpha = 0.7488, standardised alpha = 0.7560

4. Factor analysis of workgroup identity

Factor analysis was conducted for all eight items, which produced an incomprehensible result. Five items were selected and one item was reworded (the alpha coefficient for the factor was negative).

Table A 10.1.4 Factors of workgroup identity and collectivist values in the east

	Collectivism	Workgroup identity
I accept group decisions	0.42924	0.35140
I prefer to work in a group	0.77833	0.00734
Problems are better solved in a group	0.81866	0.07971
I identify strongly with group	0.27808	0.62151
I do not want to change my workgroup	−0.12447	0.83813

KMO = 0.61; cumulated pct of variance = 55.4
Collectivism: eigenvalue = 1.72086 (pct of variance = 34.4), alpha = 0.5133, standardised alpha = 0.5141
Group identity: eigenvalue = 1.05082 (pct of variance = 21.0), alpha = 0.2935, standardised alpha = 0.2979

5. Factor analysis of attribution

A factor analysis was conducted for all eleven items of external and internal attribution, which did not reveal an interpretable result. Two separate factor analyses were conducted, one for external and one for internal attribution. The analysis of external attribution produced three factors; two of those did not make any sense. A new factor analysis for the one remaining factor, 'external attribution', was conducted and the factor was computed with these new loadings (see brackets). The analysis for 'internal attribution' revealed two factors.

Table A 10.1.5 Factors of external attribution in the east

	External attribution: politics/ management	Factor 2	Factor 3
Management exploits the labour market situation with regard to the increase of workpace	0.65 (0.69)	0.22	0.04
Lack of support of politicians/ Treuhand	0.46	0.05	0.51
The politicians are causing lower wage level	0.69 (0.66)	−0.19	0.16
Management exploits the labour market situation with regard to recent pay bargaining	0.74 (0.73)	0.08	−0.15
Job losses due to lack of demand for products	−0.05	0.75	0.33
Incompetent management to be blamed for job losses	0.15	0.79	−0.25
Market competition causes job losses	−0.06	0.00	0.81

KMO = 0.59; cumulated pct of variance: 58.8
Attribution to politics/management: eigenvalue = 1.79127 (pct of variance = 25.6), alpha = 0.4322, standardised alpha= 0.4635
Factors 2, 3 make no sense (pct of variances: 17.6, 15.6)

Table A 10.1.6 Factors of internal attribution in the east

	Internal attribution: lacking workers' effort	Internal attribution: lacking solidarity of workforce
Job losses due to lacking effort of workforce (too lazy)	0.69	0.14
Job losses due to high wages	0.79	−0.11
Heavy workload due to lacking collective resistance of workforce	−0.18	0.86
Job losses due to lacking solidarity among workforce	0.41	0.64

KMO = 0.52; cumulated pct of variance: 62.1
Internal attribution to lack of individual effort at work: eigenvalue = 1.37650 (pct of variance = 34.4), alpha = 0.3245, standardised alpha = 0.3552
Internal attribution to lacking solidarity among workers: eigenvalue = 1.10810 (pct of variance = 27.7), alpha = 0.3081, standardised alpha = 0.3093

6. Factor analysis of general job issues

Since the questionnaire asked about them-and-us feelings and job satisfaction in a single section the factor analysis incorporated all nine 'job-related' items. Four factors evolved. The items were put together in one factor analysis since they formed a group in the questionnaire. (However, conducting the factor analysis separately for the two groups, dissatisfaction and them–us/trust, revealed the same factors.)

Table A 10.1.7 Factors of general job issues in the east

	General job satisfaction (comparative)	Specific job dissatisfaction (today)	Former trust relations	Current them–us
Overall work situation is better than before	0.82	−0.12	−0.11	−0.03
Capitalist firms treat workforce better than socialist firms	0.84	−0.07	−0.07	−0.09
Dissatisfied with workload today	−0.14	0.68	−0.07	0.18
Worried about job security today	−0.11	0.72	0.05	−0.23

Don't trust supervisor today	0.05	0.57	0.23	0.39
Formerly workforce was not exploited	−0.02	−0.05	0.82	0.09
Formerly you could trust supervisor	−0.17	0.13	0.76	−0.00
I am not paid a fair wage	−0.13	−0.13	−0.10	0.78
Today workforce is exploited	−0.00	0.28	0.15	0.63

KMO = 0.65; cumulated pct of variance: 61.0
General job satisfaction compared with former times: eigenvalue = 2.10404 (pct of variance = 23.4), alpha = 0.6381, standardised alpha = 0.6424
Specific job satisfaction: eigenvalue = 1.18214 (pct of variance = 13.1), alpha = 0.4290, standardised alpha = 0.4316
Trust relations (them–us compared with before): eigenvalue = 1.14835 (pct of variance = 12.8), alpha = 0.4935, standardised alpha = 0.4937
Current them–us (exploitation): eigenvalue = 1.05974 (pct of variance = 11.8), alpha = 0.2635, standardised alpha = 0.2642

Factor analysis of the west German survey

1. Factor analysis of participation items

There were six plus three additional items in the west German questionnaire, but the items still resulted in the same factors as did the east survey. The three additional items became part of organised participation.

Table A 10.1.8 Factors of participation in the west

	Organised participation	Self-initiated participation
I would protest collectively with my colleagues against layoffs.	0.61	0.11
I would actively support the works council and the GTB [in order to secure my job]	0.64	0.25
I would participate in union actions during collective bargaining	0.72	0.27
If the GTB goes on strike I will join	0.75	0.12
I try to convince others to become a union member in order to strengthen the GTB	0.58	0.49

I will definitely visit the next works council assembly	0.52	0.04
If asked I would stand for the works council election	0.14	0.87
If asked I would stand for union office	0.08	0.90
I constantly try to recruit new members	0.34	0.73

KMO= 0.81595, cum pct of variance: 56.9
Organised participation: eigenvalue 3.825 (pct of variance = 42.5), alpha 0.7603 (standardised alpha = 0.7626)
Self-initiated participation: eigenvalue 1.292 (pct of variance = 14.4), alpha 0.8289 (standardised alpha = 0.8294)

2. Factor analysis of collective instrumentality

There were eight instead of nine items (the east survey had a separate question on the former BGL) put into factor analysis which revealed the same factors as in the east.

Table A 10.1.9 Factors of collective instrumentality in the west

	Negative instrumentality of works council/union	No necessity of work council	Instrumentality of collective action
The works council is to blame, it does not put enough pressure on management	0.80	0.16	−0.05
Works council is too weak to oppose management	0.83	0.15	0.01
TB does not put enough pressure on employers	0.75	−0.12	0.09
GTB is doing too much for its East German members, we are disadvantaged (*ziehen den kuerzeren*)	0.44	0.14	−0.14

Strikes are useful means to strengthen the union during collective bargaining	0.01	−0.32	0.69
We don't need a works council because our supervisors take care of us	0.10	0.80	−0.12
I can resolve all my problems with my supervisor alone, I don't need a works council	0.13	0.82	−0.03
Works council and union are only as strong as they are actively supported by workers	−0.07	0.09	0.86

KMO = 0.67850, cum. pct of variance = 61.2
Instrumentality of works council/union: eigenvalue = 2.36432, pct of variance = 29.6, alpha = 0.6948 (standardised alpha = 0.6908)
Necessity of works council: eigenvalue = 1.49259, pct of variance = 18.7, alpha = 0.5524 (standardised alpha = 0.6021)
Instrumentality of collective activities: eigenvalue = 1.04301, pct of variance = 13.0, alpha = 0.4195 (standardised alpha = 0.4257)

3. Factor analysis of union identity

There were six items dealing with union identity (two more than in the east).
One factor was produced as in the east.

Table A 10.1.10 Factors of union identity in the west

	Union identity
I am proud to belong to the GTB	0.81
I would stay a member also when becoming unemployed	0.74
I feel closely related to the other union members in my firm	0.78
I share the values and aims of the union	0.77
Union solidarity is important for me	0.78
To be a union member also means to be active in the union	0.78

KMO = 0.87055, cum. pct of variance = 60.3
Union identity: eigenvalue = 3.61664, alpha = 0.8623 (standardised alpha = 0.8700)

4. Factor analysis of workgroup identity

The same five items that were used in the east survey were put into factor analysis
and revealed the same factors as in the east.

Table A 10.1.11 Factors of workgroup identity and collectivist values in the west

	Collectivism	Workgroup identity
I identify strongly with my workgroup	0.38	0.57
I don't want to change my workgroup	−0.09	0.90
I accept group decisions	0.64	−0.04
I prefer to work in a group	0.72	0.10
Problems are better solved in groups	0.75	0.20

KMO = 0.64088, cum. pct of variance = 56.6
Collectivism: eigenvalue = 1.811292, pct of variance = 36.3, alpha = 0.5427 (standardised alpha = 0.5423)
Workgroup identity: eigenvalue = 1.01843, pct of variance = 20.4, alpha = 0.3330 (standardised alpha = 0.3351)

5. Factor analysis of attribution

As in the east sample two separate factor analyses were conducted with similar items (some items were adapted to the west German context). The analysis of external attribution produced three factors, of which only one factor (with the highest alpha reliability) was used.

Table A 10.1.12 Factors of external attribution in the west

	Management	*(East)*	*(Market)*
The increasing Third World competition is to blame for the increase in work pace, not management	−0.10	0.12	0.81
Management exploits the labour market situation with regard to the increase of workpace	0.83	−0.01	0.13
The increasing Third World competition is to blame for the increasing job insecurity, not management	0.22	0.06	0.75
Increasing competition from east Germany	−0.03	0.83	0.17
Incompetent management	0.56	0.33	−0.27
Management exploits the labour market situation with regard to recent pay bargaining	0.80	0.03	0.11
The east German recession hinders (*erschweren*) collective bargaining in west Germany	0.14	0.78	0.03

KMO = 0.57233, cum. pct of variance = 64.1
Attribution employer: eigenvalue = 1.97359, pct of variance = 28.2, alpha = 0.5983 (standardised alpha = 0.6102)
Attribution east: eigenvalue = 1.37481, pct of variance = 19.6, alpha = 0.5468 (standardised alpha = 0.5468)
Attribution market: eigenvalue = 1.13944, pct of variance = 16.3, alpha = 0.4669 (standardised alpha = 0.4680)

Table A 10.1.13 Factors of internal attribution in the west

	Lacking workers' effort	Lacking solidarity
Heavy workload due to lacking collective resistance of workforce	0.14	0.75
Lacking effort of workforce causes job losses	0.72	0.31
Job losses due to high wages	0.86	−0.10
Job losses due to lacking solidarity among workforce	−0.00	0.76

KMO = 0.56116, cum. pct of variance = 63.0
Lacking workers' effort: eigenvalue = 1.50036, pct of variance = 37.5, alpha = 0.4388 (standardised alpha = 0.4398)
Lacking solidarity: eigenvalue = 1.02124, pct of variance = 25.5, alpha = 0.3408 (standardised alpha = 0.3416)

6. Factor analysis of general job issues

A factor analysis with all eight items (which were slightly different from the east) was possible but did not yield the same factors as the east survey. I decided therefore to drop specific job satisfaction. The factor of them-and-us feelings comprises slightly different items than in the east.

Table A 10.1.14 Factors of general job issues in the west

	Them–us	General job satisfaction
Generally satisfied with the job	0.07	0.84
No great trust in supervisors	0.62	−0.12
Natural difference of employer and labour interests	0.79	0.12
Management tries constantly to limit works councils' power	0.69	−0.24
Work climate between management and workforce is good	−0.26	0.74

KMO = 0.61309, cum. pct of variance = 57.6
Them–us: eigenvalue = 1.73734, pct of variance = 34.7, alpha = 0.5034 (standardised alpha = 0.5097)
General job satisfaction = 1.14295, pct of variance = 22.9, alpha = 0.4576 (standardised alpha = 0.4658)

A 10.2 *t*-tests of female and male members in the east and west German sample

Table A 10.2.1 *t*-test of items of collective instrumentality

| | Means | | | | Sig. T | | | |
	west males	east males	west females	east females	west/east m/m sig. T	west/east f/f sig. T	west f/m sig. T	east f/m sig. T
Instrumentality of works council								
We don't need a works council since management cares enough for us.	1.24	1.42	1.33	1.54	*	**	*	
I can solve my work problems with my supervisor alone, I don't need the works council for that.	1.74	1.77	1.95	1.90			**	
Works council does not oppose management strategies strongly enough [to secure jobs].	2.41	2.91	2.69	3.15	**	**		
Our works council is not powerful enough to negotiate better working conditions.	2.27	3.14	2.50	3.39	**	**	**	

Instrumentality of union

GTB not putting enough pressure on employers [to secure jobs].	3.23	3.63	3.12	3.68 *	**	
The GTB is not doing enough to secure the adjustment of east German wage levels./GTB is fighting more for its East German members; we lose out.	2.65	3.69	2.84	4.00 **	**	** *

Instrumentality of collective action

Works council and GTB will only be effective if they get active support from workers.	4.34	4.40	4.22	4.27		*
Strikes are an effective means to strengthen the union during collective bargaining.	4.54	3.95	4.44	3.97 **	**	*

($* = p < 0.05$, $** = p < 0.05$)

Table A 10.2.2 *t*-test of items of union identity

	Means west males	east males	west females	east females	Sig. T west/east m/m sig. T	west/east f/f sig. T	west f/m sig. T	east f/m sig. T
I share the aims and values of the union.	4.07	3.80	4.01	3.93	*			
Union solidarity is very important for me.	4.33	4.08	4.17	4.18	*		**	
I am proud of being a member of the GTB.	3.80	3.34	3.68	3.44	**	*	*	
I feel strong ties with the other union members in my plant.	3.64	3.21	3.29	3.18	**		**	
I seriously think about quitting the GTB in the future.	1.79	2.22	1.85	2.21	**	**		
I would remain in the union, even if I were unemployed.	3.43	2.98	3.32	3.13	*			

($* = p < 0.05$, $** = p < 0.05$)

Table A 10.2.3 t-test of items of group identity and them-and-us feelings

	Means				Sig. T			
	west males	east males	west females	east females	west/east m/m sig. T	west/east f/f sig. T	west f/m sig. T	east f/m sig. T
Group identity								
I accept group decisions also if I am different opinion.	4.03	4.15	4.02	4.03				
I prefer to work in groups than alone.	3.49	3.62	3.70	3.78			**	
I increasingly feel isolated in my group.	2.05	2.25	2.06	2.18				
Solidarity among colleagues diminished during recession. In the old days (GDR) group solidarity was much better.	3.46	3.77	3.46	4.22	*	**		**
I identify strongly with my group.	3.61	3.52	3.41	3.30			**	
Them-and-us feelings								
I don't have strong trust in my supervisor.	3.20	3.55	3.22	3.73	*	**		
Today workers are exploited here. Management tries constantly to reduce the influence of the works council and the union.	3.58	4.20	3.53	4.17	**	**		

($* = p < 0.05$, $** = p < 0.01$)

Table A 10.2.4 t-test of items of collective participation

	Means west males	east males	west females	east females	Sig. T west/m m sig. T	west/east f/f sig. T	west f/m sig. T	east f/m sig. T
Organised participation								
If the GTB calls a strike I would participate.	4.50	3.68	4.44	3.85	**	**		
I would take part in demonstrations/rallies during collective bargaining.	4.26	3.60	4.00	3.64	**	**	**	
I will attend the next works council assembly.	4.60	4.21	4.64	4.47	**	*		
Self-initiated participation								
If asked I would stand for the works council election.	3.53	3.31	2.69	2.80	1.7	0.27	**	**
If asked I would serve on a committee for the GTB.	3.01	2.53	2.26	2.17	**		*	*
I constantly try to recruit new members for the union.	3.38	2.62	2.85	2.42	**	**	**	
I don't see myself as a union activist.	3.19	3.68	3.49	3.76	**	*	**	

(* = p < 0.05, ** = p < 0.01)

A 10.3 Regression of antecedents of the east German survey

Table 10.3.1 Predicting four antecedents: standard regression coefficients for seventeen variables in the east

Independent variables	Instrumentality of collective activities	Union identity	External attribution	Specific job dissatisfaction
Negative instrumentality of works council/union	−0.053	−0.184**	0.229**	0.113
No necessity for works council	−0.051	−0.140**	−0.118*	−0.021
Instrumentality of collective activities		0.178**	0.140**	0.104
Union identity	0.198**		0.034	0.083
Collectivism	0.156**	0.183**	−0.015	−0.019
Workgroup identity	−0.002	0.094	−0.037	−0.110*
Former trust	−0.011	0.055	0.036	0.081
Current them–us	−0.039	0.039	0.128*	0.025
External attribution	0.166**	0.037		0.098
Int. attribution: lacking effort	−0.027	0.060	−0.079	0.127*
Int. attribution: lacking solidarity	0.012	0.056	0.157**	0.109
General job satisfaction	−0.006	−0.059	−0.129*	−0.147**
Specific job dissatisfaction	0.112	0.080	0.088	
Gender (1 = female, 2 = male)	0.043	−0.016	0.039	−0.130*
Blue/white-collar (1 = blue, 2 = white)	0.033	−0.004	0.006	−0.134*
Works council member (1 = yes, 2 = no)	0.008	−0.056	−0.057	0.013
Age	0.039	0.196**	0.002	0.004

($* = p < 0.05$, $** = p < 0.01$)
Instrumentality of collective activities: R^2 (adj.) = 0.12097 (standard error: 0.55606), residual = 323, $F = 3.91577$ (sig. $F = 0.000$); union identity: R^2 (adj.) = 0.21244 (standard error: 0.59922), residual = 323, $F = 6.71527$ (sig. $F = 0.000$); external attribution: R^2 (adj.) = 0.26214 (standard error: 0.49961), residual 323, $F = 8.52742$ (sig. $F = 0.000$); specific job dissatisfaction: R^2 (adj.) = 0.18478 (standard error: 0.53804), residual = 323, $F = 5.80242$, sig. $F = 0.000$

Notes

1 Introduction

1 'East Germany' refers to that territory after 10 March 1990. It is used as a conceptual rather than a political term. It is synonymous with 'the new German *Länder* (states)'. 'GDR' is used for the former German state. 'West Germany' means the territory of the original eleven *Länder* of the Federal Republic of Germany.

2 The literature is divided on the proper terminology for the former societal system: 'socialism', 'communism', 'state-socialism' and 'planned economy' are among the preferred options. The German literature refers to socialism and this term will be adopted in this book.

3 'Institutions' are defined as social constructs which are created for a specific cause, and determine 'what has to be done' in the long term (Lipp in Endruweit and Trommsdorff 1989: 307). They are multi-functional but with one main function, multi-dimensional, stabilise the tensions between the individual and society, and have a specific '*Leitidee*' (leading thought), at least in the German sociological tradition (e.g. Gehlen 1956; Schelsky 1952). Thus, institutions are social phenomena persisting over time and laid down in patterns of both social behaviour and social meaning with the function of providing orientation for and regulation in social interaction (Göhler 1994).

4 1993 shows a similar picture and in 1994 membership dropped by 11 per cent (Fichter 1994: 61, 1996: 12).

5 Wiesenthal (1996: 1) argues that in a precise sense institutions cannot be institutionalised, but only rules or regulations can, and that an 'institutional transfer' implies functioning institutions. However, this book will follow the mainstream of the literature and keeps the concept 'institutional transfer' separate from the question whether the institutions function ('institutionalisation').

6 Workplace relations are narrowly defined as the relations between management and worker representatives at workplace level.

7 This has now merged with the metalworkers' union.

8 In 1994 blue-collar clothing workers in the east earned on average 63 per cent of the pay of their western colleagues. In comparison the metal industry, for example, had a ratio east/west of 80 per cent (Kittner 1995: 161).

2 Workplace relations in the former socialist GDR

1 The combine was the socialist type of a 'holding', a vertically integrated conglomerate, whereby enterprises of different levels of the production of one product (e.g. textiles) were part of one holding. The combines tended to be highly autarkic in their trading patterns, had monopoly control of their market segments and boasted their own supplying companies and social services.

2 'Taylorism' is frequently used in the German literature without a precise definition. It generally refers to a highly bureaucratic, centralised organisation with a production system based on assembly lines, division of labour and 'Tayloristic' control mechanisms and personnel policies (e.g. piece-rate pay).

3 The official hierarchical centralised way of communication between departments resembled the Tayloristic and socialist ideas of centralism (Heidenreich 1991c: 424). In addition, the absence of horizontal interdependencies between the departments was fostered by the heads of the departments themselves in order to increase their autonomy (so-called 'little principalities').

4 For example, Heidenreich (1991b: 15) mentions that in one of his case-study textile firms the supervisors earned 1,100–1,200 Deutsche Mark (DM) gross (= 800 DM net, since taxes for white collars were higher), whereas good sewers earned 1,000–1,200 DM net. Similarly, Adler and Kretzschmar (1993: 114) found in their case studies that a qualified blue-collar worker earned on average 934–1,031 DM net, and a qualified white-collar worker 970–1,193 DM net. Overall, industry-wide (net) earnings of east German supervisors were on average only 8 per cent higher than that of all production workers (Heidenreich 1991b; Stephan and Wiedemann 1990: 561). Thus, there was no monetary incentive to become a supervisor (Alt *et al.* 1994: 84).

5 A good example is the long work cycles. In this book's case-study clothing firm (see Chapter 5) the sewing time in former times for one model was 100–300 minutes, i.e. 5–15 minutes per seamstress in a group comprising twenty persons. The average work cycles in western firms of 1–2 minutes were virtually unknown in the east.

6 The informal bargaining of the piece rate was particularly crucial, since basic pay was on average only 40 per cent of total earnings.

7 Longitudinal survey of 2,323 east Germans in 1991–2 and 1993.

8 Based on case studies in the tools and electrotechnical industry in Saxony during the 1980s.

9 Of people asked whether they thought they could participate at their workplace, 3 per cent answered yes, 47 per cent no (Voigt 1973: 126). On the other hand, people expressed a strong wish for co-determination on pay, piece rates, job shift, working times, the distribution of tools and work, the distribution of flats and holiday places, and the selection of brigade leaders (ibid.: 126).

10 Sample of 911 questionnaires (response rate not known) of workers of several construction sites across the GDR in 1965.

11 Based on a case study and other unspecified empirical material of a major project of the SOFI Institute Göttingen and Humboldt University Berlin.

12 He distinguishes between three meanings of the networks for the individual, which he lables '*Kollektiv*' (collective, working community), '*Vitamin B*' (connections, contacts), and '*Nische*' (niche). First, the informal networks supported and fostered the formal '*Kollektiv*'. Second, informal networks were also a source for '*Vitamin B*' which would for example better allow people to obtain goods on the black market. And, third, informal networks were also creating specific niches of privacy and security.

13 Based on an empirical study of the Institute for Economic Psychology (WIP), Dortmund, which is unfortunately not further described in this article.

14 Defined as a voluntary membership in a group with value and emotional significance attached to that membership (see Chapter 6).

3 Transforming socialist workplace relations

1 His empirical basis derives to a large extent from a joint project with Kurbjuhn in 1993 which involved interviews with seventeen east German and thirty-three west

German union officials of the sixteen unions affiliated to the DGB who were responsible for the new *Länder.*

2 There is a debate as to how far it was the political circumstances, the DGB or the FDGB that initiated the merging process (e.g. Ansorg and Hürtgen 1992; Fichter 1994: 52; Lippold *et al.* 1992).

3 See also their joint agreement to a uniform economic and social system in a unified Germany (DGB/BDA, Gemeinsame Erklärung zu einer einheitlichen Wirtschafts- und Sozialordnung in beiden deutschen Staaten, 9 March 1990 in: DGB Informationsdienst ID7).

4 In most cases each member had to declare his/her willingness to join the new (west) German union before they were taken over. However, in some unions the entire membership was collectively taken over (and their members had then a chance to leave the new union).

5 In the following the term 'worker councils' (*Arbeitsräte*) refers to spontaneous establishments before the legislation of 'works councils' (*Betriebsräte*) was introduced.

6 The German industrial relations system is often described as a 'dual system'. This means that at the industry level, interest representation is conducted on a voluntary basis through the institutions of collective bargaining between unions and employers' associations, whereas domestic/company, level negotiations are conducted on a statutory basis between works councils and individual employers. The statutory framework at the workplace is provided by the 1972 Works Constitution Act (BetrVG). Under this legislation works councils are elected in all workplaces with over five employees and are responsible for representing and protecting employee interests at the workplace. They are formally independent of the unions and are elected by the whole workforce. They have specified information, consultation and co-determination rights concerning various social, personnel and economic issues of the firm (e.g. recruitment, redundancies, overtime pay, working time) but are not allowed to bargain pay (e.g. Müller-Jentsch 1994). Alongside the statutory councils, the unions maintain a network of stewards (*Vertrauensleute*) at the workplace. Unlike the council, the body of stewards is an integral part of the union organisation and not subject to the Works Constitution Act (partly quoted from Mahnkopf 1993: 10). For further infomation on the 'dual system' of German industrial relations see Adams and Rummel (1977), Berghahn and Karsten (1987), Streeck (1984a), Thelen (1991).

7 Based on case studies in six companies in the machine industry in Saxony.

8 Expert interviews and documentary work in forty companies in Saxony and Thüringen during 1989–90 and six longitudinal case studies (mainly from interviews with works councils) in these regions, plus equivalent investigations in twenty-two companies in Berlin until 1992–3 make up their empirical underpinning.

9 Kommission für die Erforschung des sozialen und politischen Wandels in den neuen Bundesländern, Halle.

10 Mahnkopf bases her arguments on interviews with union officials and works council members in Brandenburg during 1991. We are not told how many interviews she conducted nor in which industries they took place (see Mahnkopf 1993: 1).

11 Based on twelve case studies (ninety-two interviews with managers and works councillors in these case studies and a few other companies from various industrial sectors).

12 The co-determination law requests both parties to endorse a mutually trustful and harmonious relationship and to act in the best interest of the workforce and the company (BetrVG, paragraph 2).

13 Some authors further subdivide the pre-privatisation period into more tightly specified subperiods (e.g. Alt *et al.* 1994; Mickler *et al.* 1996; Kädtler *et al.* 1997).

14 Co-operation is often defined differently: for example, that people willingly co-operate because of mutual gains (see Axelrod 1990).

15 The author of this book observed the same in a chemical company which she visited in Bitterfeld in 1993. It experienced mass redundancies without any interference from the works council or workforce, but when management once violated a specific legal (information) right of the works council, the works council organised an immediate walkout.

16 In various industries in Baden-Württemberg in 1974–5, and fifteen years later he looked at the same case studies again to measure possible changes in workplace relations.

17 An exception is Artus *et al.* (1996)'s attempt to adapt Kotthoff's typology to the east. They classified their twenty-three case-study firms (of different industrial sectors) into seven types of works council–management relations (conflictual inter-action, interest-oriented co-operation, rational co-operation (*sachrationale Koopera-tion*), co-management, integration-oriented co-operation, harmonious company pact, authoritarian–hegemonical regime).

18 Kern and Land belong to the SOFI research group which investigated one case company during 1990, about which we are not told more specific details (see Voßkamp and Wittke 1991a).

19 Kirschner bases his discussion on the SOFI case study (see above) plus two other intensive case studies (including observatory participation in the works councils of these companies for two weeks) during 1992.

20 Their study is based on surveys of twelve companies and expert interviews. No further details of these investigations are provided.

21 Based on twenty-nine intensive (two–five hours long) interviews and two days of research seminars during 1990 and 1991 with managers, engineers, union officials, works councillors and researchers.

22 Based on literature review, and interviews with eight union officials and four works councillors of two companies and one personnel manager in 1992–3.

23 Based on interviews with seven union officials of the IG Metall in Berlin, eleven works councillors and managers, as well as on an analysis of union documents.

4 Social partnership in the east German clothing industry

1 Clothing and textiles form one industrial sector in Germany and therefore statistical data are often only available for both industries together.

2 Another source speaks of 12 per cent (Rasche 1993).

3 Labour-intensive, semi-skilled work with increasing demand for quality and fast turn-round have made it difficult for many clothing firms to survive in high-wage econo-mies such as Germany's (Taplin and Winterton 1997).

4 Another source speaks of 601,747 members (Küchle and Volkmann 1993).

5 A maximum of 50 per cent reduction in the official pay level (*Tarif*) is possible, but without any staff reductions.

6 The aim of adapting the east pay level step by step to the west level (*Tarif*) was first introduced in the bargaining agreement in the metal industry in March 1991, where both bargaining partners initially agreed to an adaptation process to be finished by April 1994 (Bispinck in Kittner 1993: 172).

7 There are no differentiating data available regarding male and female earnings in the clothing industry.

8 This was confirmed by *t*-tests.

5 Transformation at enterprise level

1 To guarantee anonymity the names of the firm have been changed.
2 The idea behind that was to provide workplaces in each little village to make the transport for workers more convenient.
3 This resulted primarily from the complicated hierachical co-ordination between departments and plants. For example, at Trikotwear 450 people worked in administration. At the time of the fieldwork there were 30 people left.
4 The norm determines how many pieces a worker has to produce in a specified time in order to get 100 per cent of the pay (basic pay). They are 'scientifically' measured by workplace engineers.
5 In fact the director held a workforce meeting as the conflict escalated in order to ask whether the workforce even wanted him to stay, which seemed to have some impact.
6 The term '*Mitarbeiter*' is not directly translatable; it means something like a 'co-worker' but not as close as a 'colleague'.
7 She become chief councillor in 1995.
8 The co-determination law (BetrVG) determines the number of works council members in proporation to the size of the workforce, and also the percentage of white-collar members.
9 The GTB survey was also distributed to the Bodywear works council and was filled in by six, part-time members of the works council.
10 The average norm in the old regime (e.g. 1989) was 140–50 per cent (also 160–80 per cent was reached quite frequently), since piece-rate norms were easier, as explained before.
11 See Kotthoff (1994) who emphasised the importance of personalities in shaping workplace relations.

6 Workers' attitudes in post-socialist east Germany

1 Based on three intensive case studies of companies of the metal and steel industry in Saxony comprising open interviews (single and group) of forty-four people (managers, white- and blue-collar workers) during 1992–3.
2 Referring to the socialist firms' duties regarding the social welfare of their employees (e.g. kindergarten, holiday places, doctors, leisure facilities).
3 The qualitative interviews took place in four companies of the automobile industry during 1991 and 1993, and are part of Mickler *et al.*'s project (e.g. 1996). No more details about the type of interviews have been published.
4 Semi-structured interviews with eighty-four employees in four companies in the metal and chemical industry (two green-field sites, one Treuhand-owned, one privatised); this study is part of a large project at the SOFI institute, Göttingen, with a panel survey of 600 white- and blue-collar workers in training workshops on their views of retraining activities and on their perception and handling of the transformation as such.
5 Quantitative survey: seven companies of various industrial sectors (metal, electronic, chemical) around Dresden with questionnaires to the management and workforce (273 people, return rate 47.9 per cent) in 1990–1.
6 As mentioned before, the empirical basis is that of interviews with union officials, works councillors and managers.
7 Interviews with eighty-four employees in four companies in the metal and chemical industry (see above).
8 Kreißig belonged to the WISOC research group; his arguments here are based on a survey of employees in companies in the Chemnitz area in early 1990. Unfortunately no further details are provided.

9 This is based on yearly representative surveys of the east German population on their social situation, living and working conditions, and of people's way of thinking, attitudes and behaviour changes.

10 No differentiated figures for west and east are available.

11 Postal questionnaire to female employees of 115 companies of sixteen industrial sectors; 675 questionnaires were returned (45 per cent).

7 Methodology of the union membership surveys in the east and west German clothing industry

1 This term was used since it includes commitment to the union as well as to the works council.

2 This goes back to an idea of Fishbein (1967), who suggested that attitudes toward a specific behavioural object should be more highly related to behaviours encompassing that object than attitudes toward the class of behavioural objects into which the specific object falls.

3 They found a correlation of 0.79 between voting intent and actual voting for the union.

4 In the west 26 per cent and in the east 12 per cent were under 30 years of age, 31 per cent in the west and 37 per cent in the east were between 30 and 0 years, 25 per cent in the west and 25 per cent in the east were between 41 and 50 years and 24 per cent in the west and 20 per cent in the east were over 50 years.

5 Eleven per cent had worked in their current company for five years or less, 14.1 per cent had worked 5–10 years, 35.9 per cent 10-20 years and 39 per cent 20 years or more.

8 Collective commitment in the east and west

1 Separate data for the west and east German members of the GTV are not available.

2 However, women were less likely to stand for a union or works council post than their male colleagues (in both samples), which supports the well-known thesis of female workers' double burden.

3 It has to be noted that the survey asked for intentional behaviour only and that the structural reasons provided in the literature (such as economic recession) might inhibit actual collective activities. Yet, they did not inhibit people's declared willingness.

4 Multiple regression analysis was conducted for the two factors of participation: union identity and the necessity of works councils.

9 Theories of participation in collective activities

1 The literature is similar to the mainly US literature on unionisation (voting) and joining decisions (e.g. Barling *et al.* 1992: ch. 3; Block and Premack 1983; DeCotiis and LeLouarn 1981; Hartley 1992; Heneman and Sandver 1983; Hills 1985; Premack and Hunter 1988; Schriesheim 1978; van de Vall 1970: ch. 4; Zalesny 1985).

2 Antecedents are not predictors in a strict sense, i.e. assuming causal inferences, but are only able to support diagnostic (attributional) inferences. Strict causal inferences cannot be produced with the type of empirical data normally available (e.g. cross-sectional rather than longitudinal).

3 See for example Barling *et al.* (1992); Kelly and Kelly (1992); Klandermans (1986b).

4 For example, there is evidence that smaller rather than larger plant size facilitates collective participation (e.g. Lipset *et al.* 1956; Seidman 1953; Seidman *et al.*

1958; Spinrad 1960) and more recent studies do not find robust support for either interpretation (e.g. Allen and Stephenson 1983; Dewey *et al.* 1978; Gallie 1989: 10). Furthermore, concepts such as technology or union characteristics have not been tested sufficiently (see Nicholson and Kelly 1980).

5 Because in comparison with older workers they are less loyal to the employer, less threatened by costly victimisation, more resentful of arbitrary treatment by management and more attuned to union ideology (e.g. Shister 1956)

6 For example, younger workers have higher turnover rates, which suggests a great reduction in the value of those union benefits associated with seniority, and are less ideologically bound to union values (e.g. Perline and Lorenz 1970; Richardson and Catlin 1979). They are also likely to be with the union longer (Glick *et al.* 1977; McShane 1986; Perline and Lorenz 1970; Strauss 1977).

7 In other words a curvilinear relationship according to Guest and Dewe (1988: 183).

8 For example, younger workers are militant because of the absence of financial commitments but younger workers are less militant because of their weaker attachments to the firm and thus can resolve job dissatisfaction more easily through quitting. Some studies, however, found no relationship at all (see Klandermans 1986b).

9 If the authors of demographic variables give an explanation for their findings they commonly refer to theories such as rational choice theory. For example, Oliver (1984) argues that the restricted engagement of 'poor' workers in union activity is not due to apathy but to an acute free-rider problem in which costs of participation outweigh the individuals' share of the collective good (see also Bain and Price 1980 or Fiorito and Greer 1982 for explanations of union growth and decline and Shalev 1983 for the analysis of strike statistics).

10 An important distinction for some is made between 'individual' relative deprivation (where the individual feels personally deprived compared to other individuals) and 'collective' relative deprivation (where the individual feels that his/her group is deprived relative to other groups). Some evidence suggests that it is the perception of collective relative deprivation which has most impact on participation in collective action (Kelly and Kelly 1992: 6).

11 However, union commitment is defined in a different way, since it comprises 'moral' and 'calculative' attachment in one factor. This means that union identity does not equate with union commitment; if anything it resembles the concept of moral attachment or of union loyalty as utilised by some authors (Fullagar and Barling 1989; Kelloway *et al.* 1992).

12 Guest *et al.* (1993: 197) found evidence for different categories of identities: traditional pluralist identity, local unitarist identity and managerial identity.

13 In their study they suggest that in certain groups (e.g. those with little history of trade unionism and a high degree of contact with management) a strong sense of identification with the departmental group was synonymous with a sense of company loyalty, which, in turn, did not encourage clear differentiations between company subgroups. In addition groups were characterised by varying degrees of individualism and collectivism.

14 One might, however, question the longitudinal character of their study. It consisted of a survey conducted twice with eight months in between, a period which might be criticised as being too short for significant changes in attitudes (especially if there was no major event such as a strike occurring during that time).

10 Determinants of union membership participation in the east and west

1 This variable was only included in the analysis of the west sample because it was a negligible number in the east (8 per cent).

2 With all members (not just rank-and-file).

3 In some cases the factors comprised slightly different items in the two surveys (due to some additional questions in each survey) (see Appendix).

4 In a second step the variable was excluded from the equation which did not alter the result.

5 Works council member: R^2 (adj.) = 0.25214 (standard error = 0.79885), residual = 81, F = 3.04396 (sig. F = 0.0005); non-member: R^2 (adj.) = 0.10841 (standard error = 0.73308), residual = 225, F = 2.83156 (sig. F = 0.0003).

6 Split according to the median = 2.90: high identifier (> 2.90): R^2 (adj.) = 0.32371 (standard error = 0.75440), residual = 142, F = 5.72670 (sig. F = 0.000); low identifier ($\leqslant$ 2.90): R^2 (adj.) = 0.06549 (standard error = 0.77812), residual = 164, F = 1.78841 (sig. F = 0.0365). High identifiers yielded the same antecedents as the main equation (and in addition group collectivism and external attribution), whereas low identifiers produced two antecedents (of the main equation), instrumentality of collective activities and works-council membership.

7 However, not all measures of the theories were significant (e.g. them-and-us feelings of social identity theory).

8 A regression was conducted for each of the two types of participation in the two surveys with the three factors of collective instrumentality as independent variables. The instrumentality of collective activities was the main antecedent in both cases. Moreover, people's perception of collective action was not influenced by their perception of the institutions. This was confirmed when analysing the possible antecedents of the perception of collective action as a dependent variable (all other variables as independent). Thus, the correlation between the factors, no necessity for works council and instrumentality of collective activities, was not sufficiently strong to survive in the large-scale regression.

9 Glick *et al.* (1977) found a correlation with 'representing the union', but not with 'attending union meetings'. Klandermans (1986b) is one of the few studies which tested the instrumentality of collective action (as an item within his 'collective motives'). The 'collective motives' were significant; however, he did not report the individual beta coefficients of the separate measures of instrumentality.

10 A regression was conducted for each of the two types of participation, with the factors of social identity as the only independent variables.

11 Conducting four regression analyses with all four factors as dependent variables did not reveal any significance of them-and-us feelings.

12 Them-and-us feelings were excluded. Conducting four regression analyses with all four factors as dependent variables did not reveal any significance of them-and-us feelings.

13 The following analysis was conducted for the east sample only. First regression (workgroup identity = dependent): collectivism: beta coefficient = 0.178** (sig. T = 0.0005), union identity: beta coefficient = 0.075 (sig. T = 0.1420); R^2 (adj.) = 0.03915 (standard error = 0.70629), residual = 395, F = 9.08887 (sig. F = 0.0001); Second regression (collectivism = dependent): group identity: beta coefficient = 0.169** (sig. T = 0.0005), union identity: beta coefficient = 0.230** (sig. T = 0.000); R^2 (adj.) = 0.08616 (standard error = 0.60524), residual = 395, F = 19.71441 (sig. F = 0.000); Third regression (union identity = dependent): workgroup identity: beta coefficient = 0.073 (sig. T = 0.1420), collectivism: beta coefficient = 0.236** (sig. T = 0.000); R^2 (adj.) = 0.06284 (standard error = 0.65776), residual = 395, F = 14.30989 (sig. F = 0.000).

14 Instrumentality: R^2 (adj.) = 0.22882 (standard error = 0.52083), residual = 321, F = 6.58807 (sig. F = 0.000); identity: R^2 (adj.) = 0.26451 (standard error = 0.57907), residual = 321, F = 7.77314 (sig. F = 0.000).

15 However, excluding this independent variable from the equation did not significantly change the constellation of the other antecedents.
16 The regression was repeated for men only and did not show any difference regarding the importance of group identity.

11 Conclusion

1 Clearly, one can argue that works councillors' perceptions are just one side of the coin and a comparison of west and east German managers might be worthwhile. However, since the literature focuses on the different attitudes of east German works councils rather than managers it seemed appropriate to concentrate the discussion on works councillors alone. Moreover, the survey findings were supported by the case study which investigates works councillors' as well as managers' perceptions and behaviour.

Bibliography

Abrams, D. (1989) 'How Social is Social Identity?', paper presented at the First European Congress of Psychology, Symposium on Intergroup Relations, Amsterdam, 3 July 1989.

Adams, R. J. and Rummel, C. H. (1977) 'Workers' Participation in Management in West Germany', *Industrial Relations Journal*, 8, 1: 4–22.

Aderhold, J. *et al.* (1994) *Von der Betrubs – zur Zweckgemeinschaft. Ostdeutsche Arbeits –und Management kulturen im Transformationsprosess*, Berlin: Sigma.

Adler, F. and Kretzschmar, A. (1993) 'Ungleichheitsstrukturen in der ehemaligen DDR', in Geissler, R. *et al.* (eds) *Sozialer Umbruch in Ostdeutschland*, Frankfurt am Main: Campus.

Ajzen, I. and Fishbein, M. (1980) *Understanding Attitudes amd Predicting Social Behavior*, Englewood Cliffs, NJ: Prentice-Hall.

Albert, M. (1993) *Capitalism against Capitalism*, London: Whurr Publishers.

Allen, N. J. and Meyer, J. P. (1990) 'The Measurement and Antecedents of Affective, Continuance and Normative Commitment to the Organization', *Journal of Occupational Psychology*, 63, 1: 1–18.

Allen, P. T. and Stephenson, G. M. (1983) 'Inter-group Understanding and Size of Organisations', *British Journal of Industrial Relations*, 21: 312–29.

Allport, G. W. (1954) *The Nature of Prejudice*, Cambridge, Mass.: Addison-Wesley.

Almond, G. and Bingham Powell, G. (1978) *Comparative Politics. System, Process, and Policy*, Boston/Toronto: Little, Brown.

Almond, G. and Verba, S. (1963) *The Civic Culture: Political Attitudes and Democracy in Five Nations*, Princeton, NJ: Princeton University Press.

Almond, G. and Verba, S. (eds) (1980) *The Civic Culture Revisited*, Boston/Toronto: Little, Brown.

Alt, R., Althaus, H.-J., Deutschmann, Ch., Schmidt, W. and Warneken, B. J. (1993) 'Wandel von Arbeitsbeziehungen und Sozialpolitik in ostdeutschen Betrieben', first report, Zwischenbericht an die Hans-Böckler-Stiftung no. 92-366-3, Soziologisches Seminar der Universität Tübingen.

Alt, R., Althaus, H.-J., Schmidt, W., Deutschmann, Ch. and Warnecken, B. J. (1994) 'Vom Werktätigen zum Arbeitnehmer: Der Umbruch von Arbeitsbeziehungen und Sozialpolitik in ostdeutschen Betrieben', final report, Manuskripte der Hans-Böckler-Stiftung (142) Düsseldorf.

Altvoter, E. and Mahnkopf, B. (1993) *Gewerkscheften vor der europäischen Herausfordoung*, Münster: Westfälisches Dempfboot.

Anderson, J. C. (1978) 'Local Union Participation: a Re-examination', *Industrial Relations*, 18: 18–31.

Andretta, G., Baethge, M. and Dittmer, S. (1994) 'Übergang wohin? Schwierigkeiten ostdeutscher Industriearbeiter bei ihrer betrieblichen Neuorientierung', *SOFI Mitteilungen*, March: 1–25.

Angle, H. L. and Perry, J. L. (1986) 'Dual Commitment and Labor–Management Relationship Climates', *Academy of Management Journal*, 29, 1: 31–50.

Ansorg, L. and Hürtgen, R. (1992) '"Aber jetzt gibt es initiative Leute und die müßte man eigentlich alle an einen Tisch bringen". Die "Initiative für unabhängige Gewerkschaften" (IUG) 1989-1990', discussion paper, Arbeitshefte und Berichte zur sozialwissenschaftlichen Forschung no. 73, Freie Universität Berlin, Zentralinstitut für sozialwissenschaftliche Forschung.

Arbeitsgesetzbuch (1977) *Arbeitsgesetzbuch der Deutschen Demokratischen Republik*, Staatsverlag der Deutschen Demokratischen Republik, Berlin.

Armingeon, K. (1991) 'Ende einer Erfolgsstory? Gewerkschaften und Arbeitsbeziehungen im Einigungsprozeß', *Gegenwartskunde*, 40, 1: 29–42.

Artus, I. (1996) 'Die Etablierung der Gewerkschaften', in Bergmann, J. and Schmidt, R. (eds) op. cit., 21–48.

Artus, I., Liebold, R., Lohr, K., Schmidt, E., Schmidt, R. and Strohwald, U. (1996) 'Innerbetriebliche Interaktionsmuster in Ostdeutschland: Eine Typologie der Austauschbeziehungen zwischen Management und Betriebsrat', final report of the DFG project (Ma 607/7-1).

Augustin, W. and Sprenger, J. (1992) 'Transformation der Mitbestimmung in die neuen Bundesländer und Überlegungen zur gewerkschaftlichen Reformdebatte', sfs Beiträge (62, May 1992): Sozialforschungsstelle Dortmund Landesinstitut.

Autorenkollektiv (1978) *Ökonomisches Lexikon*, Berlin Ost (GDR).

Autorenkollektiv (1983) *Kleines politisches Wörterbuch*, Berlin Ost (GDR).

Axelrod, R. (1990) *The Evolution of Co-operation* London: Penguin.

Bain, G. and Elias, P. (1985) 'Trade Union Membership in Great Britain: an Individual Level Analysis', *British Journal of Industrial Relations*, 23, 1.

Bain, G. and Price, R. (1980) *Profiles of Union Growth*, Oxford: Basil Blackwell.

Bain, G. and Price, R. (1983) 'Union Growth: Dimensions, Determinants, and Destiny', in Bain, G. S. (ed.) *Industrial Relations in Britain*, Oxford: Basil Blackwell.

Barling, J., Fullagar, C. and Kelloway, E. K. (1992) *The Union and Its Members*, New York: Oxford University Press.

Barling, J., Wade, B. and Fullagar, C. (1990) 'Predicting Employee Commitment to Company and Union: Divergent Models', *Journal of Occupational Psychology*, 63: 49–61.

Batstone, E., Boraston, I. and Frenkel, S. (1978) *The Social Organization of Strikes*, Oxford: Basil Blackwell.

Bayer, H. (1979) 'Die Integration heterogener Mitgliedsgruppen in Industriegewerkschaften 1960–1975', *Soziale Welt*, 3.

Becker, M., Lang, R. and Wagner, D. (eds) (1996) *Personalarbeit in den neuen Bundesländern*, Munich and Mering: Rainer Hampp Verlag.

Becker, P. (1993) 'Ostdeutsche und Westdeutsche auf dem Prüfstand psychologischer Tests', *Aus Politik und Zeitgeschichte*. Beilage zur Wochenzeitung Das Parlament, B24/92, 24–27.

Beilicke, W. (1995) 'Die Transformation des VEB Pharmazeutischen Kombinat GERMED aus der Zentralverwaltungs- in die Marktwirtschaft', discussion paper, KSPW Kurzstudie, 111 (AG 01.09), Halle.

Belwe, K. (1979) *Mitwirkung im Industriebetrieb der DDR*, Opladen: Leske & Buderich.

Belwe, K. (1992) 'Zur psychosozialen Befindlichkeit der Menschen in den neuen Bundesländern', *BISS public*, 8: 5–24.

Bem, D. J. (1967) 'Self Perception: an Alternative Interpretation of Cognitive Dissonance Phenomena', *Psychological Review*, 74: 183–200.

Bem, D. J. (1972) 'Self-Perception Theory', in Berkowitz, L. (ed.) *Advances in Experimental Social Psychology*, New York: 1–62.

Berghahn, V. and Karsten, D. (1987) *Industrial Relations in West Germany*, Oxford: Berg Publishing.

Bergmann, J. (1996) 'Industrielle Beziehungen in Ostdeutschland: Transferierte Institutionen im Deindustrialisierungsprozeß', in Lutz, B. *et al.* (eds) op. cit., 257–94.

Bergmann, J. and Schmidt, R. (eds) (1996) *Industrielle Beziehungen: Institutionalisierung und Praxis unter Krisenbedingungen*, Opladen: Leske & Buderich.

Bericht der Kommission Mitbestimmung (1998) 'Mitbestimmung und neue Unternehmenskulturen – Bilanz und Perspektiven', Bertelsmann Stiftung/Hans-Böckler-Stiftung, Gütersloh: Bertelsmann Verlag.

Bertl, W., Rudat, R. and Schneider, R. (1989) *Arbeitnehmerbewußtsein im Wandel. Folgerungen für Gesellschaft und Gewerkschaft*, Frankfurt/New York: Campus.

Beyse, C. and Möll, G. (1996) 'Da braucht man wahrscheinlich den Hammer'. Probleme der Restrukturierung ostdeutscher Betriebe am Beispiel ausgegliederter Kombinatsabteilungen', in Schmidt, R. (ed.) *Reorganisation und Modernisierung der Industriellen Produktion*, Opladen: Leske & Buderich, 15–40.

Binus, G. and Groß, J. (1995) 'Veränderungen der betrieblichen Personalstruktur im Transformationsprozeß seit 1989: dargestellt am Beispiel eines noch der Treuhand unterstellten Maschinenbauunternehmens', discussion paper, KSPW Kurzstudie, 125 (AG 01.31), Halle.

Birchall, D. (1975) *Job Design: a Planning and Implementation Guide for Managers*, Epping: Gower Press.

Blanchflower, D. and Freeman, R. (1993) 'The Legacy of Communist Labor Relations', discussion paper no. 180, Centre of Economic Performance at LSE, London.

Block, R. N. and Premack, S. L. (1983) 'The Unionization Process: a Review of the Literature', *Advances in Industrial and Labor Relations*, 1: 31–70.

Bluhm, K. (1992) 'Vom gescheiterten zum nachholenden Fordismus?', in Senghaas-Knobloch, E. and Lange, H. (eds), op. cit., 44–56.

Bluhm, K. (1996) 'Regionale Strategien unter Handlungsdruck – ostdeutsche Arbeitgeberverbände im Dezentralisierungsprozeß der industriellen Beziehungen', in Bergmann, J. and Schmidt, R. (eds), op. cit., 135-60.

Blyton, P., Nicholson, N. and Ursell, G. (1981) 'Job Status and White-collar Members' Union Activity', *Journal of Occupational Psychology*, 54: 33–45.

Bochum, U. (1996) 'Produktionsmodernisierung in der ostdeutschen Industrie – Welchee Modernisierungspfade beschreiten ostdeutsche Betriebe im Prozeß der Restrukturierung?', in Schmidt, R. (ed.) 1996b, 41–140.

Boltho, A., Carlin, W. and Scaramozzino, P. (1995) 'Will East Germany Become a New Mezzogiorno?', WZB discussion papers (FS I 95-307), Wissenschaftszentrum Berlin für Sozialforschung.

Booth, A. (1986) 'Estimating the Probability of Trade Union Membership: a Study of Men and Women in Britain', *Economica*, 53, 6: 41–61.

Brähler, E. and Richter, H.-E. (1995) 'Deutsche Befindlichkeiten im Ost–West-Vergleich', *psychosozial*, 18, 59: 7–20.

Breitenacher, M., Adler, U. and Vögtle, C. (1997) 'Das Textil-, Bekleidungs- und Ledergewerbe im Freistaat Sachsen', ifo dresden studien, no. 18, Dresden: ifo Institut für Wirtschaftsforschung.

Brett, J. M. (1980) 'Behavioral Research on Unions and Union Management Systems', *Research in Organizational Behavior*, 2: 177–213.

Brett, J. M. and Hammer, T. H. (1982) 'Organizational Behavior and Industrial Relations', in Kochan, T. A., Mitchell, D. J. and Dyer, L. (eds) *Industrial Relations Research in the 1970s: Review and Appraisal*, Madison, Wis.: Industrial Relations Research Association, 221–81.

Brinkmann, U. (1996) 'Magere Bilanz: Neue Managementkonzepte (NMK) in transformierten ostdeutschen Betrieben', in Pohlmann, M. and Schmidt, R. (eds), op. cit., 215–48.

Brown, R. and Williams, J. (1984) 'Group Identification: the Same Thing to all People?', *Human Relations*, 37, 7: 547–64.

Brown, W. (1972) 'A Consideration of "Custom" and "Practice"', *British Journal of Industrial Relations*, 10: 42–61.

Brücker, H. (1995) 'Zu teuer Gezahlt?', *Die Mitgestimmung*, 7: 18–20.

Bryman, A. and Cramer, D. (1994) *Quantitative Data Analysis for Social Scientists*, London: Routledge: ch. 9.

Buechtemann, C. and Schupp, J. (1992) 'Repercussions of Reunification: Patterns and Trends in the Socio-economic Transformation of East Germany', *Industrial Relations Journal*: 90–106.

Burawoy, M. (1985) *The Politics of Production: Factory Regimes under Capitalism and Socialism*. London: Verso.

Burawoy, M. (1992) *The Radiant Future*, London.

Bust-Bartels, A. (1980) *Herrschaft und Widerstand in den DDR-Betrieben*, Frankfurt am Main: Campus.

Chalupsky, J. and Seifert, D. (1995) 'Unternehmenswandel: Umbruch, Entflechtung, Sanierung, Neustrukturierung', discussion paper, KSPW Kurzstudie, 103 (AG 01.34), Halle.

Clarke, S. (ed.) (1995) *Management and Industry in Russia: Formal and Informal Relations in the Period of Transition*, Aldershot: Edward Elgar.

Clarke, S., Burawoy, M., Fairbrother, P. and Krotov, P. (eds) (1993) *What about the Workers? Workers and the Transition to Capitalism in Russia*, London: Verso.

Clegg, H. A. (1976) *Trade Unionism under Collective Bargaining: a Theory Based on Comparisons of Six Countries*, Warwick Studies in Industrial Relations, Oxford: Basil Blackwell.

Cole, S. (1969) 'Teachers' Strike: a Study of the Conversion of Predisposition into Action', *American Journal of Sociology*, 74: 506–20.

Dalton, R. J. (1991) 'Communists and Democrats: Attitudes toward Democracy in the Two Germanies', in Annual meeting of the American Political Science Association. Washington DC.

Dastmalchian, A., Blyton, P. and Adamson, R. (eds) (1991) *The Climate of Workplace Relations*, London: Routledge.

Dathe, D. and Schreiber, T. (1993) 'Gewerkschaftliche Betriebspolitik und soziale Identitätsbildung der abhängig Beschäftigten in den neuen Bundesländern', project report (no 93-446-2), Düsseldorf: Hans-Böckler-Stiftung.

Dathe, D. and Schreiber, T. (1994) 'Das zweite Standbein wackelt: Betriebspolitik in den neuen Bundesländern', *Die Mitbestimmung*, 6: 44–6.

David, V. (1992) 'Betriebsräte als Akteure im Strukturwandel in dem NBL', in Erfahrungen und Perspektiven des Forschungsprogramms 'Arbeit und Technik in den neuen Bundesländern', Materialband Teil 2, 26/27.10.1992, Bad Schandau: 129–36.

DeCotiis, T. A. and LeLouran, J. (1981) 'A Predictive Study of Voting Behaviour in a Representative Election Using Union Instrumentality and Work Perceptions', *Organizational Behaviour and Human Performance*, 27: 103–18.

Denisow, K., Jakob, K., Steinhöfel, M. and Stieler, B. (1994) 'Personalstrategien und Überlebenschancen von Unternehmen in den NBL', discussion paper, KSPW Kurz-studie, FS I-92-33, Halle.

Deppe, R. (1991) 'Bilanz der verlorenen Zeit. Industriearbeit, Leistung und Herrschaft in der DDR und Ungarn', in Deppe, R., Dubiel, H. and Rödel, U. (eds) op. cit., 126–50.

Deppe, R. and Hoß, D. (1989) *Arbeitspolitik im Staatssozialismus: Zwei Varianten DDR und Ungarn*, Frankfurt am Main/New York: Campus.

Deppe, R., Dubiel, H. and Rödel, U. (eds) (1991) *Demokratischer Umbruch in Osteuropa*, Frankfurt am Main: Suhrkamp.

Deshpande, S. P. and Fiorito, J. (1989) 'Specific and General Beliefs in Union Voting Models', *Academy of Management Journal*, 32, 4: 883–97.

Dewey, M. E., Stephenson, G. M. and Thomas, A. C. (1978) 'Organisational Unit Size and Individual Attitudes: an Empirical Study', *Sociological Review*, 26: 125–37.

DGB Trendbarometer(1992, 1994), edited by IFEP (Institut für Sozialforschung, markanalysen und Kommunikation), Cologne.

Die Quelle (1994) Funktionärszeitschrift (magazine for trade union officials) of the DGB, June.

Diewald, M. (1995) '"Kollektiv", "Vitamin B" oder "Nische"? Persönliche Netz-werke in der DDR', in Huninink, J. and Mayer, K. U. (eds) *Lebensverläufe in der DDR*, Berlin: Akademie Verlag.

Dittrich, E. J., Haferkamper, M., Schmidt, G. and Stojanov, C. (eds) (1992) *Der Wandel der industriellen Beziehungen in Ost-Europa*, Frankfurt am Main: Campus.

DIW (1995) Deutsches Institut für Wirtschaftsforschung, Wochenberichte, Cologne.

Dollard, J. *et al.* (1939) *Frustration and Aggression*, New Haven, Conn.: Yale University Press.

Donovan (1968) 'Royal Commission on Trade Unions and Employers' Associations', report, Cmnd 3623, London: HMSO.

Dörr, G. and Schmidt, S. (1992) 'Aspekte des betrieblichen Wandels in ehemaligen Kombinatsbetrieben – eine Problemskizze aus dem Maschinenbau', in Heidenreich, M. (ed.) op. cit., 59–74.

Dubin, R. (1960) 'A Theory of Conflict and Power in Union Management Relations', *International Labor Relations Review,* 13: 501–18.

Dybowski-Johannson, G.(1980) *Die Interessenvertretung durch den Betriebsrat*, Frankfurt am Main: Campus.

Earley, P. C. (1993) 'East Meets West Meets Mideast: Further Explorations of Collectivist and Individualistic Work Groups', *Academy of Management Journal*, 36, 2: 319–48.

Edeling, T. (1992) 'Entstaatlichung und Entbürokratisierung – Strategien und Resultate der Reorganisation ostdeutscher Betriebe', in Heidenreich, M. (ed.) op. cit., 45–58.

Edwards, V. and Lawrence, P. (1994) *Management Change in East Germany: Unification and Tranformation*, London: Routledge.

Eidam, F.-M. and Oswald, H. (1993) 'Reformfähig durch den Osten?' in Leif, T., Klein, A. and Legrand, H.-J. (eds) *Reform des DGB*, Cologne: Bund Verlag, 166–82.

Eisen, A. (1996) 'Institutionenwandel und institutioneller Wandel im Transformationsprozeß', in Eisen, A. and Wollmann, H. (eds) *Institutionenbildung in Ostdeutschland: Zwischen externer Steuerung und Eigendynamik*, Opladen: Leske & Buderich, 33–62.

Eisen, A. and Wollmann, H. (eds) (1996a) *Institutionenbildung in Ostdeutschland: Zwischen externer Steuerung und Eigendynamik*, Opladen: Leske & Buderich.

Eisen, A. and Wollmann, H. (1996b) 'Institutionenbildung in Ostdeutschland: Zwischen externer Steuerung und Eigendynamik', in Eisen, A. and Wollmann, H. (eds) 1996a, 15–32.

Eiser, J. R. (1986) *Social Psychology: Attitudes, Cognition and Social Behaviour*, Cambridge: Cambridge University Press.

Ekiert, G. (1998) 'Do Legacies Matter? Patterns of Postcommunist Transitions in Eastern Europe', paper presented at the 11th International Conference of Europeanists, Baltimore.

Elster, J. (1989) *The Cement of Society: a Study of Social Order*, Cambridge: Cambridge University Press.

Endruweit, G. and Trommsdorff, G. (1989) *Wörterbuch der Soziologie*, Stuttgart: Enke.

Ermischer, I. and Preusche, E. (1992) 'Auswirkungen der Privatisierung auf die betriebliche Interessenvertretung im Prozeß der Neugestaltung industrieller Beziehungen in Chemnitzer Industriebetrieben', unpublished ms, WISOC, Chemnitz.

Ermischer, I. and Preusche, E. (1993) 'Betriebsräte zwischen Mitbestimmung und Abwicklungs- "Komanagement"', in Schmidt, R. (ed.) *Zwischenbilanz: Analysen zum Transformationsprozeß der ostdeutschen Industrie*, Berlin: Akademie Verlag, 169–92.

Ermischer, I. and Preusche, E. (1995) 'East German Works Councils: Between Co-operation and Conflict', in Hoffmann, R., Jacobi, O., Keller, B. and Weiss, M. (eds) *German Industrial Relations under the Impact of Structural Change, Unification, and European Integration*, Düsseldorf: Hans-Böckler-Stiftung, 53–61.

Ettl, W. and Heikenroth, A. (1995) 'Strukturwandel, Verbandsabstinenz, Tarifflucht: Zur Lage ostdeutscher Unternehmen und Arbeitgeberverbände', AG TRAP working paper, no 95/3, Humboldt Universität Berlin.

Ettl, W. and Wiesenthal, H. (1994) 'Tarifautomonie in de-industriaalisiertem Gelände: Report und Analyse eines Institutionentransfers im Prozeß der deutschen Einheit', AG TRAP working paper, no. 94/2, Humboldt Universität Berlin.

Etzel, J. M. and Walker, B. J. (1974) 'Effects of Alternative Follow-up Procedures on Mail Survey Response Rates', *Journal of Applied Psychology*, 59, 219–21.

Etzioni, A. (1975) *A Comparative Analysis of Complex Organizations*, New York: The Free Press.

Fantasia, R. (1988) *Cultures of Solidarity: Consciousness, Action and Contemporary American Workers*, Berkeley: University of California Press.

Farber, H. S. and Saks, D. H. (1980) 'Why Workers Want Unions: the Role of Relative Wages and Job Characteristics', *Journal of Political Economy*, 88, 2: 349–69.

FAZ (Frankfurter Allgemeine Zeitung), various issues.

Feather, N. T. (1982) *Expectations and Actions: Expectancy–Value Models in Psychology*, Hillsdale, NJ: Lawrence Erlbaum.

Feist, U., Hartenstein, W., Rudat, R., Schneider, R. and Schmid, M. (1989) *Wandel der Industriegesellschaft und Arbeitsbewußtsein. Untersuchungen in ausgewählten Wirtschaftszweigen Nordrhein-Westfalens*, Frankfurt/New York: Campus.

Feminist Review (ed.) (1991) *Shifting Territories: Feminism and Europe*, 39, special issue, London: Routledge.

Ferree, M. M. and Miller, F. (1985) 'Mobilization and Meaning: toward an Integration of Social Psychological and Resource Perspectives on Social Movements', *Sociological Inquiry*, 55, 1: 38–61.

Fichter, M. (1991) 'From Transmission Belt to Social Partnership? The Case of Organized Labor in Eastern Germany', *German Politics and Society*, 23: 21–39.

Fichter, M. (1994) 'Revamping Union Structures: Does Eastern Germany Count?', in International Industrial Relations Association (ed.) *4th European Regional Congress, volume 4, Transformation of the Industrial Relations in Central and Eastern Europe*, Helsinki, Finland: 47–68.

Fichter, M. (1996) 'Unions in the new Länder: Evidence for the Urgency of Reform', working paper, Free University Berlin.

Fichter, M. (1997a) 'Unions in the New Länder: Evidence for the Urgency of Reform', in L. Turner (ed.) *Negotiating the New Germany: Can Social Partnership Survive?*, Ithaca, NY: ILR Press.

Fichter, M. (1997b) 'Trade Union Members: a Vanishing Species in Post-Unification Germany?', draft, forthcoming in *German Studies Review*.

Fichter, M. and Kurbjuhn, M. (1993) 'Spurensicherung. Der DGB und seine Gewerkschaften in den neuen Bundesländern 1989–1991', HBS-Manuskripte, 120, Düsseldorf: Hans-Böckler-Stiftung: 1–126.

Fiorito, J. and Greer, C. (1982) 'Determinants of US Unionism: Past Research and Future Needs', *Industrial Relations*, 21: 1–32.

Fiorito, J. and Greer, C. (1986) 'Gender Differences in Union Membership, Preferences, and Beliefs', *Journal of Labor Research*, 7, 2: 145–64.

Fiorito, J., Gallagher, D. G. and Fukami, C. V. (1988) 'Satisfaction with Union Representation', *Industrial and Labor Relations Review*, 41, 2: 294–307.

Fireman, B. and Gamson, W. H. (1979) 'Utilitarian Logic in the Resource Mobilization Perspective', in Zald, M. N. and McCarthy, J. D. (eds) *The Dynamics of Social Movements*, Cambridge, Mass.: Winthrop Publishers, 8–45.

Fishbein, M. (ed.) (1967) *Readings in Attitude Theory and Measurement*, New York, London: Wiley.

Fishbein, M. and Ajzen, I. (1975) *Belief, Attitude, Intention and Behavior*, Reading, Mass.: Addison-Wesley.

Flanagan, R. J., Strauss, G. and Ulman, L. (1974) 'Worker Discontent and Workplace Behaviour', *Industrial Relations*, 13, 2: 101–23.

Förster, H. and Röbenack, S. (1996) 'Wendel Getrieblicher Interessenvertrelungen im Ostdeutschland', KSPW – working paper, Halle.

Fosh, P. (1981) *The Active Trade Unionist: a Study of Motivation and Participation at the Branch Level*, Cambridge: Cambridge University Press.

Freeman, R. (1993) 'What Direction for Labour Market Institutions in Eastern and Central Europe?', discussion paper no 157, Centre for Economic Performance, LSE, London.

Frege, C. M. (1996) 'Workplace Relations in East Germany after Unification: Explaining Worker Participation in Trade Unions and Works Councils', Ph.D. thesis, London: London School of Economics and Political Science.

Frege, C. M. (1997) 'Does Economic Transformation Undermine Union Collectivism? The Case of East German Textile Workers', *Industrial Relations Journal*, 28, 3: 163–75.

Frege, C. M. and Tóth, A. (1999) 'Institutions Matter: the Case of Union Solidarity in Hungary and East Germany', forthcoming in *British Journal of Industrial Relations*.

Friedman, D. (1983) 'Why Workers Strike: Individual Decisions and Structural Constraints', in Hechter, M. (ed.) *The Microfoundations of Macrosociology*, Philadelphia: University Press, ch. 9, 250–83.

Fritze, L. (1993a) *Innenansicht eines Ruins: Gedanken zum Untergang der DDR*, Munich: Olzog Verlag.

Fritze, L. (1993b) 'Kommandowirtschaft: Ein wissenschaftlicher Erlebnisbericht über Machtverhältnisse, Organisationsstrukturen und Funktionsmechanismen im Kombinat', *Leviathan*, 174–204.

Fuchs, D. and Roller, E. (1994) 'Cultural Conditions of the Transition to Liberal Democracy in Central and Eastern Europe', WZB discussion paper FS III-94-202, Berlin: Wissenschaftszentrum Berlin für Sozialforschung.

Fukami, C. V. and Larson, E. W. (1984) 'Commitment to Company and Union: Parallel Models', *Journal of Applied Psychology*, 69, 3: 367–71.

Fullagar, C. (1986) 'A Factor Analytic Study on the Validity of a Union Commitment Scale', *Journal of Applied Psychology*, 71, 1: 129–36.

Fullagar, C. and Barling, J. (1987) 'Toward a Model of Union Commitment', *Advances in Industrial and Labor Relations*, 4: 43–78.

Fullagar, C. and Barling, J. (1989) 'A Longitutional Test of a Model of the Antecedents and Consequences of Union Loyalty', *Journal of Applied Psychology*, 74: 213–27.

Fullagar, C., McCoy, D. and Shull, C. (1992) 'The Socialization of Union Loyalty', *Journal of Organisational Behaviour*, 13: 13–26.

Gabriel, O. (1993) 'Institutionenvertrauen im vereinigten Deutschland', *Aus Politik und Zeitgeschichte*, Beilage zur Wochenzeitung Das Parlament, B43, 3–12.

Gallagher, D. C. and Strauss, G. (1991) 'Union Membership Attitudes and Participation', in Strauss, G., Gallagher, D.G. and Fiorito, J. (eds) *The State of the Unions*, Madison, Wis: Industrial Relations Research Association: ch. 4, 139–74.

Gallagher, D. C., Parks, J. and Wetzel, K. (1987) 'Methodological Considerations in the Measurement of Union Participation: The Issue of a Multi-Dimension Construct', Proceedings of the 19th Annual Meeting of the Decision Sciences Institute, Boston, Mass.: 530–3.

Gallie, D. (1989) 'Trade Union Allegiance and Decline in British Urban Labour Markets', ESRC working paper no. 9.

Gamson, W. A. (1975) *The Strategy of Social Protest*, Homewood, Ill.: Dorsey Press.

Geare, A. J., Herd, J. J. and Howells, J. H. (1979) *Women in Trade Unions: a Case Study of Participation in New Zealand*, Wellington: Victoria University of Wellington.

Gebbert, C. and Gebbert, V. (1993) 'Neuanfang oder Niedergang? Transformationsprobleme der ostdeutschen Bekleidungsindustrie', in Schmidt, R. (ed.) op. cit., 215–29.

Gehlen, A. (1956) *Urmensch und Spätkultur*, Bonn.

Geiger, T. (1949) *Klassengesellschaft im Schmelztiegel*, Cologne.

Gensicke, T. (1992) 'Mentalitätsentwicklungen im Osten Deutschlands seit den 70er Jahren', Speyer Forschungsberichte, no 109, Speyer: Forschungsinstitut für Öffentliche Verwaltung.

Gensicke, T. (1992) 'Wertstrukturen im Osten und Westen Deutschlands', *BISS public*, 8: 45–53.

Gensior, S. (1992) 'Die Bedeutung von Gruppenstrukturen und sozialer Bindung: Frauenerwerbstätigkeit in ostdeutschen Betrieben', in Heidenreich, M. (ed.) op. cit., 273–82.

George, K. D. *et al.* (1977) 'The Size of the Work Unit and Labour Market Behaviour', *British Journal of Industrial Relations*, 15, 2: 265–78.

Geschwender, J. (1964) 'Social Structure and the Negro Revolt: an Examination of Some Hypothses', *Social Forces*, 43: 250–6.

Giesen, B. and Leggewie, C. (1997) 'Sozial wissenschaften vis-à-vis: Die deutsche Vereinigung als sozialer Großversuch', in Giesen, B. and Leggewie, C. (eds) *Experiment Vereinigung*, Berlin:Rotbuch: 7–18.

Gill, U. (1989) *Der Freie Deutsche Gewerkschaftsbund (FDGB)*, Opladen: Westdeutscher Verlag.

Gill, U. (1991) FDGB: *Die DDR-Gewerkschaft von 1945 vis zu ihrer Auflosung 1990*, Cologne: Bund Verlag.

Glaesner, G.-J. (1989) *Die andere deutsche Republik*, Opladen: Westdeutscher Verlag.

Glick, W., Mirvis, P. and Harder, D. (1977) 'Union Satisfaction and Participation', *Industrial Relations*, 16, 2: 145–51.

Glotz, P. and Ladensack, K. (1995) 'Reorganisation des Managements in ausgewählten Unternehmen der NBL', discussion paper, KSPW Kurzstudie, FS I-92-75/1, Halle.

Glotz, P. and Ladensack, K. (1996) 'Personalarbeit und Führungskräfteentwicklung', in Becker, M., Lang, R. and Wagner, D. (eds) op. cit., 229–46.

Göhler, G. (ed.) (1994) *Die Eigenart der Institutionen. Zum Profil politischer Institutionentheorie*, Baden-Baden: Nomos.

Gordon, M. E. and Ladd, R. T. (1990) 'Dual Allegiance: Renewal, Reconsideration, and Recantation', *Personnel Psychology*, 43: 37–69.

Gordon, M. E., Beauvais, L. L. and Ladd, R. T. (1984) 'The Job Satisfaction and Union Commitment of Unionized Engineers', *Industrial and Labour Relations Review*, 37, 359–70.

Gordon, M. E., Philpot, J. W., Burt, R. E., Thompson, C. A. and Spiller, W. E. (1980) 'Commitment to the Union: Development of a Measure and an Examination of Its Correlates', *Journal of Applied Psychology Monograph*, 65, 4: 479–99.

Grabher, G. (1993) 'Rediscovering the Social in the Economics of Interfirm Relations', in Grabher, G. (ed.) *The Embedded Firm: on the Socioeconomics of Industrial Networks*, London: Routledge: 1–33.

Grabher, G. (1995) 'The Elegance of Incoherence: Economic Transformation in East Germany and Hungary', in Dittrich, E. J., Schmidt, G. and Whitley, R. (eds) *Industrial Transformation in Europe*, London: Sage, 33–53.

Graf, H.-W. and Miethe, H. (1990) 'Wechselwirkungen zwischen Produktionskonzeptionen und subjektiven Verhaltenspotentialen der Beschäftigten in der ehemaligen DDR und Konsequenzen für den Transformationsprozeß', unpublished manuscript, Berlin.

Granovetter, M. (1985) 'Economic Action and Social Structure: the Problem of Embeddedness', *American Journal of Sociology*, 91: 481–510.

Grant, D. S. (1992) 'Japanese Manufacturers in the UK Electronics Sector: the Impact of Production Systems on Employee Attitudes and Behaviour', Ph.D. thesis, London: London School of Economics and Political Science.

Guest, D. E. and Dewe, P. (1988) 'Why Do Workers Belong to a Trade Union?: A Social Psychological Study in the UK Electronics Industry', *British Journal of Industrial Relations*, 26, 2: 178–93.

Guest, D. E. and Dewe, P. (1991) 'Company or Trade Union: Which Wins Workers' Allegiance? A Study of Commitment in the UK Electronics Industry', *British Journal of Industrial Relations*, 29, 1: 75–95.

Guest, D., Peccei, R. and Thomas, A. (1993) 'The Impact of Employee Involvement on Organizational Commitment and "Them–Us" Attitudes', *Industrial Relations Journal*, 24, 3: 191–200.

Gurney, J. N. and Tierney, K. T. (1982) 'Relative Deprivation and Social Movements: a Critical Look at Twenty Years of Theory and Research', *Sociological Quarterly*, 23: 33–47.

Gurr, T. (1970) *Why Men Rebel*, Princeton, NJ: Princeton University Press.

Gut, P., Heering, W., Rudolph, J. and Schroeder, K. (1993) 'Normative Regulierung von Arbeit: Zum Wandel betrieblicher Arbeitsbeziehungen in Unternehmen der ehemaligen DDR', apt-paper (1/93), Arbeitsstelle Politik und Technik, Freie Universität Berlin: 1–63.

Hackman, J. R. and Lawler, E. E. (1971) 'Employee Reactions to Job Characteristics', *Journal of Applied Psychology*, 55: 259–86.

Hamner, W. C. and Smith, F. J. (1978) 'Work Atttitudes as Predictors of Unionization Activity', *Journal of Applied Psychology*, 63, August: 415–21.

Handelsblatt, no. 22, issue 2, February 1993.

Haraszti, M. (1974) 'Fragen an eine Brigade', *Kursbuch*, 38: 139–51.

Haraszti, M. (1977) *A Worker in a Workers' State: Piece-rates in Hungary*, Harmondsworth: Penguin.

Hartley, J. (1984) 'Industrial Relations Psychology', in Gruneberg, M. and Wall, T. (eds) *Social Psychology and Organisational Behaviour*, Chichester: Wiley, 149–81.

Hartley, J. (1989) 'Leadership and Decision Making in a Strike Organization', *International Social Movements Research*, 2: 241–65.

Hartley, J., Jacobson, D., Klandermans, B. and van Vuuren, T. (1991) *Job Insecurity: Coping with Jobs at Risk*, London: Sage.

Hartley, J. (1992) 'Joining a Trade Union', in Hartley, J. and Stephenson, G. M. (eds) *Employment Relations: the Psychology of Influence and Control at Work*, Oxford: Blackwell, 163–83.

Heering, W. and Schroeder, K. (1992) 'Hohe Motivation und Verhaltener Optimismus: Ergebnisse einer Befragung von Belegschaften und Geschäftsleitungen ostdeutscher Betriebe', apt-papers (1/92), Arbeitsstelle Politik und Technik, Freie Universität, Berlin.

Heering, W. and Schroeder, K. (1995) 'Vom Arbeitskollektiv zur Sozialpartnerschaft', in Schmidt, R. and Lutz, B. (eds) op. cit., 159–80.

Heidenreich, E. (1991a) 'Thesen zu gewerkschaftlichen Entwicklungspotentialen?', in Friedrich-Ebert Stiftung (ed.) *Industriebetriebe an der Schwelle zur Marktwirtschaft*, Cologne: Bund.

Heidenreich, M. (1991b) 'Plan und Flexibilität. Zur institutionellen Struktur sozialistischen Wirtschaftens', working paper, no. 59, Forschungsschwerpunkt Zukunft der Arbeit, Universität Bielefeld, Fakultät Soziologie.

Heidenreich, M. (1991c) 'Zur Doppelstruktur planwirtschaftlichen Handelns in der DDR', *Zeitschrift für Soziologie*, 20, 6: 411–29.

Heidenreich, M. (ed.) (1992) *Krisen, Kader, Kombinate: Kontinuität und Wandel in ostdeutschen Betrieben*, Bonn: Sigma.

Heidenreich, M. (1993) 'Transformationsprobleme betrieblicher Produkt-, Organisations- und Personalkonzepte in Ostdeutschland', *Cologneer Zeitschrift für Soziologie und Sozialpsychologie*, 45, 1, 76–96.

Heidenreich, M. (1994) 'Industrial Relations in East German Enterprises', paper presented paper at the XII World Congress of Sociology, Bielefeld, 18–23 July.

Heidenreich, M. (1996) 'Betriebliche Sozialordnungen im ostdeutschen Transformationsprozeß', in Schmidt, R. (ed.) 1996b, 141–52.

Heider, F. (1958) *The Psychology of Interpersonal Relations*, New York: Wiley.

Heneman III, H. G. and Sandver, M. H. (1983) 'Predicting the Outcome of Union Certification Elections: a Review of the Literature', *International Labor Relations Review*, 36, 4: 537–59.

Henneberger, F. (1993) 'Transferstart: Organisationsdynamik und Strukturkonservatismus westdeutscher Unternehmerverbände – Aktuelle Entwicklungen unter besonderer Berücksichtigung des Aufbauprozesses in Sachsen und Thüringen', *Politische Vierteljahreszeitschrift*, 34, 4: 640–73.

Henrich, R. (1989) *Der vormundschaftliche Staat*, Reinbeck: Rowohlt.

Hentze, J. and Lindert, K. (1991) *Manager im Vergleich: Daten aus Ostdeutschland und Osteuropa*, Stuttgart: Haupt Verlag.

Hertle, H.-H. (1990) 'Transmissionsriemen ohne Mission. Der FDGB im Umwälzungsprozeß der DDR', discussion paper no. 20, Berliner Arbeitshefte und Berichte zur sozialwissenschaftlichen Forschung, Zentralinstitut für sozialwissenschaftlichen Forschung, Freie Universität Berlin.

Hertle, H.-H. and Weinert, R. (1991) 'Die Auflösung des FDGB und die Auseinandersetzung um sein Vermögen', discussion paper no. 45, Berliner Arbeitshefte und Berichte zur sozialwissenschaftlichen Forschung, Zentralinstitut für sozialwissenschaftlichen Forschung, Freie Universität Berlin.

Héthy, L. (1991) 'Industrial Relations in Eastern Europe: Recent Developments and Trends', in Adams, R. (ed.) *Comparative Industrial Relations*, London: HarperCollins, 124–139.

Héthy, L. (1994) 'Tripartism in Eastern Europe', in Ferner, A. and Hyman, R. (eds) *New Frontiers in European Industrial Relations*, Oxford: Blackwell.

Héthy, L. and Csuhaj, V. I. (1990) *Labour Relations in Hungary*, Budapest: Institute of Labour Research.

Hewstone, M. (1989) *Causal Attribution: From Cognitive Processes to Collective Beliefs*, Oxford: Blackwell.

Hildebrandt, E. (1990) 'Annäherung an einen untergehenden Betrieb', in Blanke, T. and Erd, R. (eds) *DDR – Ein Staat vergeht*, Frankfurt am Main: Fischer, 92–113.

Hill, S. (1974) 'Norms, Groups and Power: The Sociology of Workplace Industrial Relations', *British Journal of Industrial Relations*, 12: 213–35.

Hills, S. (1985) 'The Attitudes of Union and Nonunion Male Workers toward Union Representation', *Industrial and Labor Relations Review*, 38, 2: 179–94.

Hinkle, S. W. and Brown, R. J. (1990) 'Intergroup Comparisons and Social Identity: Some Links and Lacunae', in Abrams, D. and Hogg, M. A. (eds) *Social Identity Theory: Constructive and Critical Advances*, London: Harvester Wheatsheaf, 44–70.

Hirschman, A. (1982) *Shifting Involvements: Private Interest and Public Action*, Princeton, NJ: Princeton University Press.

Hoffmann, R., Kluge, N., Linne, G. and Mezger, E. (eds) (1994) *Problemstart: politischer und sozialer Wandel in den neuen Bundesländern*, Cologne: Bundverlag.

Hoffmann, W., Neumann, U. and Schäfer, W. (1987) 'Entwicklungsbedingungen kollektiver Interessenvertretung im Industriebetrieb unter den Bedingungen klein- und mittelbetrieblicher Verhältnisse', research report, SOFI-Forschungsbericht, Göttingen.

Hofmann, M. and Rink, D. (1993) 'Die Auflösung der ostdeutschen Arbeitermilieus: bewältigungsmuster und Handlungsspielräume ostdeutscher Industriearbeiter im Transformationsprozeß', *Aus Politik und Zeitgeschichte*, Beilage zur Wochenzeitung Das Parlament, B 26-27 (1), 29-36.

Holst, C. (1991) 'Ein Jahr Umfragen in den Neuen Bundesländern: Themen und Tendenzen', WZB discussion paper P 91-102, Berlin: Wissenschaftszentrum Berlin für Sozialforschung.

Housner, J. Jessop, B. and Nielsen, K. (eds) *Strategic Choice and Path-Dependency in Post-Socialism*, Aldershot: Edward Elgar.

Howson, C. and Urbach, P. (1990) *Scientific Reasoning: the Bayesian Approach*, LaSalle: Open Court.

Hürtgen, R. (1992) 'Der Wandel regionaler Organisationsstrukturen soziopolitischer Interessenvermittlung im Raum Frankfurt/Oder. Teil 2: Gewerkschaften und Betriebsräte in Frankfurt/Oder', report for the KSPW (Kommission für die Erforschung des sozialen und politischen Wandels in den neuen Bundesländern), Halle.

Huszczo, G. E. (1983) 'Attitudinal and Behavioural Variables Related to Participation in Union Activities', *Journal of Labour Research*, 4: 289–97.

Hyman, R. (1996) 'Institutional Transfer: Industrial Relations in Eastern Germany', *Work, Employment and Society* 10, 2: 601–39.

Ingham, G. K. (1970) 'Size of Industrial Organisation and Worker Behaviour', *Cambridge Papers in Sociology*, no. 1, Cambridge: Cambridge University Press.

Ingham, G. K. (1974) *Strikes and Industrial Conflict*, London: Macmillan.

ISDA (1992), Umfrage.

IWH (1994) Institut für Wirtschaftsforschung in Halle, Herbstgutachten.

Jacoby, W. (1994) 'Industrial Relations in Eastern Germany: the Politics of Imitation', paper presented at the American Political Science Association Annual Meeting, New York, September 1994.

Jacoby, W. (1995) 'Dissertation Chapter Outline' of 'The Politics of Institutional Transfer: Two Postwar Reconstructions in Germany, 1945–1995', Ph.D. thesis, Boston: MIT, 1996.

Jander, M. and Lutz, S. (1991a) 'Betriebsräte in der ehemaligen DDR – eine vernachlässigte Institution', discussion paper, no 66, Berliner Arbeitshefte und Berichte zur sozialwissenschftliche Forschung, Zentralinstitut für sozialwissen-schafltiche Forschung, Freie Universität Berlin.

Jander, M. and Lutz, S. (1991b) 'Betriebsräte ratlos?! Erste Einschätzungen zu betrieblichen Interessenvertretern der Arbeitnehmer in Ostberliner Betrieben', in Meyer, H. (ed.) *Soziologen-Tag Leipzig: Soziologie in Deutschland und die Transformation großer gesellschaftlicher Systeme*, Berlin: Akademie Verlag, 406–23.

Jander, M. and Lutz, S. (1992) 'Die Grünolung des Betrübsrotes war eigentlich ein Mißverständnis', *Berliner Arbeitschefte und Berichte, 77*.

Jander, M. and Lutz, S. (1993a) 'Vor einer krisenhaften Veränderung der industriellen Beziehungen in der Bundesrepublik Deutschland?', unpublished manuscript, Zentralinstitut für sozialwissenschaftliche Forschung, Freie Universität Berlin.

Jander, M. and Lutz, S. (1993b) 'Ostdeutsche "Betriebsräteinitiative" vor dem Ende?', *links*, 7/8: 5–7.

Jander, M. and Voß, T. (1991) 'Mangel an Perspektiven: Die bundesdeutschen Gewerkschaften im Vereinigungsprozeß', in Gatzmaga, D.. Voß, T. and Westermann, K. (eds) *Auferstehen aus den Ruinen, Arbeitswelt und Gewerkschaft in der früheren DDR*, Marburg: Schüren, 147–55.

Jander, M., Kädtler, J., Kottwitz, G. and Lutz, S. (1992) 'Überforderung oder Chance? Betriebsräte in der "Zwickmühle" zwischen betrieblicher Modernisierung und sozialer Interessenvertretung', unpublished manuscript, Halle: WISOC.

Jenkins, J. C. (1983) 'Resource Mobilization Theory and the Study of Social Movements', *Annual Review Sociology*, 9: 527–53.

Jürgens, U. Klinzing, L. and Turner, L. (1993) 'The Transformation of Industrial Relations in Eastern Germany', *Industrial and Labor Relations Review*, 46, 2: 229–44.

Kädtler, J. (1991a) 'Probleme bei der Analyse real noch nicht existierender industrieller Beziehungen in der ehemaligen DDR', unpublished manuscript, Universität Göttingen.

Kädtler, J. (1991b) 'Betriebliche Interessenvertretung im Umbruch – Anmerkungen zu Möglichkeiten und Grenzen der empirischen Analyse noch nicht existierender industrielle Beziehungen', in Meyer, H. (ed.) *Soziologen-Tag Leipzig: Soziologie in Deutschland und die Transformation großer gesellschaftlicher Systeme*, Berlin: Akademie Verlag, 412–23.

Kädtler, J. (1993) 'Arbeitnehmerinteressenvertretung durch Marktwirtschaft – oder: Kommt der Interessengegensatz in die Betriebe zurück?', in report of the DFG Schwerpunkt "Strukturwandel industrieller Beziehungen" workshop, Berlin, June 1993: 1–13.

Kädtler, J. and Kottwitz, G. (1990) 'Betriebsräte zwischen Wende und Ende in der DDR', discussion paper, no. 42, Berliner Arbeitshefte und Berichte, Zentralinstitut für sozialwissenschaftliche Forschung, Freie Universität Berlin.

Kädtler, J. and Kottwitz, G. (1991) 'Betriebsräte zwischen Wende und Ende in der DDR', in Gatzmaga, D. Voß, T. and Westermann, K. (eds) *Auferstehen aus den Ruinen, Arbeitswelt und Gewerkschaft in der früheren DDR*, Marburg: Schüren.

Kädtler, J. and Kottwitz, G. (1992) 'Wie kommt der Interessengegensatz in den Betrieb zurück? Entwicklungsprobleme der betrieblichen Arbeitnehmerinteressenvertretung in Ostdeutschland', unpublished lecture manuscript, Universität Göttingen.

Kädtler, J. and Kottwitz, G. (1994) 'Industrielle Beziehungen in Ostdeutschland: Durch Kooperation zum Gegensatz von Kapital und Arbeit?', *Industrielle Beziehungen*, 1, 1: 13–38.

Kädtler, J., Kottwitz, G. and Weinert, R. (1997) *Betriebsräte in Ostdeutschland: Institutionenbildung und Handlungskonstellationen 1989–1994*, Opladen:Westdeutscher Verlag.

Kelley, H. H. and Michela, J. L. (1980) 'Attribution Theory and Research', *Annual Review of Psychology*, 31: 457–503.

Kelloway, E. K., Catano, V. M. and Southwell, R. R. (1992) 'The Construct Validity of Union Commitment: Development and Dimensionality of a Shorter Scale', *Journal of Occupational and Organizational Psychology*, 65: 197–211.

Kelly, C. (1993) 'Group Identification, Intergroup Perceptions and Collective Action', *European Review of Social Psychology*, 4: 59–83.

Kelly, C. and Kelly, J. (1994) 'Who Gets Involved in Collective Action? Social Psychological Determinants of Individual Participation in Trade Unions', *Human Relations*, 47, 1: 63–88 (quoted pages in text refer to the draft version).

Kelly, J. (1996a) *Rethinking Industrial Relations: Mobilization, Collectivism and Long Waves*, manuscript, subsequently published 1998, London: Routledge.

Kelly, J. (1996b) 'Does the Field of Industrial Relations Have a Future?', unpublished manuscript, Industrial Relations Department, London School of Economics.

Kelly, J. and Kelly, C. (1991) ' "Them and Us": Social Psychology and "The New Industrial Relations" ', *British Journal of Industrial Relations*, 29, 1: 25–44.

Kelly, J. and Kelly, C. (1992) 'Industrial Action', in Hartley, J. and Stevenson, G. M. (eds) *Employment Relations: the Psychology of Influence and Control at Work*, Cambridge, Mass.: Basil Blackwell.

Kelly, J. and Kelly, C. (1993) 'Union Participation: the Roles of Value Expectancy and Social Identity', unpublished manuscript, Industrial Relations Department, London School of Economics.

Kelly, J. and Nicholson, N. (1980) 'The Causation of Strikes: a Review of Theoretical Approaches and the Potential Contribution of Social Psychology', *Human Relations*, 33, 12: 853–83.

Kempe, M. (1995) 'Ueckermünde fast ent industrielisiert', *Die Mitgestimmung*, 10: 9.

Kern, H. and Land, R. (1991) 'Der "Wasserkopf" oben und die "Taugenichtse" unten. Zur Mentalität von Arbeitern und Arbeiterinnen in der ehemaligen DDR', *Frankfurter Rundschau*, 13 February 1991: 16–17.

Kern, H. and Schumann, M. (1985) *Industriearbeit und Arbeitsbewußtsein*, Frankfurt am Main: Suhrkamp.

Kern, H. and Voskamp, U. (1994) 'Bocksprungstrategie – Überholende Mdernisierung zur Sicherung ostdeutscher Industriestandorte', discussion paper, Göttingen: SOFI Mitteilungen, 21: 98–138.

Kirschner, L. (1991) 'Betriebliche Mitbestimmung und Interessenwahrnehmung im Osten Deutschlands – eine rechtssoziologische Interpretation der gegenwärtigen Transformations-prozesse', in Meyer, H. (ed.) *Soziologen-Tag Leipzig: Soziologie in Deutschland und die Transformation großer gesellschaftlicher Systeme*, Berlin: Akademie Verlag, 1033–42.

Kirschner, L. (1992) 'Transformation von Interessenwahrnehmung und Mitbestimmung – Fallstudien aus Unternehmen und Betrieben der neuen Bundesländer', research report (3/2) for KPSW (Kommission für die Erforschung des politischen und sozialen Wandels in den neuen Bundesländern), Halle.

Kittner, M. (ed.) (1993) *Gewerkschaftsjahrbuch 1993*, Cologne: Bund.

Kittner, M. (ed.) (1994) *Gewerkschaften heute 1994*, Cologne: Bund.

Kittner, M. (ed.) (1995) *Gewerkschaften heute 1995*, Cologne: Bund.

Klandermans, B. (1984a) 'Mobilization and Participation in Trade Union Action: an Expectancy–Value Approach', *Journal of Occupational Psychology*, 57: 107–20.

Klandermans, B. (1984b) 'Mobilization and Participation: Social-Psychological Expansions of Resource Mobilization Theory', *American Sociological Review*, 49: 583–600.

Klandermans, B. (1986a) 'Perceived Costs and Benefits of Participation in Union Action', *Personnel Psychology*, 39: 379–97.

Klandermans, B. (1986b) 'Psychology and Trade Union Participation: Joining, Acting, Quitting', *Journal of Occupational Psychology*, 59: 189–204.

Klandermans, B. (1988) 'The Formation and Mobilization of Consensus', in Klandermans, B., Kriesi, H. and Tarrow, S. (eds) *From Structure to Action: Comparing Movement Participation across Cultures*, Greenwich, Conn. JAI Press.

Klandermans, B. (1989) 'Union Commitment: Replications and Tests in the Dutch Context', *Journal of Applied Psychology*, 74, 6: 869–75.

Klandermans, B. (1992) 'Trade Union Participation', in Hartley, J. and Stephenson, G. M. (eds) *Employment Relations: the Psychology of Influence and Control at Work*, London: Blackwell, 184–99.

Klandermans, B. (1995) 'Ideology and the Social Psychology of Union Participation', unpublished manuscript (chapter of an Anthology on Ideology and Labour Unions), Free University of Amsterdam, Dept. of Social Psychology.

Klandermans, B., van Vuuren, T. and Jacobson, D. (1991) 'Employees and Job Insecurity', in Hartley, J. Jacobson, D., Klandermans, B. and van Vuuren, T. (eds), op. cit., 40–64.

Klinzing, L. (1992) 'Zwischen Anpassung und Öffnung – Gewerkschaftsstrukturen im beigetretenen Teil Deutschlands', report, KSPW Kurzstudie, 7/1, Kommission für die Erforschung des politischen und sozialen Wandels in den neuen Bundesländern, Halle.

Knowles, K. J. (1952) *Strikes – a Study in Industrial Conflict*, Monograph, University of Oxford, Institute of Economics and Statistics, no. 3, Oxford: Basil Blackwell.

Koch, T. (1993) '"Selbst-Unternehmertum" und "Aufschwung Ost"', *Politik und Zeitgeschichte*, Beilage zur Wochenzeitung Das Parlament, B24: 37–45.

Koch, T. (1997) 'Ostdeutsche Identitätsbildungen in der dualistischen Gesellschaft: Fokus – Phänomenologie – Forschungsfragen', *Berliner Debatte Initial*, 8, 3: 93–108.

Kochan, T. A. (1979) 'How American Workers View Labor Unions', *Monthly Labor Review*, 102, April: 23–31.

Kochan, T. A. (1980) *Collective Bargaining and Industrial Relations*, Homewood, Ill.: R. D. Irwin.

Köhler, T. (1995) 'Erhebung zur Arbeitsmarktsituation, zur Berufsbiographie und Karriere mobilität von Menagon und Führungskräften', KSPW–working paper, Halle.

Kolchin, M. G. and Hyclak, T. (1984) 'Participation in Union Activites: a Multi-variate Analysis', *Journal of Labor Research*, 5: 255–62.

Kollmorgen, R. (1996) 'Schöne Aussichten? Eine Kritik integrativer Transformationstheorien', in Kollmorgen, R., Reißig, R. and Weiß, J. (eds) op. cit., 281–332.

Kollmorgen, R., Reißig, R. and Weiß, J. (eds) (1996) *Sozialer Wandel und Akteure in Ostdeutschland*, Opladen: Leske & Buderich.

Kornai, J. (1986) *Contradictions and Dilemmas*, Cambridge, MA.: MIT Press.

Kotthoff, H. (1981) *Betriebsräte und betriebliche Herrschaft*, Frankfurt am Main: Campus.

Kotthoff, H. (1994) *Betriebsräte und Bürgerstatus*, Mering: Rainer Haampp Verlag.

Kottwitz, G. (1991) 'Betriebsratsgründungen in Leipzig und Dresden', in Meyer, H. (ed.) *Soziologen-Tag Leipzig: Soziologie in Deutschland und die Transformation großer gesellschaftlicher Systeme*, Berlin: Akademie Verlag, 417–23.

Kreißig, V. (1990) 'Gewerkschaftliche Organisationsprobleme und Mitbestimmungsentwicklung in den ostdeutschen Bundesländern – empirische befunde und erste theoretische Verallgemeinerungen', working paper, Chemnitz: WISOC.

Kreißig, V. (1992) '"Realsozialistische" betriebliche Machtstrukturen und Industrielle Beziehungen im Transformationsprozeß zur Marktwirtschaft', working paper, Chemnitz: WISOC.

Kreißig, V. (1993) '"Realsozialistische" betriebliche Machtstrukturen und industrielle Beziehungen im Transformationsprozeß zur Marktwirtschaft', in Schmidt, R. (ed.) op. cit., 109–30.

Kreißig, V. and Preusche, E. (1994) 'Industrial Relations in the Process of Transformation from Planned to Market Economy in East Germany', paper presented at the IIRA, 4th European Congress, Helsinki, September.

Krieger, H., Liepelt, K., Schneider, R. and Schmid, M. (1989) *Arbeitsmarktkrise und Arbeitnehmerbewußtsein*, Frankfurt am Main/New York: Campus.

Küchle, H. and Volkmann, G. (1993) 'Sanierungsverläufe ostdeutscher Textilunternehmen', project report, no. 92-369-2, Düsseldorf: Hans-Böckler-Stiftung.

Kuhn, J. W. (1961) *Bargaining in Grievance Settlement: the Power of Industrial Work Groups*, New York: Columbia University Press.

Kurbjuhn, M. and Fichter, M. (1993) 'Auch im Osten brauchen die Gewerkschaften Gestaltungskompetenz', *Gewerkschaftliche Monatshefte*, 1: 36–45.

Kuruvilla, S., Gallagher, D. G., Fiorito, J. and Wakabayashi, M. (1990) 'Union Participation in Japan: Do Western Theories Apply?', *Industrial and Labor Relations Review*, 43, 4: 374–89.

Lang, R. (1992) 'Sozialisation und Wertorientierungen ostdeutscher Führungskräfte', in Heidenreich, M. (ed.) op. cit., 125–42.

Lang, R. (1994) 'Führungskräfte in Ostdeutschland', project report, SOKULT 92, Arbeitspapier 03, Technische Universität Chemnitz-Zwickau, Lehrstuhl für Organisation und Arbeitswissenschaft.

Lange, H. (1992) 'Loyalitätsarbeit und Ersatzarbeit. Realsozialistische Verformungen beruflicher Standards', in Senghaas-Knobloch, E. and Lange, H. (eds) op. cit., 102–20.

Lawrence, E. (1994) *Gender and Trade Unions*, London: Taylor and Francis.

Lecher, W. (1990) 'Gewerkschaften in Deutschland: Ost–West-Zukunft', *WSI Mitteilungen*, 5: 320–27.

Lehmbruch, G. (1993) 'Der Staat des vereinigten Deutschland und die Transformations-dynamik der Schnittstellen von Staat und Wirtschaft in der ehemaligen DDR', *BISS public*, 10: 21–41.

Lehmbruch, G. (1996) 'Die ostdeutsche Transformation als Strategie des Institutionentransfers: Überprüfung und Antikritik', in Eisen, A. and Wollmann, H. (eds) 1996a, 63–78.

Liebold, R. (1996) 'Innerbetriebliche Beziehungen in ostdeutschen Industriebetrieben: Die (ost)deutsche Einheit zwischen Management und Betriebsrat', in Bergmann, J. and Schmidt, R. (eds) op. cit., 213–36.

Lind, J. (1996) 'Trade Unions: Social Movement or Welfare Apparatus?', in Leisink, P., van Leemput, J. and Vilrokx, J. (eds) *The Challenges to Trade Unions in Europe: Innovation or Adaptation*, Cheltenham: Edward Elgar, 105–22.

Lippold, S., Lohr, K., Neudel, J. and Schmidt, E. (1992) 'Anpassung oder Modifikation industrieller Beziehungen im Transformationsprozeß', final report, KSPW Halle and Humboldt Universität Berlin, Institut für Soziologie.

Lipset, S. M., Trow, M. A. and Coleman, J. S. (1956) *Union Democracy: the Internal Politics of the International Typographical Union*, Glencoe, Ill.: Free Press.

Lohr, K. (1992) 'Management und Belegschaft im wirtschaftlichen Wandel: Brüche und Kontinuitäten', in Heidenriech, M. (ed.) op. cit., 159–71.

Luhmann, N. (1987) *Soziale Aufklärung* (4th edn) Opladen: Westdeutscher Verlag.

Luhmann, N. (1989) *Die Wirtschaft der Gesellschaft*, Frankfurt am Main: Suhrkamp.

Lungwitz, R. E. (1994) 'Transformation als subjektive Realität – Alltagsvorstellungen von Produktionsarbeitern der ostdeutschen Automobilindustrie', in Bieszcz-Kaiser, B., Lungwitz, R.-E. and Preusche, E. (eds) *Transformation, Privatisierung, Akteure*, Munich and Mering: Rainer Hampp Verlag, 297–309.

Lungwitz, R. E. and Preusche, E. (1994) 'Mängelwesen und Diktator? Ostdeutsche Industriemanager als Akteure betrieblicher Transformationsprozesse', *Industrielle Beziehungen*, 1, 1: 219–38.

Lungwitz, R. E. and Preusche, E. (1996) 'Betriebliche Interessenvertretung und die Konstitutierung von Gemeinschaftlichkeit – Situationsdeutungen und Handlungsorientierungen ostdeutscher Betriebsräte', in Becker, M. *et al.* (eds) op. cit., 121–38.

Lutz, B. and Grünert, H. (1996) 'Der Zerfall der Beschäftigungsstrukturen der DDR 1989–1993', in Lutz, B., Nickel, H. M., Schmidt, R. and Sorge, A. (eds) op. cit., 69–117.

Lutz, B., Nickel, H. M., Schmidt, R. and Sorge, A. (eds) (1996) *Arbeit, Arbeitsmarkt und Betriebe*, Opladen: Leske & Buderich.

Lutz, S. (1991) 'Probleme der Interessenvertretung der Arbeitnehmer bei der Übernahme des westdeutschen Modells der Arbeitsbeziehungen in der DDR, untersucht auf der Betriebsebene', M.Sc. thesis (*Diplomarbeit*), Freie Universität Berlin.

Maaz, H.-J. (1991) *Das gestürzte Volk: die unglückliche Einheit*, Berlin: Argon Verlag.

McAdam, D. (1986) 'Recruitment to High-Risk Activism: the Case of Freedom Summer', *American Journal of Sociology*, 92: 64–90.

McAdam, D. (1988) 'Micromobilization Contexts and Recruitment to Activism', *International Social Movements Research*, 1: 125–54.

McAdam, D., McCarthy, J. D. and Zald, M. N. (1988) 'Social Movements', in Smelser, N. J. (ed.) *Handbook of Sociology*, London, 695–739.

McPhail, C. (1971) 'Civil Disorder Participation: a Critical Examination of Recent Research', *American Sociological Review*, 36: 1058–73.

McShane, S. L. (1986) 'The Multidimensionality of Union Participation', *Journal of Occupational Psychology*, 59: 177–87.

Mahnkopf, B. (1991) 'Vorwärts in die Vergangenheit? Pessimistische Spekulationen über die Zukunft der Gewerkschaften in der neuen Bundesrepublik', in Westphal, A. *et al.* (eds) *Wirtschaftspolitische Konsequenzen der deutschen Vereinigung*, Frankfurt/New York: Campus.

Mahnkopf, B. (1992) 'Die Gewerkschaften im West-Ost-Spagat', *Forschungsjournal NSB*, 3: 33–42.

Mahnkopf, B. (1993) 'The Impact of Unification on the German System of Industrial Relations', WZB discussion paper, no. FS I 93-102, Berlin: Wissenschaftszentrum Berlin für Sozialforschung.

Makó, C. and Simonyi, A. (1987) 'Can Taylorism be applied in Hungary?', in Braczyk, H.-J., Schmidt, G. and Tacke, V. (eds) *The Present Situation and Problems of Applied Industrial Sociology in the Countries of Eastern Europe and in the Federaal Republic of Germany*, Bielefeld: ASIF Forschungsberichte, 105–19.

Martens, H. (1992) 'Gewerkschaftlicher Organisationsaufbau und Mitbestimmung in Ostdeutschland – De-Modernisierung oder Modernisierungsimpulse?', *Arbeit*, 1, 4: 368–86.

Martens, H. (1994) 'Gewerkschaftlicher Organisationsaufbau und Mitbestimmung in Ost-deutschland – 17 Thesen', in Hoffmann, R. *et al.* (eds) op. cit., 311–30.

Martens, H. (1996) 'Zur Institutionalisierung von Mitbestimmung in Ostdeutschland im Kontext der Modernisierung der industriellen Beziehungen in der Bundesrepublik Deutschland', in Kollmorgen, R. *et al.* (eds) op. cit., 165–79.

Martin, J. E. (1986) 'Predictors of Individual Propensity to Strike', *Industrial and Labor Relations Review*, 39, 2: 214–27.

Marz, L. (1992a) 'Beziehungsarbeit und Mentalität', in Senghaas-Knobloch, E. and Lange, H. (eds) op. cit., 75–90.

Marz, L. (1992b) 'Geständnisse und Erkenntnisse – Zum Quellenproblem empirischer Tranformationsforschung', in Heidenreich, M. (ed.) op. cit., 215–38.

Marz, L. (1993a) 'Dispositionskosten des Transformationsprozesses', *Politik und Zeitgeschichte*, Beilage zur Wochenzeitung Das Parlament, 24, 3–10.

Marz, L. (1993b) 'System-Zeit und Entökonomisierung. Zu Zeit/Macht-Dispositiven und mentalen Dispositionen in realsozialistischen Wirtschaften', in Schmidt, R. (ed.) op. cit., 73–108.

Matthäi, I. (1996) 'Die neuen Unternehmer in Ostdeutschland – Träger eines neuen Mittelstandes? Orientierungen des Managements beim Auf- und Umbau innerbetrieblicher Strukturen', in Pohlmann, M. and Schmidt, R. (eds) op. cit., 137–76.

Matthies, H., Mückenberger, U., Offe, C., Peter, E. and Raasch, S. (1994) *Arbeit 2000*, Reinbeck: Rowohlt.

Mayntz, R. (1994) 'Die deutsche Vereinigung als Prüfstein für die Leistungsfähigkeit der Sozialwissenschaften', *BISS public*, 4, 13: 21–4.

Melich, J. S. (1997) 'The Post-Communist Mind: Socio-Psychological and Cultural Aspects of the Communist Legacy and the Transformation Processes in Eastern Europe', in Sevic, Z. and Wright, G. (eds) *Transition in Central Eastern Europe*, Belgrade: Yugoslav Association of Sasakawa Fellows, 20–41.

Mense-Petermann, U. (1996) 'Die Vertrieblichung der industriellen Beziehungen in Ostdeutschland', *Industrielle Beziehungen*, 3, 1: 65–79.

Merkel, W. (1995) 'Theorien der Transformation: Die demokratische Konsolidierung postautoritärer Gesellschaften', in von Beyme, K. and Offe, C. (eds) *Politische Theorien in der Ära der Transformation*, Opladen: Westdeutscher Verlag.

Mickler, O., Engelhard, N., Lungwitz, R. and Walker, B. (1992) 'Ein Aufstieg wie Phönix aus der Asche? Nach Abriß nun Wiederaufbau der ostdeutschen Automobilindustrie. Die Betriebsräte im Konflikt zwischen Schutzinteressen un Modernisierungspartnerschaft', unpublished manuscript, Universität Hannover.

Mickler, O., Engelhard, N., Lungwitz, R. and Walker, B. (1996) *Nach der Trabi-Ära: Arbeiten in schlanken Fabriken*, Berlin: Edition Sigma.

Miethe, H. *et al.* (1989) 'Probleme der Erhöhung der sozialen Wirksamkeit der komplexen Automatisierung im Rahmen umfassender Intensivierung', research report, Akademie der Wissenschaften der DDR, Institut für Soziologie und Sozialpolitik, Ost-Berlin.

Mishler, W. and Rose, R. (1997) 'Trust, Distrust and Scepticism: Popular Evaluations of Civil and Political Institutions in Post-Communist Societies', *The Journal of Politics*, 59, 2: 418–51.

Morgenroth, C., Niemeyer, E. and Hollmann, R. (1994) *Realistische Utopien: Beteiligungsgewerkschaft als Zukunftsperspektive*, Cologne: Bund Verlag.

Mowday, R. T., Porter, L. W. and Steers, R. M. (1982) *Employee–Organization Linkages: the Psychology of Commitment, Absenteeism, and Turnover*, New York: Academic Press.

Müller-Jentsch, W. (1994) 'Germany: from Collective Voice to Co-management', in Rogers, J. and Streeck, W. (eds) *Works Councils: Consultation, Representation and Cooperation in Industrial Relations*, Chicago: University of Chicago Press, 97–152.

Neier, A. (1991) 'Die Revolution entläst ihre Theoretiker', in Giesen, B. and Leggewie, C. (eds) *Experiment Vereinigung*, Berlin: Rotbuch: 28–37.

Neubauer, R. (1992) 'Warnsignale von der Basis', *Die Zeit*, 26 July.

Newton, L. A. and McFarlane Shore, L. (1992) 'A Model of Union Membership: Instrumentality, Commitment, and Opposition', *Academy of Management Review*, 17, 2: 275–98.

Nicholson, N., Ursell, G. and Blyton, P. (1981) *The Dynamics of White Collar Unionism: a Study of Local Union Participation*, London: Academic Press.

Nickel, W. (1972) *Zum Verhältnis von Arbeiterschaft und Gewerkschaft. Eine soziologische Untersuchung über die qualitative Struktur der Mitglieder und des Mitgliederpotentials der Gewerkschaften in der Bundesrepublik*, Cologne: Bund Verlag.

Niebur, J. (1992) 'Zwischen Stillegung und Privatisierung – Die Sanierung eines Stahlstandorts', in Heidenreich, M. (ed.) op. cit., 95–108.

Nolte, D. and Sitte, R. (1995) 'Ostdeutschland als Dependenzökonomie – einige Bermerkungen zur Qualität des Wachstums in den neuen Bundesländern', *WSI Mitteilungen*, 48, 5: 300–7.

Oberschall, A. (1973) *Social Conflict and Social Movements*, Englewood Cliffs, NJ: Prentice-Hall.

Offe, C. (1994) *Der Tunnel am Ende des Lichts: Erkundungen der politischen Transformation im Neuen Osten*, Frankfurt am Main: Campus.

Offe, C. (1995) 'Designing Institutions for East European Transitions', in Hausner, J., Jessop, B. and Nielsen, K. (eds) *Strategic Choice and Path Dependency in Post-Socialism*, Aldershot: Edward Elgar.

Oliver, P. (1984) 'If You Don't Do It, Nobody Will. Action and Token Contributors to Local Collective Action', *A Sociological Review*, 49: 601–10.

Olson, J. M., Herman, C. P. and Zanna, M. P. (eds) (1986) *Relative Deprivation and Social Comparison*, Hillsdale, NJ.

Olson, M. (1971) *The Logic of Collective Action*, Cambridge, Mass.: Harvard University Press.

Ost, D. and Weinstein, M. (forthcoming) 'Unionists against Unions: towards Hierarchical Management in Postcommunist Poland', *East European Politics and Societies*.

Paul Lazarfeld Society (1994), New Democratic Barometer, Vienna.

Parkin, F. (1967) 'Working-class Conservatives: a Theory of Political Deviance', *British Journal of Sociology*, 18: 278–90.

Peiperl, M. and Estrin, S. (1998) 'Managerial Markets in Transition in Central and Eastern Europe: a Field Study and Implications', *The Internationaal Journal of Human Resource Management*, 9, 1: 58–77.

Perline, M. M. and Lorenz, V. R. (1970) 'Factors Influencing Member Participation in Trade Union Activities', *American Journal of Economics and Sociology*, 29: 425–37.

Pirker, T., Hertle, H. H., Kädtler, J. and Weinert, R. (1990a) *FDGB – Wende zum Ende*, Cologne: Bund Verlag.

Pirker, T. *et al.* (1990b) *Wende zum Ende: Auf dem Weg zu unabhängigen Gewerkschaften*, Cologne: Bund Verlag.

Pohlmann, M. and Gergs, H. J. (1996) 'Manageriale Eliten im Transformationsprozeß', in Pohlmann, M. and Schmidt, R. (eds) op. cit., 63–136.

Pohlmann, M. and Schmidt, R. (eds) (1996) Management inder Ostdeutschen Industrie, Opladen: Leske und Buderich.

Pohlmann, M. and Schmidt, R. (1996) 'Management in Ostdeutschland und die Gestaltung des wirtschaftlichen und sozialen Wandels', in Lutz, B., Nickel, H. M., Schmidt, R. and Sorge, A. (eds) *Arbeit, Arbeitsmarkt und Betriebe*, Opladen: Leske & Buderich, 191–225.

Polanyi, K. (1978) *The Great Transformation*, Frankfurt am Main: Suhrkamp.

Pollack, D. (1991) 'Sozialstruktur und Mentalität in Ostdeutschland', in Meyer, H. (ed.) *Soziologen-Tag Leipzig: Soziologie in Deutschland und die Transformation großer gesellschaftlicher Systeme*, Berlin: Akademie Verlag, 272–85.

Popitz, H. et. al. (1957) *Das Gesellschaftsbild des Arbeiters*, Tübingen.

Prais, S. J. (1977) 'The Strike Proneness of Large Plants in Britain', discussion paper (no. 5), National Institute for Economic and Social Research.

Premack, S. L. and Hunter, J. E. (1988) 'Individual Unionization Decisions', *Psychological Bulletin*, 103, 2: 223–34.

Preusche, E. (1994) 'Ostdeutsches Management im betrieblichen Transformationsprozeß – empirische Befunde', in Bieszcz-Kaiser, A., Lungwitz, R.-E. and Preusche, E. (eds) *Transformation, Privatisierung, Akteure*, Munich and Mering: Rainer Hampp Verlag, 253–96.

Promberger, M. (1991) 'Strukturen und Prozesse in der betrieblichen Interessenvertretung. Eine Fallstudie', discussion paper, Institut für praxisorientierte Sozialforschung und Beratung, Erlangen.

Prott, J. (1993) 'Beweggründe für den Austritt aus der Gewerkschaft HBV in Hamburg', report, Hamburg: Gewerkschaft HBV.

Purcell, K. (1979) 'Militancy and Acquiescence amongst Women Workers', in Burman, S. (ed.) *Fit Work for Women*, London: Croom Helm, 112–33.

Purcell, T. V. (1953) *The Worker Speaks his Mind on Company and Union*, Cambridge, Mass.

Rasche, E. (1993) 'Der Verband der Nord-Ostdeutschen Textilindustrie e.V.', in Bieszcz-Kaiser, A., Preusche, E. and Raasche, E. (eds) *Regionale Akteure im Transformationsprozeß*, WISOC bulletin, no. 21/1993, Chemnitz: WISOC.

Reißig, R. (1993) 'Paradigmenwechsel im ostdeutschen Transformations- und deutschen Integrationsprozeß', *BISS public*, 10: 5–20.

Reißig, R. (1996) 'Perspektivenwechsel in der Transformationsforschung', in Kollmorgen, R., Reißig, R. and Weiß, J. (eds) op. cit., 245–62.

Revans, F. W. (1956) 'Industrial Morale and Size of Unit', *Political Quarterly*, 27, 303–11.

Richardson, R. and Catlin, S. (1979) 'Trade Union Density and Collective Agreement Patterns in Britain', *British Journal of Industrial Relations*, 17: 376–85.

Röbenack, S. (1992) 'Institutionalisierung industrieller Beziehungen im betrieblichen Umstrukturierungsprozeß in Ostdeutschland, in Eichener, V. *et al.* (eds) *Organisierte Interessen in Ostdeutschland*, Marburg: Metropolis, 195–210.

Röbenack, S. (1996) 'Betriebe und Belegschaftsvertretungen', in Bergmann, J. and Schmidt, R. (eds) op. cit., 161–212.

Rokeach, M. (1969) *Beliefs, Attitudes, and Values*, San Francisco: Jossey-Bass.

Roller, E. (1992) 'Ideological Basis of the Market Economy: Attitudes toward Distribution Principles and the Role of Government in Western and Eastern Germany', WZB discussion paper FS III 92-206, Berlin: Wissenschaftszentrum Berlin für Sozialforschung.

Rose, R., Zapf, W., Seifert, W. and Page, E. (1993) 'Germans in Comparative Perspective', *Studies in Public Policy*, no. 218, University of Strathclyde.

Rosenbaum, W. and Weinert, R. (1991) 'Entstehung und Entwicklung von Betreibsräten in Betrieben der ehemaligen DDR', project proposal for the DFG, Universität Göttingen/Freie Universität Berlin.

Röske, V. and Wassermann, W. (1991) 'Mitbestimmung im Osten – eine Aufbaupartnerschaft', *Die Mitbestimmung*, 2: 142–44.

Ross, A. M. and Hartman, P. T. (1960) *Changing Patterns of Industrial Conflict*, New York, London: Wiley.

Rottenburg, R. (1991) '"Der Sozialismus braucht den ganzen Menschen" Zum Verhältnis vertraglicher und nichtvertraglicher Beziehungen in einem VEB', *Zeitschrift für Soziologie*, 20, 4: 305–22.

Rottenburg, R. (1992) 'Welches Licht wirft die volkseigene Erfahrung der Werktätigkeit auf westliche Unternehmen?', in Heidenreich, M. (ed.) op. cit., 239–72.

Ruppert, B. (1994) 'Wandel betrieblicher Interessenvertretung in einem ostdeutschen Betrieb', in Hoffmann, R., Kluge, N., Linne, G. and Mezger, E. (eds) *Problemstart: politischer und sozialer Wandel in den neuen Bundesländern*, Cologne: Bund, 281–310.

Sayles, L. (1958) *Behavior of Industrial Work Groups: Prediction and Control*, New York: Wiley, Chapman & Hall.

Sayles, L. R. and Strauss, G. (1953) *The Local Union*, Chicago: Harcourt, Brace and World.

Schelsky, H. (1952) 'Über dü Stobilität von Institutionen', *Jahrbuch für Sozielwissenschaften*, 3: 1–21.

Schienstock, G. (1982) *Industrielle Arbeitsbeziehungen*, Opladen: Westdeutscher Verlag.

Schünstock, G. and Traxler, F. (1994) 'Economic Transformation and Institutional Change: a cross-national study in the Conversion of Union Structures and Politics in Eastern Europe', paper presented at the IIRA, 4th European Congress, Helsinki.

Schmid, J. and Blancke, S. (1995) 'Gelungene Anpassung oder prekäre Normalisierung und erfolgreiches Scheitern? Gewerkschaften im Prozeß der Einheit', *Gewerkschaftliche Monatshefte*, 9.

Schmidt, R. (ed.) (1993) *Zwischenbilanz: Analysen zum Transformationsprozeß der ostdeutschen Industrie*, Berlin: Akademie Verlag.

Schmidt, R. (1996a) 'Einleitung', in Bergmann, J. and Schmidt, R. (eds) *Industrielle Beziehungen: Institutionalisierung und Praxis unter Krisenbedingungen*, Opladen: Leske & Buderich, 11–20.

Schmidt, R. (ed.) (1996b) *Reorganisation und Modernisierung der Industriellen Produktion*, Opladen: Leske & Buderich.

Schmidt, R. and Lutz, B. (1995) *Chancen und Risiken der industriellen Restrukturierung in Ostdeutschland*, Berlin: Akademie Verlag.

Schmidt, W. (1995) 'Metamorphosen des Betriebskollektivs. Zur Transformation der Sozialordnung in ostdeutschen Betrieben', in Schmiede, R. (ed.) *Arbeit und Subjektivität*, Bonn: Informationszentrum Sozialwissenschaften.

Schmidt, W. (1996) 'Das Management betrieblicher Sozialintegration als Problem des Transformationsprozesses', report in KSPW-Berichtsband, Halle.

Schöbel, C. (1993) 'Sozialisation in unterschiedlichen Systemen. Zum Profil der Persönlichkeitstypen in West- und Ost-Berlin', WZB discussion paper FSIII 93-204, Berlin: Wissenschaftszentrum Berlin für Sozialforschung.

Schrager, L. S. (1986) 'Private Attitudes and Collective Action', *American Sociological Review*, 50: 858–9.

Schreiber, W. (1995) 'Durch Gemeinschaftsgröße individuellen Nutzen stiften: Der gewerkschaftliche Mitgliedsausweis als Wertpapier', *WSI Mitteilungen*, 2: 175–81.

Schriesheim, C. A. (1978) 'Job Satisfaction, Attitudes toward Unions, and Voting in a Union Representation Election', *American Psychological Association*, 63, 5: 548–52.

Schroeder, W. (1994) 'Die Unternehmerverbände: Programmatik, Politik, Organisation', in Kittner, M. (ed.) op. cit., 623–42.

Schroeder, W. (1996) 'Westdeutsche Prägung – ostdeutsch Bewährungsproben: Industrielle Beziehungen in der Metall- und Elektroindustrie', in Bergmann, J. and Schmidt, R. (eds) op. cit., 101–34.

Schuldt, K. (1994) 'Qualifizieren, Rekrutieren, Selektieren, Entlassen – Typisierung personalwirtschaftlicher Strategien im Rekrutierungsprozeß von Kombinaten', WZB discussion paper FS I 94-102, Berlin: Wissenschaftszentrum Berlin für Sozialforschung.

Schwartz, M. (1976) *Radical Protest and Social Structure*, New York: Academy Press.

Scott, W. H. *et. al.* (1963) *Coal and Conflict*, Liverpool: Liverpool University Press.

Seibel, W. (1996) 'Innovation, Imitation, Persistenz: Muster staatlicher Institutionenbildung in Ostdeutschland seit 1990', in Eisen, A. and Wollmann, H. (eds) 1996a, 359–416.

Seidman, J. (1953) 'Democracy in Labor Unions', *Journal of Political Economy*, 61.

Seidman, J., London, J., Karsh, B. and Tagliacozzo, D. L. (1958) *The Worker Views his Union*, Chicago: University of Chicago Press.

Seifert, W. and Rose, R. (1994) 'Lebensbedingungen und Politische Einstellungen im Transformationsprozess: Ostdeutschland und Osteuropa im Vergleich', WZB discussion paper P 94-104, Berlin: Wissenschaftszentrum Berlin für Sozialforschung.

Senghaas-Knobloch, E. (1992) 'Notgemeinschaft und Improvisationsgeschick: Zwei Tugenden im Transformationsprozeß', in Heidenreich, M. (ed.) op. cit., 295–312.

Senghaas-Knobloch, E. and Lange, H. (1992) *DDR-Gesellschaft von Innen: Arbeit und Technik im Transformationsprozess*, Forum Humane Technikgestaltung, 5, Düsseldorf: Friedrich-Ebert Stiftung.

Shalev, M. (1983) 'Strikes and the Crises: Industrial Conflict and Unemployment in the Western Nations', *Economic and Industrial Democracy*, 4: 417–60.

Shiller, R. J., Boycko, M. and Korobov, V. (1991) 'Popular Attitudes toward Free Markets: the Soviet Union and the United States Compared', *American Economic Review*, 81, 2: 385–400.

Shiller, R. J., Boycko, M. and V. Korobov (1992) 'Hunting for Homo Sovieticus: Situational versus Attitudinal Factors in Economic Behavior', *Brookings Papers on Economic Activity*, 1: 127–94.

Shister, J. (1956) 'The Logic of Union Growth', *Journal of Political Economy*, 61: 410–35.

Shorter, E. and Tilly, C. (1974) *Strikes in France, 1830–1968*, Cambridge: Cambridge University Press.

Sills, D. E. (ed.) (1968) *International Encyclopedia of the Social Sciences*, New York: Macmillan/Free Press.

Snow, D. A., Burke Rochford, E. Jr., Worden, S. K. and Benford, R. D. (1986) 'Frame Alignment Processes, Micromobilization, and Movement Participation', *American Sociological Review*, 51, August: 464–81.

Snyder, R. A., Verderber, K. S. and Morris, J. H. (1986) 'Voluntary Union Membership of Women and Men: Differences in Personal Characteristics, Perceptions and Attitudes', *Journal of Occupational Psychology*, 59: 205–16.

Sosa, E. and Tooley, M. (eds) (1993) *Causation*, Oxford: Oxford University Press.

Spangenberg, A. (1993) 'Was ist vom "Kollektiv der Werktätigen" geblieben?', *Die Mitbestimmung*, 1: 20–3.

Specht, L. (1993) 'Transformation of Property Rights in Former Soviet Socialist Systems', paper presented at Second Workshop of the Agenda Group, Vienna, 1–3 July.

Spinrad, W. (1960) 'Correlates of Trade Union Participation: a Summary of the Literature', *American Sociological Review*, 25: 237–44.

Stagner, R. and Eflal, B. (1982) 'Internal Union Dynamics during a Strike: a Quasi-Experimental Study', *Journal of Applied Psychology*, 67, 1: 37–44.

Stark, D. (1992a) 'Path Dependence and Privatization Strategies in East Central Europe', *East European Politics and Societies*, 6, 1: 17–54.

Stark, D. (1992b) 'The Great Transformation? Social Change in Eastern Europe', *Contemporary Sociology*, 21, 3: 299–304.

Stark, D. (1995) 'Not by Design: the Myth of Designer Capitalism in Eastern Europe', in Hausner, J., Jessop, B. and Nielsen, K. (eds) *Stratgic Choice and Path-Dependency in Post-Socialism*, Aldershot: Edward Elgar, 67–80.

Stark, D. and Bruszt, L. (1998) *Postsocialist Pathways: Transforming Politics and Property in East Central Europe*, Cambridge: Cambridge University Press.

Statistisches Bundesamt, Wiesbaden, various issues

Stephan, H. and Wiedemann, E. (1990) 'Lohnstruktur und Lohndifferenzierung in der DDR. Ergebnisse der Lohndatenerfassung vom September 1988', *MittAB*, 23, 4: 550–62.

Stratemann, I. (1991) *Psychologische Aspekte des wirtschaftlichen Wiederaufbaus in den neuen Bundesländern*, Göttingen.

Stratemann, I. (1993) 'Psychologische Bedingungen des wirtschaftlichen Aufschwungs in den neuen Bundesländern', *Politik and Zeitgeschichte*, Beilage zur Wochenzeitung Das Parlament, 24: 15–26.

Strauss, G. (1977) 'Union Government in the US: Research Past and Future', *Industrial Relations*, 16, 2: 215–42.

Streeck, W. (1981) *Gewerkschaftliche Organisations probleme in der Sozialstaatlichen Demokratie*, Köngistein: Athenäum.

Streeck, W. (1984) 'Co-determination: the Fourth Decade', in Wilpert, B. and Sorge, A. (eds) *International Yearbook of Organizational Democracy*, New York: John Wiley and Sons, 391–422.

Streeck, W. (1995) 'German Capitalism: Does it Exist? Can it Survive?', in Crouch, C. and Streeck, W. (eds) *Modern Capitalism or Modern Capitalisms?*, London: Frances Pinter.

Streeck, W. (1997) 'German Capitalism: Does it Exist? Can it Survive?', *New Political Economy*, 2, 2: 237–56.

Suckut, S. (1982) *Die Betriebsrätebewegung in der Sowjetisch Besetzten Zone Deutschlands (1945–1948)*, Frankfurt: Haag and Herchen.

Summers, T. P., Betton, J. H. and DeCotiis, T. A. (1986) 'Voting for and against Unions: a Decision Model', *Academy of Management Review*, 11: 643–55.

Swartz, R. (1990) 'Die Deutschstunde', *Kursbuch*, 100: 11–21.

Széll, G. (ed.) (1992) *Labour Relations in Transition in Eastern Europe*, Berlin, New York: W. de Gruyter.

Sztompka, P. (1993a) *The Sociology of Social Change*, Oxford: Blackwell.

Sztompka, P. (1993b) 'Civilizational Incompetence: the Trap of Post-Communist Societies', *Zeitschrift für Soziologie*, 22, 2: 85–95.

Sztompka, P. (1994) 'Society as Social Becoming: beyond Individualism and Collectivism', in Sztompka, P. (ed.) *Agency and Structure. Reorienting Social Theory*, Amsterdam, 251–82.

Tajfel, H. (ed.) (1982) *Social Identity and Intergroup Relations*, Cambridge: Cambridge University Press.

Tajfel, H. and Turner, J. C. (1986) 'The Social Identity Theory of Intergroup Behavior', in Worchel, S. and Austin, W. G. (eds) *Psychology of Intergroup Relations*, Monterey, Calif.: Brooks Cole.

Tannenbaum, A. S. (1965) 'Unions', in March, J. G. (ed.) *Handbook of Organizations*, Chicago: Rand-McNally.

Tannenbaum, A. S. and Kahn, R. L. (1958) *Participation in Local Unions*, Evanston, Ill.: Row, Peterson.

Taplin, I. M. and Winterton, J. (1997) *Rethinking Global Production: a Comparative Analysis of Restructuring in the Clothing Industry*, Aldershot: Ashgate.

Taylor, D. M. and Moghaddam, F. M. (1987) *Theories of Intergroup Relations: International Social Psychological Perspectives*, New York, London: Praeger.

Thelen, K. A. (1991) *Union of Parts: Labour Politics in Postwar Germany*, Ithaca, NY: Cornell University Press.

Thompson, M., Ellis, R. and Wildavsky, A. (1990) *Cultural Theory*, Boulder, Colo.: Westview Press.

Tóth, A. (1997) 'The Invention of Works Councils in Hungary', *European Journal of Industrial Relations*, 3, 2: 161–82.

Treuhandanstalt (1992) Prospectus 'Entschlossen Sanieren', Berlin.

Treuhandanstalt (1994) Information brochure, Dokumentation 1990–1994, Berlin.

Triandis, H. C., Bontempo, R., Villareal, M. J., Asat, M. and Lucca, N. (1988) 'Individualism and Collectivism: Cross-cultural Perspectives on Self–Ingroup Relationships', *Journal of Personality and Social Psychology*, 54: 323–8.

Trinczek, R. (1987) 'Zur Struktur innerbetrieblicher Aushandlungsprozesse', working paper, Institut für praxisorientierte Sozialforschung und Beratung, Erlangen.

Trinczek, R. (1989) 'Betriebliche Mitbestimmung als soziale Interaktion', *Zeitschrift für Soziologie*, 8.

Trinczek, R. (1993) 'Management und innerbetriebliche Mitbestimmung. Eine Typologie kollektiver Orientierungsmuster', Ph.D. thesis (Habilitation), Universität Erlangen.

Trommsdorff, G. (ed.) (1994) *Psychologische Aspekte des sozio-politischen Wandels in Ostdeutschland*, Berlin: de Gruyter.

Turner, L. (1991) *Democracy at Work: Changing World Markets and the Future of Labor Unions*, Ithaca, NY: Cornell University Press.

Turner, L. (1992) 'Institutional Resilience in a Changing World Economy: German Unions between Unification and Europe', *WZB discussion paper* FS I 92-6, Wissenschaftszentrum Berlin für Sozialforschung.

Turner, L. (ed.) (1997) *Negotiating the New Germany: Can Social Partnership Survive?*, Ithaca, NY: ILR Press.

Turner, L. (1998) *Fighting for Partnership: Labor and Politics in Unified Germany*, Ithaca, NY: Cornell University Press.

van de Vall, M. (1970) *Labour Organizations*, Cambridge: Cambridge University Press.

van der Veen, G. and Klandermans, B. (1989) '"Exit" Behavior in Social Movement Organizations', *International Social Movements Research*, 2: 179–98.

van Vuuren, T., Klandermans, B., Jacobson, D. and Hartley, J. (1991) 'Employees' Reactions to Job Insecurity', in Hartley, J. *et al.* (eds) op. cit., 79–103.

Vickerstaff, S. A., Thirkell, J. and Scase, R. (1994) 'Transformation of Labour Relations in Eastern Europe and Russia: a Comparative Assessment', paper presented at the International Industrial Relations Association, 4th European Regional Congress, Helsinki, Finland.

Voigt, D. (1973) *Montagearbeiter in der DDR*, Darmstadt: Westdeutscher Verlag.

Voigt, D. (1985) 'Arbeitsbeziehungen in der DDR', in Endruweit, G. *et al.* (eds), *Handbuch der Arbeitsbeziehungen*, Berlin, 463–82.

Voskamp, U. and Wittke, V. (1990) 'Fordismus im ünem Land – Das Produktions – modell der DDR', in *SOWI – Mitteilungen*, 3.

Voskamp, U. and Wittke, V. (1991a) 'Aus Modernisierungsblockaden werden Abwärts-spiralen – zur Reorganisation von Betrieben und Kombinaten der ehemaligen DDR', *Berliner Journal für Soziologie*, 1: 17–39.

Voskamp, U. and Wittke, V. (1991b) 'Industrial Restructuring in the Former GDR: Barriers to Adaptive Reform become Downward Development Spirals', *Politics and Society*, 19, 3: 341–71.

Waddington, J. and Whitston, C. (1995) 'Collectivism in a Changing Context: Union Joining and Bargaining Preferences among White-Collar Staff', in Leisink, P., van Leemput, J. and Vilrokx, J. (eds) *The Challenges to Trade Unions in Europe*, Cheltenham: Edward Elgar: 153–70.

Walker, I. and Pettigrew, T. F. (1984) 'Relative Deprivation Theory: an Overview and Conceptual Critique', *British Journal of Social Psychology*, 57: 79–86.

Walton, R. E. (1985) 'From Control to Commitment in the Workplace', *Harvard Business Review*, (March/April): 77–84.

Warr, P., Cook, J. and Wall, T. (1980) 'Scales for the Measurement of Some Work Attitudes and Aspects of Psychological Well-being', *Journal of Occupational Psychology*, 52: 129–48.

Weber, M. (1979) *Wirtschaft und Gesellschaft*, Tübingen: Mohr.

Weick, K. E. (1969) *The Social Psychology of Organizing*, Reading, Mass.

Weiner, B. (1985) '"Spontaneous" Causal Thinking', *Psychological Bulletin*, 97: 74–84.

Weinert, R. (1984) 'Betriebsräte und technischer Wandel. Kooperation und Konflikt bei technisch-organisatorischen Umstellungen in Betrieben des privaten Versicherungs-gewerbes und der Druckindustrie', thesis (Dissertation), Freie Universität Berlin.

Weinert, R. (1993) 'Probleme betrieblicher und gewerkschaftlicher Interessenvertretung in Ostdeutschland', proposal for a research conference, 11/12.6.1993, DFG-Schwerpunkt 'Strukturwandel industrieller Beziehungen', Freie Universität Berlin.

Weischer, C. (1993) 'Gewerkschaftsorganisation auf dem Prüfstand. Eine Bilanz der gewerkschaftssoziologischen Diskussion', in Leif, T., Klein, A. and Legrand, H.-J. (eds) *Reform des DGB*, Cologne: Bund Verlag: 89–144.

Weltz, F. (1988) 'Die doppelte Wirklichkeit der Unternehmen und ihre Konsequenzen für die Industriesoziologie', *Soziale Welt*, 1: 97–103.

Weßels, B. (1992) 'Bürger und Organisationen – Ost-und Westdeutschland: vereinigt und doch verschieden?', WZB discussion papers FS III 92-204, Berlin: Wissenschaftszentrum Berlin für Sozialforschung.

Wheeler, L., Reis, H. T. and Bond, M.H. (1989) 'Collectivism–Individualism in Everyday Social Life: the Middle Kingdom and the Melting Pot', *Journal of Personality and Social Psychology*, 57: 79–86.

Wicker, A. (1969) 'Attitudes vs. Action: the Relationship of Verbal and Overt Behavioral Responses to Attitude Objects', *Journal of Social Issues*, 25: 41–78.

Wiedenhofer, H. *et al.* (1979) *Probleme gewerkschaftlicher Interessenvertretung: Beispiel der Gewerkschaft Nahrung, Genuß, Gaststätten*, Bonn: Verlag Neue Gesellschaft.

Wiesenthal, H. (1993) 'Institutionelle Dynamik und soziale Defensive', *BISS public*, 3, 11: 5–23.

Wiesenthal, H. (1994) 'East Germany as a Unique Case of Societal Transformation: Main Characteristics and Emergent Misconceptions', working paper, AG TRAP no. 94/8. Max-Planck-Gesellschaft, Arbeitsgruppe Transformationsprozesse in den neuen Bundesländern.

Wiesenthal, H. (1995) 'Die Transformation Ostdeutschlands: Ein (nicht ausschließlich) privilegierter Sonderfall der Bewältigung von Transformationsproblemen', in Wollmann, H., Wiesenthal, H. and Bönker, F. (eds) *Transformation sozialistischer Gesellschaften: Am Ende des Anfangs*, Opladen: Westdeutscher Verlag, 134–62.

Wiesenthal, H. (1996) 'Contingencies of Institutional Reform: Reflections on Rule Change, Collective Actors, and Political Governance in Postsocialist Democracies', working paper, AG TRAP, no. 96/10, Humboldt Universität Berlin.

Wilke, M. and Müller, H.-P. (1991) *Zwischen Solidarität und Eigennutz: Die Gewerkschaften des DGB im deutschen Vereinigungsprozeß*, St. Augustin: Konrad-Adenauer Stiftung.

Windolf, P. (1997) 'The Transformation of the East German Economy', unpublished manuscript, University of Trier.

Windolf, P. and Wegener, B. (1993) 'Manager in Ostdeutschland. Transformation der ökonomischen Elite auf dem Gebiet der ehemaligen DDR', funding application report, Trier/ Berlin.

Winkler, G. (1993) *Social report 1993*, Berlin: Morgenbuch.

Wittke, V., Voskamp, U. and Bluhm, K. (1993) 'Den Westen überholen, ohne ihn einzuholen? – Zu den Schwierigkeiten bei der Restrukturierung der ostdeutschen Industrie und den Perspektiven erfolgreicher Reorganisationsstrategien', in Schmidt, R. (ed.) op. cit., 131–54.

Woderich, R. (1992) 'Mentalitäten zwischen Anpassung und Eigensinn', *Deutschland Archiv*, 25, 1: 21–32.

Woderich, R. (1996) 'Peripherienbildung und kulturelle Identität', in Kollmorgen, R., Reißig, R. and Weiß, J. (eds) *Sozialer Wandel und Akteure in Ostdeutschland*, Opladen: Leske & Buderich, 81–102.

Wollmann, H., Wiesenthal, H. and Bönker, F. (eds) (1995) *Transformation sozialistischer Gesellschaften: Am Ende des Anfangs*, Opladen: Westdeutscher Verlag.

Woolfson, C. and Foster, J. (1988) *Track Record: the Story of Caterpillar Occupation*, London: Verso.

WSI Tarifarchiv (research institute of the DGB, Düsseldorf), various issues.

Zalesny, M. D. (1985) 'Comparison of Economic and Noneconomic Factors in Predicting Faculty Vote Preference in a Union Representation Election', *Journal of Applied Psychology*, 70, 243–356.

Zapf, W. (ed.) (1969) *Theorien des sozialen Wandels*, Cologne: Kiepenheuer & Witsch.

Zapf, W. (1991) 'Der Untergang der DDR und die soziologische Theorie der Modernisierung', in Giesen, B. and Leggewie, C. (eds) *Experiment Vereinigung: Ein sozialer Großversuch*, Berlin: Rotbuch, 38–51.

Zapf, W. (1992) 'Die Transformation in der ehemaligen DDR und die soziologische Theorie der Modernisierung', WZB discussion paper P 92-104, Berlin: Wissenschaftszentrum Berlin für Sozialforschung.

Zapf, W. (1994) 'Zur Theorie der Transformation', *BISS public*, 13: 5–10.

Zech, R. (1993) 'Probleme der individuellen und kollektiven Partizipation an der Organisationspolitik der Gewerkschaft Erziehung und Wissenschaft', final report, Hans-Böckler-Stiftung, Düsseldorf.

Zoll, R. (1979) *Streik und Arbeitsbewußtsein*, Frankfurt am Main: Europäische Verlagsanstalt.

Zoll, R. (ed.) (1981) *Arbeitsbewußtsein in der Wirtschaftskrise, 1. Bericht: Krisenbetroffenheit und Wahrnehmung*, Cologne: Bund Verlag.

Zoll, R. (1984a) ' *"Die Arbeitslosen, die könnt" ich alle erschießen!'*, Cologne: Bund Verlag.

Zoll, R. (1984b) *'Hauptsache ich habe meine Arbeit'*, Cologne: Bund Verlag.

Zurcher, L. A. and Snow, D. A. (1981) 'Collective Behavior: Social Movements', in Rosenberg, M. and Turner, R. (eds) *Social Psychology, Sociological Perspectives*, New York: Basic Books, ch. 15, 447–82.

Index